Filtering THE News

Filtering THE News

Essays *On* Herman and Chomsky's Propaganda Model

Jeffery Klaehn, editor

Montreal/New York/London

Black Rose Books No. II335

National Library of Canada Cataloguing in Publication Data

Filering the news : essays on Herman and chomsky's propaganda model /
Jeffery Klaehn, editor

Includes bibliographical references and index.

ISBN: 1-55164-261-1 (bound)   ISBN: 1-55164-260-3 (pbk.)

(alternative ISBNs 9781551642611 [bound]   9781551642604 [pbk.])

1. Press and propaganda. 2. Press and politics. I. Klaehn, Jeffery

P95.8.F54 2005   302.23   C2004-907115-7

Cover design: Associés libres

C.P. 1258	2250 Military Road	99 Wallis Road
Succ. Place du Parc	Tonawanda, NY	London, E9 5LN
Montréal, H2X 4A7	14150	England
Canada	USA	UK

To order books:

In Canada: (phone) 1-800-565-9523 (fax) 1-800-221-9985
email: utpbooks@utpress.utoronto.ca

In United States: (phone) 1-800-283-3572 (fax) 1-651-917-6406

In the UK & Europe: (phone) 44 (0)20 8986-4854 (fax) 44 (0)20 8533-5821
email: order@centralbooks.com

Our Web Site address: http://www.web.net/blackrosebooks

A publication of the Institute of Policy Alternatives of Montréal (IPAM)

Printed in Canada

The Canada Council | Le Conseil des Arts
for the Arts | du Canada

Contents

Respectfully dedicated to the memory of
Dr. Robert Everton
(1952–2004)

Notes On Contributors

ROBERT BABE holds the Jean Monty/BCE Chair in Media Studies at the University of Western Ontario in London. His publications include *Communication and the Transformation of Economics* (1995) and *Canadian Communication Thought: Ten Foundational Writers* (2000). He is, as well, a contributor to *Radical Mass Media Criticism: A Cultural Genealogy* (2005), and a forthcoming book entitled *Cultural Ecology: Communication, Environment and Development*.

PETER EGLIN, Ph.D., is Professor of Sociology at Wilfrid Laurier University in Waterloo where, for the last twenty-seven years, he has taught courses in Human Rights, Ethnomethodology, Theory and Practice, and the Sociology of Crime. During that time, he was, as well, Humboldt Research Fellow at the Universitat Konstanz, 1980-1981, and Visiting Senior Lecturer in Sociology at Newcastle-upon-Tyne Polytechnic, 1985-1987. He is the author of *Talk and Taxonomy: A Methodological Comparison of Ethnosemantics and Ethnomethodology* (1980), and co-author, with Stephen Hester, of *The Montreal Massacre: A Story of Membership Categorization Analysis* and *A Sociology of Crime* (1992), and co-editor of *Culture in Action: Studies in Membership Categorization Analysis* (1997). He is currently working a book on intellectual responsibility.

ROBERT EVERTON (1952–2004) taught extensively in both Communication Studies and Latin American Studies since first instructing at Simon Fraser University in 1992. As well as an academic, he was a social and political activist for over two decades. Involved in the efforts to demand government accountability to its citizenry, he participated widely in citizen efforts to make the so-called free trade agreements both transparent and accountable. His doctoral dissertation was entitled "Democracy in Action: Communicative Action."

ROBERT JENSEN, Ph.D., teaches media law, ethics, and politics at the University of Texas. Prior to his academic career, he worked as a professional journalist and continues to write for the popular media, both alternative and mainstream. His opinion and analytic pieces on such subjects as foreign policy, politics, and race have appeared in papers around the country. He is also involved with a number of activist groups working against U.S. military and economic domination of the rest of the world. Jensen is author of *Writing Dissent: Taking Radical Ideas from the Margins to the Mainstream* (2001), co-author, with Gail Dines and Ann Russo, of *Pornography: The Production and Consumption of Inequality* (1998), and co-editor, with David S. Allen, of *Freeing the First Amendment: Critical Perspectives on Freedom of Expression* (1995).

JEFFERY KLAEHN's work has been published in a wide range of scholarly journals, including the *European Journal of Communication, Gazette: The International Journal for Communication Studies, Portuguese Studies Review, Cultural Dynamics, Journalism Studies,* and the *Canadian Review of Sociology and Anthropology.* He is the editor of the forthcoming *Bound by Power: Intended Consequences* (2005) and of *Studies in Popular Culture: Comic Books and Comic Book Culture* (2006). His substantive areas of interest include media, pop culture, theory, social inequality, and political economy. In his spare time, he enjoys watching anime and Japanese horror films and playing video games (RPGs).

VALERIE SCATAMBURLO-D'ANNIBALE is an award-winning educator (recipient of the 2001-2002 Faculty of Arts and Social Sciences Teaching Award) who teaches at the University of Windsor. Her first book entitled *Soldiers of Misfortune: The New Right's Culture War and the Politics of Political Correctness* (1998), received the American Educational Studies Association's 2000 Critics Choice Award. Her work on social and cultural theory and critical pedagogy has been published in *Current Perspectives in Social Theory, Cultural Studies/Critical Methodologies,* the *Journal of Educational Philosophy and Theory* and in books including the *Dictionary of Cultural Theorists; Alienation, Ethnicity and Postmodernism;* and *Bringing Capitalism Back for Critique by Social Theory.* A recent article was translated into Spanish and appeared in one of the largest Latin-American journals, *Herramienta.* Her current research focuses on internet activism and social movements.

JAMES WINTER is Professor of Communication Studies at the University of Windsor and the author of numerous books, including *Common Cents: Media Portrayal of the Gulf War and Other Events* (1992), *Democracy's Oxygen: How the Corporations Control the News* (1997), *MediaThink* (2000), and, most recently, *Lies the Media Tell Us* (2005). He is also a contributor to *Radical Mass Media Criticism* (2005) and to the forthcoming *Bound by Power: Intended Consequences* (2005).

Chapter One

A Critical Review And Assessment Of Herman And Chomsky's 'Propaganda Model'[1]

Jeffery Klaehn

MASS MEDIA PLAY AN ESPECIALLY IMPORTANT role in democratic societies. They are presupposed to act as intermediary vehicles that reflect public opinion, respond to public concerns and make the electorate cognizant of state policies, important events and viewpoints. The fundamental principles of democracy depend upon the notion of a reasonably informed electorate.

The 'propaganda model' of media operations laid out and applied by Edward Herman and Noam Chomsky in *Manufacturing Consent: The Political Economy of the Mass Media* postulates that elite media interlock with other institutional sectors in ownership, management and social circles, effectively circumventing their ability to remain analytically detached from other dominant institutional sectors.[2] The model argues that the net result of this is self-censorship without any significant coercion.

Media, according to this framework, do not have to be controlled nor does their behaviour have to be patterned, as it is assumed that they are integral actors in class warfare, fully integrated into the institutional framework of society, and act in unison with other ideological sectors, ie., the academy, to establish, enforce, reinforce and 'police' corporate hegemony.[3]

It is not a surprise, then, given the interrelations of the state and corporate capitalism and the 'ideological network,' that Herman and Chomsky's propaganda model has routinely been mis-characterized if not ignored altogether. The model is generally excluded from scholarly debates on patterns of media behaviour.

This chapter provides a critical review and assessment of the propaganda model and seeks to encourage debate regarding the interrelations between corporate power and ideology. Highly descriptive in nature, the chapter is concerned with the question of whether media can be seen to play a hegemonic role in society oriented toward legitimization, political accommodation and ideological management.

Initially referred to as a 'general theory of the Free Press,' the propaganda model contends that America's elite agenda-setting mass media play an important role in establishing cultural hegemony, primarily by establishing a general framework for the news that is adhered to by lower-tiered media. For Herman and Chomsky, there is a clear demarcation between elite media—the *New York Times* and the *Washington Post*—and the 'quality press'—a term they use to refer to more 'populist' newspapers, such as the *Boston Globe*, the *Los Angeles Times*, and the *Philadelphia Inquirer*, among others.[4] Chomsky remarks that the extent to which ideological constraints typically relax varies according to the geographic proximity of particular media organizations to the centres of economic and political power.

> What happens in areas that are marginal with respect to the exercise of power doesn't matter so much. What happens in the centres of power matters a great deal. Therefore the controls are tighter to the extent that you get closer to the centre.[5]

Within the geographic nexus of corporate-state power, however, ideological control is generally extremely tight.

The propaganda model contends that agenda-setting media function as mechanisms of propaganda in several ways. Elite media determine what topics, issues and events are to be considered 'newsworthy' by lower-tier media and establish the general premises of official discourse.[6] Furthermore, elite media establish limitations on the range of debate and general boundaries for subsequent interpretation.[7]

> They determine, they select, they shape, they control, they restrict—in order to serve the interests of dominant, elite groups in the society.[8]

Herman and Chomsky do not claim that media function only to circulate propaganda.[9] The authors do, however, assert that the propaganda function is an important aspect of media performance, and their propaganda model seeks to describe 'the forces that cause the mass media to play a propaganda role.'[10] Right-wing think-tanks, such as the Fraser and C.D. Howe Institutes in Canada, and the PR industries worldwide, more generally, can be seen to be ideologically significant, in relation to what Herman and Chomsky call 'manufacturing consent,' beyond the direct control that owners exert over their 'outlets.'

First and foremost, the propaganda model constitutes an institutional critique of media performance. Herman and Chomsky argue that media serve the political and economic interests of dominant elites and charge that 'the workings of the media...serve to mobilize support for the special interests that dominate the state and private activity.'[11]

> Perhaps this is an obvious point, but the democratic postulate is that media are independent and committed to discovering and reporting the truth, and that they do not merely reflect the world as powerful groups wish it to be perceived. Leaders of the media claim that their news choices rest on unbiased professional and objective criteria, and they have support for this contention within the intellectual community. If, however, the powerful are able to fix the premises of discourse, to decide what the general populace is allowed to see, hear, and think about, and to "manage" public opinion by regular propaganda campaigns, the standard view of how the system works is at serious odds with reality.[12]

The propaganda model argues that regularities of misrepresentation in news accounts flow directly from the concentration of private power in society. It holds that elite media interlock with other institutional sectors in ownership, management, and social circles, effectively circumventing their ability to remain analytically detached from the power structure of society, of which they themselves are an integral part. The net result of this, the authors contend, is self-censorship without any significant coercion. Media performance, then, is understood as an outcome of market forces.

> Most biased choices in the media arise from the preselection of right-thinking people, internalized preconceptions, and the adaptation of personnel to the constraints of ownership, organization, market and political power. Censorship is largely self-censorship, by reporters and commentators who adjust to the realities of source and organizational media requirements, and by people at higher levels within media organizations who are chosen to implement, and have usually internalized, the constraints imposed by proprietary and other market and government centres of power.[13]

The model argues that media serve *'political ends'* by mobilizing bias, patterning news choices and marginalizing dissent, and by allowing 'the government and dominant private interests to get their messages across to the public.'[14] Herman and Chomsky state that media serve to foster and enforce an intellectual and moral culture geared toward protecting wealth and privilege 'from the threat of public understanding and participation.'[15]

> The general picture is of a media machine acting as a self-regulating system where propaganda is produced voluntarily and in a decentralized way by media personnel who censor themselves on the basis of an internalized sense of political correctness.[16]

Market Forces In Action: The Five 'Filter Elements' (Constraints) Explained

Herman and Chomsky argue that the 'raw material of news' passes through a series of five inter-related filter constraints, 'leaving only the cleansed residue fit to print.'[17] These five elements continuously 'interact with and reinforce one another' and have multilevel effects on media performance.[18] They identify the central elements of the filter constraints as follows:

> (1) the size, concentrated ownership, owner wealth, and profit orientation of the dominant mass-media firms; (2) advertising as the primary income source of the mass media; (3) the reliance of the media on information provided by government, business, and "experts" funded and approved by these primary sources and agents of power; (4) "flak" as a means of disciplining the media; and (5) "anticommunism" as a national religion and control mechanism.[19]

The first filter constraint emphasizes that media are closely interlocked and share common interests with other (dominant) institutional sectors (corporations, the state, banks).[20] As Herman and Chomsky note: 'the dominant media firms are quite large businesses; they are controlled by very wealthy people or by managers who are subject to sharp constraints by owners and other market-profit-oriented forces.'[21]

The second filter highlights the influence of advertising values on the news production process. To remain financially viable, most media must sell markets (readers) to buyers (advertisers). This dependency can directly influence media performance. Chomsky remarks that media content reflects 'the perspectives and interests of the sellers, the buyers, and the product.'[22]

The third filter notes that dominant elites routinely facilitate the news gathering process: providing press releases, advance copies of speeches, periodicals, photo opportunities and ready-for-news analysis.[23] Thus, government and corporate sources are attractive to the media for purely economic reasons. Such sources are favoured and are routinely endorsed and legitimized by media because they are recognizable and typically viewed as prima facie credible. Information provided to media by corporate and state sources does not require fact checking or costly background research and is typically portrayed as accurate. Herman and Chomsky highlight not only the symbiotic nature of the relationship between journalists and their sources, but the reciprocity of interests involved in the relationship. The third filter stresses that the opinions and analyses expounded by corporate and state sources are typically adapted to dominant class interests and market forces. Thus,

> Because of their services, continuous contact on the beat, and mutual dependency, the powerful can use personal relationships, threats, and rewards to further influence and coerce the media. The media may feel obligated to carry extremely dubious stories and mute criticism in order not to offend their sources and disturb a close relationship. It is very difficult to call authorities on whom one depends for daily news liars, even if they tell whoppers. Critical sources may be avoided not only because of their lesser availability and higher cost of establishing credibility, but also because the primary sources may be offended and may even threaten the media using them.[24]

Importantly, the authors contend that bias may be structured into news discourse as a result of the dominance of official sources who are identified as 'experts.' In this way, news discourse 'may be skewed in the direction desired by the government and "the market".'[25] Concurrently, *preferred* readings structured into news discourse are typically 'those that are functional for elites.'[26]

Flak, the fourth filter, observes that dominant social institutions (most notably the state) possess the power and requisite organizational resources to pressure media to play a propagandistic role in society. Herman and Chomsky explain that "Flak" refers to negative responses to a media statement or program...It may be organized centrally or locally, or it may consist of the entirely independent actions of individuals.'[27]

In sum, the authors maintain that there are powerful interests that routinely encourage right-wing bias in media. According to the propaganda model, these filter constraints are the most dominant elements in the news production process, and they continuously interact with one another and operate on an individual and institutional basis.[28] Herman and Chomsky comment that the filter constraints excise the news that powerful interests deem not fit to print.

Since the publication of *Manufacturing Consent*, the demise of Communism in the former Soviet Union has brought about radical changes in the world political landscape. According to Chomsky, the last filter, formerly anti-communism, still functions in the post-Cold War period, but now in the form of a dichotomy of *'otherness.'*[29] Chomsky remarks,

> ...it's the idea that grave enemies are about to attack us and we need to huddle under the protection of domestic power. You need something to frighten people with, to prevent them from paying attention to what's really happening to them. You have to somehow engender fear and hatred, to channel the kind of fear and rage—or even just discontent— that's being aroused by social and economic conditions.[30]

Herman concedes that the filter perhaps should have been originally termed *'the dominant ideology,'* so as to include elements of the dominant ideology that are referred to at various points throughout *Manufacturing Consent;* these include the merits of private enterprise, or the benevolence of one's own government.[31] In the end, however, *anti-communism* was selected, primarily because the authors wished to emphasize the ideological elements that have been most important in terms of disciplinary and control mechanisms. As it is laid out in *Manufacturing Consent*, the description of the fifth filter is vague and is already veering toward the newly revised definition. For example, Herman and Chomsky originally wrote that:

> This ideology helps mobilize the populace against an enemy, and because the concept is fuzzy it can be used against anybody advocating policies that threaten property interests or support accommodation with Communist states and radicalism.[32]

Herman and Chomsky state that these five filter constraints capture the essential elements of the propaganda model. The authors argue that there is 'a systematic and highly political dichotomization in news coverage based on serviceability to important domestic power interests.'[33] They charge that this dichotomy is routinely observable in 'choices of story and in the volume and quality of coverage,' that choices for publicity and suppression are bound to the five filter constraints.[34] Their model suggests that media shape public opinion by controlling how ideas are presented to the public, and also by limiting the range of credible alternatives. As Herman and Chomsky write,

> The five filter constraints narrow the range of news that passes through the gates, and even more sharply limit what can become "big news," subject to sustained news campaigns. By definition, news from primary establishment sources meets one major filter requirement and is readily accommodated by the mass media. Messages from and about dissidents and weak, unorganized individuals and groups, domestic and foreign, are at an initial disadvantage in sourcing costs and credibility, and they often do not comport with the ideology or interests of the gatekeepers and other powerful parties that influence the filtering process.[35]

Media: Threatening Democracy, Inducing Avoidance, Self-Indulgently Hypocritical?

The propaganda model argues that the elite agenda-setting media legitimize dominant ideological principles and social institutions by systematically defending the principal 'economic, social and political agendas' of dominant elites and social institutions.[36] In Chomsky's view, it is not surprising that the media fulfill this function in the capitalist democracies,

> If you look at the institutional structure of media and the pressures that act on them and so forth and so on, you would tend on relatively uncontroversial assumptions to expect that the media would serve this function.[37]

Herman and Chomsky's view of media as an ideological apparatus for elites mirrors the thesis put forth by William Domhoff in his book, *The Powers That Be: Processes of Ruling Class Domination in America* (published 9 years before *Manufacturing Consent*). On the ideology process, Domhoff writes that,

> The ideology process consists of the numerous methods through which members of the power elite attempt to shape the beliefs, attitudes and opinions of the underlying population...Free and open discussion are claimed to be the hallmarks of the process, but past experience shows that its leaders will utilize deceit and violence in order to combat individuals and organizations which espouse attitudes and opinions that threaten the power and privileges of the ruling class...The ideology pro-

cess is necessary because public opinion does not naturally and automatically agree with the opinions of the power elite.[38]

Like Herman and Chomsky, Domhoff stresses that the ideological network is both 'extremely diverse and diffuse,'[39] and such that media interact with other institutional sectors in circulating knowledge and shaping public opinion on a range of foreign policy and key domestic issues, such as the functioning of the economy.[40]

It bears noting that Herman and Chomsky appropriated the phrase *'manufacturing consent'* from the influential American journalist, Walter Lippman, who advocated consent engineering early in this century. For Lippman, the *'manufacture of consent'* was both necessary and desirable, predominantly because, in Lippman's view, *'the common interests'*—meaning, presumably, issues of concern to all citizens in democratic societies—'very largely elude public opinion entirely.' Lippman postulated that *'the common good'* ought to be *'managed'* by a small 'specialized class.'[41] Lippman recommended that the role of the electorate—the *'bewildered herd,'* as he called them—be restricted to that of *'interested spectators of action.'*[42]

Lippman predicted that the 'self-conscious art of persuasion' would eventually come to preface every 'political calculation' and 'modify every political premise' and stressed that consent engineering is not historically inconsistent with the overall *'practice of democracy.'* In his own words,

> The creation of consent is not a new art. It is a very old one which was supposed to have died out with the appearance of democracy. But it has not died out. It has, in fact, improved enormously in technique, because it is now based on analysis rather than on rule of thumb. As so, as a result of psychological research, coupled with the modern means of communication, the practice of democracy has turned a corner. A revolution is taking place, infinitely more significant than any shifting of economic power.[43]

In 1947, in an article entitled 'The Engineering of Consent,' published in the *Annals of the American Academy of Political and Social Science*, Edward Bernays put forth a similar argument in support of *'the manufacture of consent.'* Like Walter Lippman, Bernays declares that the interests of *'democracy'* are particularly well served by 'the application of scientific principles and tried practices' to *'the engineering of consent.'* Bernays asserts that consent engineering is at the heart of democracy and characterizes it as 'among our most valuable contributions to the efficient functioning of society.'

> The engineering of consent is the very essence of the democratic process, the freedom to persuade and suggest. The freedoms of speech, press, petition, and assembly, the freedoms to make the engineering of consent possible, are among the most cherished guarantees of the Constitution of the United States.[44]

In Chomsky's view, the effectiveness of 'thought control' in contemporary democratic societies owes much to the fact that ideological indoctrination is combined with a general impression that society is relatively open and free.

> In brief, it is necessary to ensure that those who own the country are happy, or else all will suffer, for they control investment and determine what is produced and distributed and what benefits will trickle down to those who rent themselves to the owners when they can. For the homeless in the streets, then, the highest priority must be to ensure that the dwellers in the mansions are reasonably content. Given the options available within the system and the cultural values it reinforces, maximization of short-term individual gain appears to be the rational course, along with submissiveness, obedience, and abandonment of the public arena. The bounds on political action are correspondingly limited. Once the forms of capitalist democracy are in place, they remain very stable, whatever suffering ensues—a fact that has long been understood...[45]

The propaganda model argues that because *'thought control'* is virtually invisible in democratic societies, the propaganda system is actually more effective and efficient than it is in totalitarian states.

This view of dominant social institutions as autocratic, oppressive, deterministic and coercive can be understood as the bedrock upon which the foundations of the propaganda model are constructed. Herman and Chomsky, in arguing that the mass media mobilize support for corporate and state monied interests, contend that media play a key role in engineering or manufacturing consent. Thus, it is important to highlight their argument that media performance is *'guided'* by market forces and elite interests. Media content is directly relevant to the 'manufacture of consent.' Herman and Chomsky state that there is a 'systematic and highly political dichotomization in news coverage,' 'based on serviceability to important domestic power interests.'[46] They maintain that the propaganda function of media is observable in choices of story selection, in quantity and quality of coverage, and in modes of handling some stories as opposed to others. The authors explain that 'modes of handling favoured and inconvenient materials (placement, tone, context, fullness of treatment) differ in ways that serve political ends.'[47] The propaganda model argues that media content serves *'political ends'* by *'mobilizing interest and outrage'* and by generating interest and sympathetic emotion in some stories while diverting attention from others.

Central Methodological Assumptions of the Propaganda Model

This section provides an overview of the main methodological assumptions of the propaganda model. As noted, the model argues that the news media serve to 'mobilize support for special interests that dominate the state and private activity.'[48] It contends that media choices pertaining to treatment of particular news stories and events are fundamentally political ones and predicts that the treatment accorded certain news stories and events varies in ways that effectively serve political ends and reflect the multifaceted (geo)political-economic interests of corporate and state monied elites. The model identifies several areas of import, and these will be examined below.

The propaganda model, then, predicts that in certain cases media will exemplify tendencies toward ideological closure and hypothesizes that news coverage will be aligned with elite interests. The model predicts a range of debate, but a narrow one. As Chomsky puts it,

> Debate cannot be stilled, and indeed, in a properly functioning system of propaganda, it should not be, because it has a system-reinforcing character if constrained within proper bounds. What is essential is to set the bounds firmly. Controversies may rage as long as it adheres to the presuppositions that define the consensus of elites, and it should furthermore be encouraged within these bounds, thus helping to establish the doctrines as the very conditions of thinkable thought while reinforcing the belief that freedom reigns...In short, what is essential is the power to set the agenda.[49]

The propaganda model has its own methodological approach to news analysis and makes a range of predictions concerning patterns of media behavior. These include first-order, second-order and third-order predictions. Each of these are explored below. As Chomsky explains,

> The propaganda model makes predictions at various levels. There are first-order predictions about how the media function. The model also makes second-order predictions about how media performance will be

discussed and evaluated. And it makes third-order predictions about the reactions to studies of media performance. The general prediction, at each level, is that what enters into the mainstream will support the needs of established power.[50]

The propaganda model argues that media suppress and distort, advocate and promote, in the interests of establishing ideologically serviceable consensus that will 'legitimize' and facilitate corporate and state monied interests. It predicts that media behavior will reflect political-economic interests of dominant elites.

This is a first-order prediction of Herman and Chomsky's propaganda model.

In a world of concentrated wealth and major conflicts of class interest, to fulfill this role requires systematic propaganda.[51]

Herman and Chomsky charge that news coverage devoted to government (state) policy in general (foreign and domestic) is typically *framed* in order to effectively legitimize and facilitate elite (geo)political-economic interests and prevent opposition to corporate hegemony. The authors write that the 'modes of handling favoured and inconvenient materials (placement, tone, context, fullness of treatment) differ in ways that serve political ends.'[52] On news discourse devoted to foreign policy issues, Herman and Chomsky add that media can be seen to share a 'close interest in the Third World, and their interconnections with the government in these policies are symbiotic.'[53] Therefore, on fairly logical grounds, one could expect to find a high degree of 'closure' in foreign and international news coverage.

The propaganda model predicts that media typically treat victims of oppression and state terrorism differently, depending upon the perpetrator(s). How the victims of state-sponsored violence/terrorism are represented in media discourse is of central importance to the model's overall methodological approach to the study of news discourse. It predicts that there will be qualitative and quantitative differences in treatment in the Western media accorded *'unworthy victims'* (victims of oppression and/or state terrorism perpetrated by us—*Canada, the U.S., and the other capitalist democracies), and 'worthy victims'* (victims of oppression and/or state terrorism perpetrated by official enemy states). Differences in treatment will be observable in sourcing of stories, in how stories are evaluated by media, and also in the 'investigatory zeal in the search for…villainy and the responsibility of high officials,' such that worthy victims are accorded more news coverage, more prominent coverage, and more humanistic treatment in media accounts.[54] Conversely, unworthy victims will typically 'merit only slight detail, minimal humanization, and little context that will excite and enrage.'[55] Chomsky explains,

In the case of enemy crimes, we find outrage; allegations based on the flimsiest evidence, often simply invented, and uncorrectable, even when conceded to be fabrication; careful filtering of testimony to exclude contrary evidence while allowing what may be useful; reliance on official U.S. sources, unless they provide the wrong picture, in which case they are avoided (Cambodia under Pol Pot is a case in point); vivid detail; insistence that the crimes originate at the highest level of planning, even in the absence of evidence or credible argument; and so on. Where the locus of responsibility is at home, we find precisely the opposite: silence or apologetics; avoidance of personal testimony and specific detail; world-weary wisdom about the complexities of history and foreign cultures that we do not understand; narrowing of focus to the lowest levels of planning or understandable error in confusing circumstances; and other forms of evasion.[56]

The propaganda model predicts a systematic and political dichotomization in news discourse, observable in story selection choices and in editorial choices pertaining to story construction, headlines, fullness of context and story treatment.

We would expect different criteria of evaluation to be employed, so that what is villainy in enemy states will be presented as incidental background fact in the case of oneself and friends. What is on the agenda in treating one case will be off the agenda in discussing the other.[57]

The model predicts that the elite, agenda-setting Western media reporting on the democracies (and their allies and client states) will feature the 'uncritical acceptance of premises' and will rely almost exclusively upon information provided by official state sources. It predicts further that ideologically serviceable themes and facts will be heavily promoted whereas *inconvenient* truths will not. Victims of state-sponsored terrorism/violence perpetuated by the democracies, its allies and/or client states will be accorded treatment that can be seen to serve the ideological and political ends of dominant elites. The model also emphasizes the importance of delineating the absence of historical context in news reporting and treats as significant the degree to which news is isolated from prior and subsequent events.

Chomsky employs two methodological techniques to test the model. The first is to study *'paired examples'* of historical events during the same period of time. Disparities in treatment can lend insight into interpreting media behavior. The second method of testing the propaganda model, and that which is most favored by Chomsky in his polemical writings, is to explore the 'boundaries of the expressible' on crucial topics.

> One appropriate method is to consider the spectrum of opinion allowed expression. According to the propaganda model, one would expect the spectrum to be bounded by the consensus of powerful elites while encouraging tactical debate within it.[58]

This approach highlights the importance of scrutinizing media content, sources, framing, and representation in news discourse. The first-order predictions of the propaganda model are exclusively concerned with the observable patterns of media behavior.

The second and third order predictions of the model are concerned with the role that the ideological institutions play in policing the boundaries of intellectual debates. More specifically, they are concerned with how social institutions, and the professional classes working within them, serve to foster and reinforce an intellectual environment that effectively prevents opposition to the dominant ideology and structures of ideological rule. Both predictions speak to the issue of civil liberties and academic freedom within the institutional setting of the academy and within the broader intellectual culture.

The second-order prediction of the propaganda model is that studies and analysis of news media which prove that the model is correct in its first-order predictions will be effectively excluded from intellectual debate(s) on media discourse and media behavior. This is predictable under a thesis of corporate hegemony. Chomsky explains,

> One prediction of the model is that it will be effectively excluded from discussion, for it questions the factual assumption that is most serviceable to the interests of established power: namely, that the media are cantankerous, perhaps excessively so. However well-confirmed the model may be, then, it is inadmissible, and, the model predicts, should remain outside the spectrum of debate over media. Note that the model has a rather disconcerting feature. Plainly, it is either valid or invalid. If invalid, it may be dismissed; if valid, it will be dismissed.[59]

That the propaganda model typically *is* excluded from academic and intellectual debates on media and patterns of media behavior seems to confirm the model's second-order prediction.

It is rare to discover in the mainstream any recognition of the existence
or possibility of analysis of the ideological system in terms of a propaganda model, let alone to try and confront it on rational grounds.[60]

Moreover,

By and large, the possibility of studying the functioning of the media in
terms of a propaganda model is simply ignored.[61]

The propaganda model's third-order prediction is that intellectual and academic
analyzes and studies, however well grounded in logical argument and coupled
with an adequate amount of supporting evidence, which prove that the PM's
first-order predictions are correct, will be bitterly condemned.

On the crucial third-order prediction, Chomsky comments that,

...the model predicts that such inquiry will be ignored or bitterly condemned, for it conflicts with the needs of the powerful and the privileged.[62]

Chomsky's critique of intellectuals (and academics) as servants of power has been
well documented.[63] In sum, Chomsky contends that the liberal-intelligentsia have
been assimilated into the 'establishment' and are fully integrated into the institutional nexus of state and corporate power. Chomsky believes that contemporary
intellectuals play important roles in establishing and legitimizing cultural hegemony, and maintains that universities, like the other ideological institutions,
function to manage and police ideologized spectrums of opinion.

Chomsky stresses that intellectual dissenters are often 'filtered out' at the
graduate-school level, when they are particularly vulnerable to outside pressures,
if they are unwilling or unable to conform, or if they are unwilling to subordinate
social, political and class-based commitments.

To confront power is costly and difficult; high standards of evidence and
argument are imposed, and critical analysis is naturally not welcomed
by those who are in a position to react vigorously and to determine the
array of rewards and punishments.[64]

In Chomsky's view, however, the writer is invested with a *moral* responsibility to
tell the truth. Chomsky writes,

About the responsibility to try to find and tell the truth...it is often
hard, and can be personally costly, particularly for those who are more
vulnerable. That is true even in societies that are very free; in others the
cost can be severe indeed.

The responsibility of the writer as a *moral agent* is to try to bring
the truth about *matters of human significance* to an *audience that can do
something about them.* This is part of what it means to be a moral agent
rather than a monster. It is hard to think of a less contentious proposal
than this truism...

Unfortunately, that is not quite the case, for a simple reason: the
standard practice of the intellectual communities to which we (more or
less) belong rejects this elementary moral principle, with considerable
fervor and passion, in fact.[65]

Nexus: Interrelations of State and Corporate Capitalism and the Corporate Media

In sum, the propaganda model constitutes an institutional critique of mass media. It highlights the multilevel ways in which money and power can be seen to
influence overall media performance. Herman and Chomsky suggest that media
interests and choices routinely 'amount to propaganda campaigns' and contend
that media performance reflects the fact that dominant media firms share interlocks and common interests with other institutional sectors.[66]

> Societies differ, but in ours, the major decisions over what happens in the
> society—decisions over investment and production and distribution and
> so on—are in the hands of a relatively concentrated network of major
> corporations and conglomerates and investment firms. They are also the
> ones who staff the major executive positions in the government. They're
> the ones who own the media and they're the ones who have to be put in
> a position to make the decisions. They have an overwhelmingly domi-
> nant role in the way life happens...Within the economic system, by law
> and in principle, they dominate. The control over resources and the need
> to satisfy their interests imposes very sharp restraints on the political
> system and on the ideological system.[67]

It is upon this conception of social organization that the foundations of the propaganda model are constructed.

The propaganda model stresses that there are correlations between patterns
of media behaviour and broader institutional and market imperatives. Its theoretic underpinnings stress that elites are over-represented in government and big
business sectors and that elites are the major initiator of action in society. Fur-

thermore, the model can be seen to assume that elites dominate economic decision-making processes and that elites share common interests and goals that are largely integrated. For Chomsky, there is a clear demarcation between the 'state' and the 'government.' Chomsky asserts that the state comprises institutions that set the conditions for public policy and is relatively stable. The state constitutes the 'actual nexus of decision-making power...including investment and political decisions, setting the framework within which the public policy can be discussed and is determined.'[68] In contrast, Chomsky views government as more visible, consisting of 'whatever groups happen to control the political system, one component of the state system, at a particular moment.'[69]

Herman and Chomsky acknowledge that elites can disagree but stress that such disagreements are largely confined to tactics on how they can achieve common goals. They acknowledge that such disagreement over tactics will be reflected in media discourse.

> The mass media are not a solid monolith on all issues. Where the powerful are in disagreement, there will be a certain diversity of tactical judgments on how to attain shared aims, reflected in media debate. But views that challenge fundamental premises or suggest that the observed modes of exercise of state power are based on systemic factors will be excluded from the mass media even when elite controversy over tactics rages fiercely.[70]

The authors acknowledge that a careful and thorough reading of various media typically bears this out but emphasize that 'the filter constraints are so powerful, and built into the system in such a fundamental way, that alternative bases of news choices are hardly imaginable.'[71] They suggest that the illusion of genuine debate serves to reinforce the overall effectiveness of the overall propaganda system in society.[72] While emphasizing its extensive reach and resiliency, Chomsky describes the propaganda system as 'inherently unstable,' and notes that this instability can create 'space' or openings for dissent. In this context, Chomsky comments that the system is intrinsically unstable: 'Any system that's based on lying and deceit is inherently unstable.'[73] Even so, the authors contend that the filter constraints have powerful effects, such that media interests and choices serve class interests on a consistent basis.

In conclusion, it is important to highlight that Herman and Chomsky's model encourages intellectual and political opposition to fundamental trends that accommodate the established order and structures of ideological rule.[74] Chomsky suggests that individuals can actively combat the propaganda system and states that the first step is to develop a 'sceptical reflex.' 'It's got to get to the point where it's like a reflex to read the first page of the Los Angeles *Times* and to count the lies and distortions and to put it in some sort of rational framework.'[75]

Mounting such a course of intellectual self-defence requires sufficient motivation and intellectual resources. Chomsky believes that combatting the propaganda system requires the ability to think independently and desire to think critically. Intellectual self-defence also requires hard work. To defend against the propaganda system and gain an understanding of many issues, Chomsky says, 'you're going to have to read exotic newspapers, and you're going to have to compare today's lies with yesterday's lies and see if you can construct some rational story out of them. It's a major effort.'[76]

To do this, Chomsky warns that: 'you have to decide to become a fanatic...You have to work, because nobody's going to make it easy for you.'[77] Thus, in terms of motivation, desire is a major prerequisite. Beyond this, intellectual self-defence entails a 'willingness to look at the facts with an open mind, to put simple assertions to the test, and to pursue an argument to its conclusions.[78]

On what resources are required to undertake this, Chomsky remarks: 'I frankly don't think that anything more is required than ordinary common sense...A willingness to use one's native intelligence and common sense to analyze and dissect and compare facts with the way in which they're presented is really sufficient.'[79] 'With a little industry and application, anyone who is willing to extricate himself [sic] from the system of shared ideology and propaganda will readily see through the modes of distortion developed by substantial segments of the intelligentsia. Everyone is capable of doing this.'[80]

In Chomsky's view, individuals who wish to actively pursue a course of intellectual self-defence will also need to gain access to independent media whenever possible. This is crucial, Chomsky suggests, because the mass media routinely block information and reproduce dominant representations. Chomsky contends that individuals do not require political scientists to explain 'political affairs' to them. 'The alleged complexity, depth and obscurity of these questions is part of the illusion propagated by the system of ideological control, which aims to make these issues seem remote from the general population and to persuade them of their capacity to organize their own affairs and understand the social world in which they live without the tutelage of intermediaries.[81]

In the preface to the collection of his Massey Lectures on CBC, entitled *Necessary Illusions: Thought Control in Democratic Societies*, Chomsky states that: 'My

personal feeling is that citizens of the democratic capitalist societies should undertake a course of intellectual self-defence to protect themselves from manipulation
and mind control.'[82] Elsewhere, Chomsky comments that 'An independent mind
must seek to separate itself from official doctrine, and from criticism advanced by
its alleged opponents; not just from the assertions of the propaganda system, but
from its tacit presuppositions as well, expressed by critic and defender. This is a
far more difficult task.'[83]

Concluding Remarks

Herman and Chomsky's institutional critique of media behaviour is forceful and
convincing, as is their analysis of the ideological formation of public opinion and
of the 'Orwellian' abuse of language in western democracies. 'Brainwashing under freedom' is Chomsky's catch-phrase for the hypocrisy of western liberal opinion and its relationship to power. The thesis put forth in *Manufacturing Consent*,
that consent in a free society is manufactured through manipulation of public
opinion, even more so now then when the book was first published, bespeaks
journalistic self-censorship in an era in which corporate ownership of media has
never been as concentrated, right-wing pressure on public radio and television is
increasing, the public relations industries are expanding exponentially, and advertising values dominate the news production process.

    If ever there was a time for Herman and Chomsky's 'propaganda model' to
be included in scholarly debates on patterns of media performance, it is now.

NOTES
1. This chapter was first published as " A Critical Review and Assessment of Herman and
   Chomsky's Propaganda Model of Media Operations" in *The European Journal of Communication*, 2002, Vol. 17(2): 147–182. Reprinted by permission of Sage Publications Ltd.
2. It bears noting in this context that Ed Herman was the principle author of the first chapter of
   Manufacturing Consent, in which the five filter mechanisms are laid out.
3. This view echoes Miliband, who wrote that: 'There is nothing particularly surprising about the
   character and role of the major mass media in advanced capitalist society. Given the economic
   and political context in which they function, they cannot fail to be, predominantly, agencies
   for the dissemination of ideas and values which affirm rather than challenge existing patters
   of power and privilege, and thus to be weapons in the arsenal of class domination.' Miliband,
   as cited in Wallace Clement, *Canadian Corporate Elite: Analysis of Economic Power* (Toronto:
   McClelland and Stewart, 1975), 278.
4. Noam Chomsky, *The Chomsky Reader*, ed. James Peck (New York: Pantheon, 1997), 135.
5. Noam Chomsky, Language and Politics (Montreal: Black Rose, 1988), p. 629.
6. Vivian and Maurin note that agenda-setting occurs at various levels: (1) creating awareness,
   (2) establishing priorities and (3) perpetuating issues. See John Vivian and Peter J. Maurin, *The
   Media of Mass Communication* (Toronto: Allyn and Bacon, Canada, 2000), 302. For analysis of

Canadian media coverage of the Persian Gulf conflict, and other cases, see James Winter, *Common Cents: media portrayal of the Gulf War and other events* (Montreal: Black Rose, 1992).

7. Edward S. Herman and Noam Chomsky, *Manufacturing Consent: The Political Economy of the Mass Media* (New York: Pantheon, 1988), 1-2.

8. Noam Chomsky, cited in Peter Wintonick and Mark Achbar, *Manufacturing Consent: Noam Chomsky and the Media* (Montreal: Black Rose, 1994), 55.

9. In the Preface to *Manufacturing Consent* Herman and Chomsky write: 'We do not claim this is all the mass media do, but we believe the propaganda function to be a very important aspect of their overall service.' See Herman and Chomsky, xi.

10. Herman and Chomsky, 1988:xi-xii.

11. Herman and Chomsky, xi.

12. Herman and Chomsky, xi.

13. Herman and Chomsky, xii.

14. Herman and Chomsky, 2.

15. Noam Chomsky, *Necessary Illusions: Thought Control in Democratic Societies* (Toronto: CBC Enterprises, 1989), 14.

16. Milan Rai, *Chomsky's Politics* (New York: Verso), p. 46.

17. Herman and Chomsky, 1-35.

18. Herman and Chomsky, 2.

19. Herman and Chomsky, 2.

20. Herman and Chomsky, 3-14.

21. Herman and Chomsky, 14.

22. Chomsky, *Necessary Illusions*, 8.

23. Herman and Chomsky, 19.

24. Herman and Chomsky, 22.

25. Herman and Chomsky, 23.

26. Herman and Chomsky, 23.

27. Herman and Chomsky, 26.

28. Herman and Chomsky, 2; Rai, 40.

29. The filter constraint suggests that media generate fear. It also suggests that media redirect fear that already exists. For discussion of the latter, see Noam Chomsky, *Class Warfare*, Interviews with David Barsamian (Vancouver, New Star, 1997), 91-2.

30. Noam Chomsky, *The Common Good*, Interviews with David Barsamian (Berkeley, CA: Odonian, 1998), 41.

31. Herman, cited in Wintonick and Achbar, 108.

32. Herman and Chomsky, 29.

33. Herman and Chomsky, 35.

34. Herman and Chomsky, 35.

35. Herman and Chomsky, 31.

36. Herman and Chomsky, 298.

37. Source: Transcript, 'Noam Chomsky Meets the Washington Press,' National Press Club, DC, 11 April 1989, p. 2.

38. William G. Domhoff, *The Powers That Be: Processes of Ruling Class Domination in America* (New York: Vintage), 169.

39. Domhoff, 173.

40. Domhoff, 179-183. Domhoff asserts that the sum total of special interest is class rule, ie., 'what is *not* done and *not* debated defines ruling-class domination even if the class as a whole does not act consciously to realize its will and to subordinate other classes.' See Domhoff, 57.

41. Lippman, cited in Wintonick and Achbar, 40.

42. Lippman, cited in Rai, 23.

43. Lippman [1922], cited in Wintonick and Achbar, 40.

44. Bernays [1947], cited in Wintonick and Achbar, 41.

45. Chomsky, *Necessary Illusions*, 22.

46. Herman and Chomsky, 35.

47. Herman and Chomsky, 35.

48. Herman and Chomsky, xi.

49. Chomsky, *Necessary Illusions*, 48.

50. Chomsky, 153.

51. Herman and Chomsky, 2.

52. Herman and Chomsky, 35.

53. Herman and Chomsky, 13-14.

54. Herman and Chomsky, 34-35.

55. Herman and Chomsky, 35.

56. Chomsky, *Necessary Illusions*, 137.

57. Herman and Chomsky, 34.

58. Chomsky, 59.

59. Chomsky, 11.

60. Chomsky, 151.

61. Chomsky, 145.

62. Chomsky, 153.

63. Most notably, by Russell Jacoby, *The Last Intellectuals: American Culture in the Age of the Academe* (New York: Noonday Press, 1987), 182-200.

64. Chomsky, 8-9.

65. Noam Chomsky, *Perspectives on Power: Reflections on Human Nature and the Social Order* (Montreal: Black Rose, 1997), 55-6.

66. Herman and Chomsky, 2.

67. Chomsky, cited in Wintonick and Achbar, 51.

68. Chomsky, cited in Rai, 91.

69. Chomsky, cited in Rai, 91.

70. Herman and Chomsky, xiii.

71. Herman and Chomsky, 2.

72. Herman and Chomsky, 298.

73. Chomsky, cited in Jeffery Klaehn, "A Critical Review and Assessment of Herman and Chomsky's 'Propaganda Model'," *European Journal of Communication*, 2002, Vol. 17(2), 172.

74. See Chomsky, *The Common Good*, 138-48.

75. Chomsky, *Language and Politics*, 740.

76. Chomsky, *Ibid.*, 717.

77. Chomsky, *Ibid.*, 742.

78. Chomsky, cited in Klaehn, 'A Critical Review...,' 172.

79. Chomsky, cited in Rai, 53.

80. Chomsky, cited in Rai, 53.

81. Chomsky, cited in Rai, 53.

82. Chomsky, *Necessary Illusions*, vii.

83. Noam Chomsky, *Towards a New Cold War: Essays on the Current Crisis and How We Got There* (London: Sinclair Browne, 1982), 81.

Chapter Two

In 'Sync': Bush's War Propaganda Machine And The American Mainstream Media

Valerie Scatamburlo-D'Annibale

IN *MANUFACTURING CONSENT: THE POLITICAL Economy of the Mass Media*, Edward Herman and Noam Chomsky offered their "propaganda model" (PM) as a framework for analyzing and comprehending the inner-workings, behavior and performance of the American mainstream media. Their work helped to draw attention to the incompatibility between corporate media and an ostensibly democratic society. One of their major claims was that the media tended to behave predictably in terms of their reportage on certain issues—particularly those concerning U.S. foreign policy. The authors contended that the media operated within restricted assumptions, rarely transcending what Chomsky later called the "bounds of the expressible" given their dependence on 'elite' information sources, the commercial underpinnings of the corporate media structure, and other structural factors which impacted on the production of 'news.'[1]

The PM was presented as an alternative paradigm for understanding media operations and the role which the media played in maintaining and indeed, manufacturing consent, to dominant social and political arrangements and power relations. In distinct contrast to the prevailing mainstream explanations that existed at the time—both liberal and conservative—which focused primarily on journalistic practices, norms, etc., Herman and Chomsky's model provided an institutional critique of media performance that emphasized structural dynamics and which clearly situated the media in the larger market system. The model suggested that there was a multi-leveled capability of powerful business and government entities and collectives to exert considerable control over the flow of information in a manner which furthered the interests of dominant elites. The model conceded that while the powerful may have individual objectives and private agendas, the dominant elite generally shared common political, economic and social interests.

Since the PM first appeared on the scene of media criticism, it has garnered considerable attention and criticism. Some have gone to ridiculous lengths in portraying Herman and Chomsky as "conspiracy" theorists while other criticisms, undoubtedly more measured, have suggested that the model excludes analysis of mediating variables—including journalistic values and norms, and media professionalism and notions of objectivity (cf. Hallin, 1994). Rather than regurgitate those debates here, I would point my readers in the direction of Herman's (effective, in my opinion) rebuttal to various critics of the PM as well as Jeffery Klaehn's thorough and effective reassessment of the model's enduring relevance.[2] While it is certainly the case that valid criticisms have been launched, and while I would concede that the PM is more applicable in some contexts than in others, it provides a powerful framework for analyzing the media behavior to be explored in this paper—namely the mainstream media coverage of the recent "war on Iraq." As Herman notes, the model does

> ...suggest that the mainstream media, as elite institutions, commonly frame news and allow debate only within the parameters of elite interests; and that where the elite is really concerned and unified, and/or where ordinary citizens are not aware of their own stake in an issue or are immobilized by effective propaganda, the media will serve elite interests uncompromisingly.[3]

As the arguments in *Manufacturing Consent* suggest, capitalist news media generally function to generate support for elite policies rather than attempting to empower people to make informed political decisions. Such was the case, as I will argue, during the build-up to the war and in the subsequent media coverage of it.[4] By extrapolating key themes/concepts from the PM, this chapter will analyze the role of the mainstream media, especially television, in transmitting, promoting, and legitimizing the most recent U.S. military aggression in Iraq. Accordingly, I will provide an analysis and critique of how the media represented the alleged crisis in Iraq prior to the invasion and then how they covered the war itself. As I write, the occupation of Iraq continues. While a transfer to "full sovereignty" for Iraq is scheduled for June 30, 2004, the gesture is largely symbolic insofar as the U.S. will essentially retain sovereignty as long as it "maintains its military, monetary, and administrative domination of the country."[5] Contrary to pre-war administration assertions that the occupation would be short-lived, officials have now admitted that American troops will be stationed in Iraq for years to come. At last count, 837 U.S. service members had died since the beginning of military operations in Iraq; thousands of others have been permanently maimed. The estimated number of Iraqi civilian casualties stands at more than 10,000 and the region remains in tatters. In many parts of Iraq, basic services including access to water and electricity are scarce or sporadic at best. Daily car bombings have become the norm. No weapons of mass destruction have been found.

In recent months, the media have begun to ask questions about the rationale initially provided by the Bush administration to justify their unprecedented pre-emptive war—namely, Iraq's possession of weapons of mass destruction (WMD) and Saddam Hussein's apparent links to Al Qaeda—in light of damning reports that have shed considerable doubt on most pre-war declarations. While this is a welcome development—after an "astonishing two years of cowardice" and media collusion with an "unconscionable level of administrative deception"[6] —that could potentially lead to some critical discourse now that more complex perceptions of the event are beginning to emerge, it does not absolve the media of their complicity in parroting the official line in the days, weeks, and months leading to the war—a line which was, at best, based on a combination of willfully gross exaggerations and brazen lies. With few exceptions, the bulk of media coverage, from headline news on television to the front pages of major newspapers, repeated the administration's 'talking points' unquestioningly. As Wicker noted, "Bush administration spokesmen have made several cases for waging war against Iraq, and the U.S. press has tended to present all those cases to the public as if they were gospel."[7] During the almost surreal run-up to "Operation Iraqi Freedom," the American media—and particularly mainstream media networks—were transmogrified into hollow echo chambers that gleefully valorized U.S. military might and an unthinking patriotism. In many ways, media docility played a key role in "manufacturing consent" and "selling the war" to the American population.

On the War Path

If this were a dictatorship, it would be a heck of a lot easier, just so long as I'm the dictator. —George W. Bush, Dec. 18, 2000, Washington, D.C., during his first visit to Washington as President-elect

Why, of course the people don't want war...But, after all, it is the leaders of the country who determine the policy, and it is always a simple matter

to drag the people along, whether it is a democracy, or a fascist dictatorship, or a parliament, or a communist dictatorship...Voice or no voice, the people can always be brought to do the bidding of the leaders. That is easy. All you have to do is tell them they are being attacked, and denounce the pacifists for lack of patriotism and exposing the country to danger.
—Hermann Goering, Nazi leader, at the Nuremberg Trials after WWII

Given the historical record, one could certainly argue that the American mainstream media tend to assume an obedient, not to mention, obsessive patriotic tone during times of international 'conflict.'[8] Yet the coverage of the current Bush administration's drive to war (as it was in relation to Afghanistan) appears to be especially insidious in this regard. For the most part, it was largely devoid of historical context, lacked substantive debate, and often times served to buttress the Manichean (i.e., good versus evil) worldview served up by the Commander-in-Chief. This propensity for 'going soft' on Bush, however, dates back to the days of his presidential campaign, the 2000 election debacle, and his subsequent 'appointment' to the White House by the Supreme Court.[9] After the tragic events of September 11th, the mainstream media became even more acquiescent to an administration that had clearly capitalized on the culture of fear created in the aftermath of the terrorist attacks.[10] From color-coded risk alerts and duct tape frenzy to warnings about the "axis of evil" and Iraq's weapons of mass destruction (WMD), a majority of the American population has been cowering in fear and the current administration has manipulated that fear brilliantly.[11] With few exceptions, the mainstream media have been used as propagandistic mouthpieces for Bush's "war on terror" and have greatly assisted in generating and maintaining the kind of fear necessary to whip up patriotic fervor and populist support for military aggression.[12] As Schechter maintains:

> There is an intimate link between the media, the war, and the Bush administration...Few administrations have been as adept at using polling, focus groups, "perception managers," spinners and I.O. or "information operations" specialists to sell slogans to further a "patriotically correct" climate. Orchestrating media coverage is one of their most well-honed skills, aided and abetted by professional PR firms, corporate consultants, and media outlets.[13]

In addition and not surprisingly, the media have been quick to bolster the claims of the Bush administration no matter how ridiculous or fallacious. Parry has aptly noted that:

> Bush and his advisers have grasped that they face few limits on how far
> they can push their political/media advantage. Protected by an army of
> media allies, who either share a conservative ideology or see financial
> gain in playing along, Bush has learned that he stands little risk no mat-
> ter how over-the-top his imagery or assertions.[14]

This was clearly the case in the buildup to, and the subsequent, war in Iraq. The
context in which this war was waged is particularly interesting in terms of the
parallels with the first Gulf War. By early 2002, George W. Bush faced a situation
akin to what his father had faced in the aftermath of the Gulf War. Despite the
"victory" against the Taliban (a claim that seems even more dubious at this date
given the re-emergence of 'warlords' in war-torn Afghanistan and recent indica-
tions that the Bush administration is wheeling and dealing with the Taliban in an
effort to bring them back into the Afghan government),[15] the limited success of
the war in Afghanistan was coming to light. While Bush had promised, in typical
bellicose mode, to smoke out the terrorists and capture Osama bin Laden—dead or
alive—the 'enemy' proved to be more elusive than the administration had anticipated. The failure to "get" bin Laden coupled with a weakening economy posed a
serious threat to Bush's re-election. What Bush needed was both a dramatic media spectacle and a decisive 'war' victory to bolster his chances of being re-elected.
To this end, Saddam Hussein once again provided a practical target.[16]

In his January 29, 2002 State of the Union address, George W. Bush identified the infamous "axis of evil" constituted by North Korea, Iran and Iraq. Bush
then suggested that Iraq "continued to flaunt its hostility toward America and to
support terror" and further added that in seeking out weapons of mass destruction, Iraq was poised to arm terrorists. This, of course, was also among Bush's
first attempts to link the terrorist attacks to Iraq and, particularly, to Saddam
Hussein. As has since been revealed with the publication of David Frum's book *The
White House in the Right Time: The Surprise Presidency of George W. Bush*, Frum was
contacted by chief presidential speechwriter Mike Gerson in late December 2001.
His task was simple: he was to provide a justification for a war on Iraq. And
hence, the infamous "axis of evil" phrase was born. Key Bush cabinet members
had been clamoring for a confrontation with Iraq for quite some time—long before the events of September 11th. To confirm this, one need only peruse the un-
settling canon of PNAC (Project for the New American Century).[17] There in plain
sight, one can find Bush's blueprint for the establishment of *Pax Americana*. A report entitled *Rebuilding American's Defenses: Strategy, Forces and Resources for a*

New Century, penned in September 2000 by a cabal of far-right intellectuals and think tank mandarins has, in effect, been wholeheartedly adopted as the Bush administration's foreign policy since September 11, 2001. The plan called for regime change in Iraq and the events of 9/11 were pressed into service towards that aim. In short, the attacks on the World Trade Center and the Pentagon provided the needed justification for adopting and implementing the plan (that had been years in the making) detailed in the document. Indeed, prior to 9/11, PNAC (which is chaired by arch conservative William Kristol and whose staunchest supporters include Donald Rumsfeld, Dick Cheney, Richard Perle, and Paul Wolfowitz)[18] hypothesized that the United States could not attempt to conquer the globe without some "catastrophic and catalyzing event, like a new Pearl Harbor." As 'luck' would have it, 9/11 was the Pearl Harbor they had hoped for.[19] Within hours of the attacks, Rumsfeld was "ordering his staff to find something that could be used to pin the blame on Iraq" and Condoleeza Rice instructed her staff to "consider the opportunities 9/11 provided" in order to "justify the vigorous extension of U.S. hegemony."[20] On September 20, 2001, the PNAC sent a letter to George W. Bush encouraging regime change in Iraq.[21]

Not surprisingly, such connections were never made nor investigated by the dominant media who were rather content to out-do one another in lavishing effusive praise on Bush for his performance. After the speech, Dan Rather proclaimed that the speech was a "solid, even eloquent address." CBS's Rather, one may recall, had been reduced to blubbering on national television while making an appearance on the *David Letterman Show* shortly after 9/11. It was in that context that Rather told Letterman that "George W. Bush is my president" and that he would do whatever he was told by the Commander-in-Chief.[22] On NBC, Andrea Mitchell, declared the speech "amazing." Not to be bested, CNN featured commentator immediately after the State of Union speech was none other than William Bennett (the self-proclaimed guardian of morality and Western civilization) who praised the "moral" dimensions of Bush's address:

> It was a very interesting and powerful speech...It was a speech replete with morality, morally confident...This was a speech of moral confidence, of tremendous sense of commitment and forward looking.

CNN senior political analyst William Scheider (who also happens to be a resident fellow at the right-wing American Enterprise Institute and hardly a neutral observer)[23] also chimed in:

This president has a particular strength and it is a strength of character. It's a strength of that, more than other presidents, when he makes a personal commitment and shows resolve, it's an example to the country...His strongest appeal to Americans is his strength of character. At one point he called for a new culture of responsibility in the country. I think it was the president's personal commitment and personal resolve that stood as an example to the American people.[24]

Schneider's pandering would be comical if it were not a tragic indication of the typical media coverage of Bush Junior. Here was a man (i) who had been involved in a number of financial scandals and had looted the public purse in Texas; (ii) who had his father, George Sr., pull strings so that he could avoid service in the Vietnam War and who then went AWOL for a year after he got into the Texas National Guard; (iii) who was a heavy alcohol and drug abuser (iv) whose family had extensive business dealings with the bin Laden family,[25] and; (v) who had left Texas in ruins after his tenure as governor—being portrayed as a paragon of virtue, the epitome of character and responsibility.[26] The next morning, the fawning continued in newspaper commentary and columns that almost "universally applauded the speech."[27] The push for another war, this time on Iraq, was in full swing.

As 2002 unfolded, the Bush administration ratcheted up the rhetoric and intensified its ideological war against Iraq. The real public relations campaign to sell the war, however, arguably began on September 7, 2002 when George Bush and Tony Blair mugged for the cameras at Camp David. The timing of the meeting was well- planned for as White House chief of staff Andrew Card had indicated earlier: "From a marketing point of view, you don't introduce new products in August." Rather, the marketing campaign to sell the war (apparently like any other commodity) was timed to coincide with the emotional anniversary of September 11. It was at Camp David that both politicians cited a "new" report from the UN's International Atomic Energy Agency that allegedly stated that Iraq was "six months away" from building a nuclear weapon. Bush declared: "I don't know what more evidence we need." Of course, the IAEA possessed no evidence that Iraq was reconstituting its nuclear program yet, with few exceptions, virtually no one in the media bothered to check the story.[28] In fact, the following day, more "evidence" suddenly appeared—on the front page of that so-called bastion of liberalism—the *New York Times*. On September 8, Judith Miller and Michael Gordon essentially helped to "co-launch the Bush II sales campaign for Saddam-change."[29] In a shameful example of fear-mongering, the reporters began their article with a dramatic opening salvo: "Iraq has stepped up its quest for nuclear weapons and has embarked on a worldwide hunt for materials to make atomic bombs, Bush administration officials said today." Subsequently, the authors claimed (once again according to anonymous "administration officials") that "acquiring nuclear arms is again a top Iraqi priority." Gordon and Miller referred to aluminum tubes that had "persuaded American intelligence experts that they were meant for Iraq's nuclear program." Iraq, we were told, had been trying to buy tubes specifically designed as "components of centrifuges to enrich uranium" for nuclear weapons.[30]

Predictably, that same Sunday morning, Dick Cheney appeared on NBC's Meet the Press and cited (while giving proper credit to the *New York Times* piece)[31] the aluminum tubes as proof of Saddam's nuclear threat. Cheney also recited a well-worn litany of Saddam Hussein's crimes, reiterated long-discredited ties between Iraq and the Al Queda terrorist network, and even tried to insinuate that Iraq had had a hand in the anthrax attacks—despite the fact, that all evidence then pointed to U.S. weapons-grade facilities. Donald Rumsfeld and Condoleeza Rice also appeared on the political talk show circuit that day to trumpet the discovery of the tubes and Iraq's apparent nuclear threat. In the months that followed, the notion that aluminum tubes were being used as part of a revived nuclear weapons program was discredited but the *Times* never published a clarification and administration representatives were never really taken to task for presenting falsehoods as undeniable facts.[32]

In the weeks that followed, with the anniversary of 9/11 still fresh in the minds of most Americans, in various speeches and interviews, administration officials also reiterated the claim that there were ties between Saddam Hussein and Al Queda. In an interview on September 25, 2002, Rice adamantly insisted that "there were in the past and have been contacts between senior Iraqi officials and members of al-Qaida going back for actually quite a long time." She added that "there clearly are contacts between Al-Qaida and Iraq that can be documented. There clearly is testimony that some of these contacts have been important contacts and there's a relationship here."[33] On the same day, speaking at a photo op with visiting Colombian President Alvaro Uribe, Bush warned that the danger lied in al Queda becoming "an extension of Saddam's madness and his hatred and his capacity to extend weapons of mass destruction around the world."[34] Such statements, which the mainstream dutifully reported with little or no regard as to their accuracy, were daily fodder on television news, political commentary talk shows, and in the press.[35] By November 2002, poll after poll indicated that the

Bush administration was winning the domestic debate about Iraq as large percentages of Americans believed that Iraq posed a threat to the United States and that Saddam Hussein was developing weapons of mass destruction.[36] What was missing, of course, was any type of contextual information. That the comrades in George W's administration—many of whom served under the Reagan and Bush I regimes—had once viewed Saddam as an ally and had happily provided him with aid and the means to develop WMD was clearly a slice of history that was conveniently ignored.[37]

In *Manufacturing Consent*, Herman and Chomsky noted that during the Cold War, there were many occasions where the American mainstream media were especially critical and analytical of claims made by so-called "enemies" and other nations when it came to geopolitical issues. However, they were generally reluctant to apply the same critical and analytical standards when it came to their "own" politicians and their own country and, therefore, tended to be more supportive of the authorities. Under the guise of being "objective" by simply reporting what leaders are saying, the mainstream media often, and perhaps, unwittingly, promote the official line of propaganda. At times, the propaganda is subtle but on some occasions even blatant propaganda often goes uncontested by the mainstream media. Two recent examples would include President Bush's 2003 State of the Union address and Colin Powell's February address to the United Nations Security Council where both leaders were able to make dubious claims that were basically unchallenged (at least at the time) by the media.

By January 2003, the United States had already deployed thousands of troops poised for war and a confrontation with Iraq seemed likely despite all the posturing about hopes for a peaceful resolution. On January 28, in his State of Union Speech, Bush—while stopping short of declaring war—used numerous scaremongering tactics to make the case for war. He also made his case to the public by using discredited information. It took the media well over six months to discover that many of his statements were questionable. For example, one of more dubious claims made in the speech—namely Iraq's presumed attempt to obtain uranium from Niger—only came under scrutiny several months after Bush's oration. In the subsequent coverage, the media tended to focus on the infamous and misleading "sixteen words" and while much media hand-wrenching was on display, the narrow focus on that one egregious example of blatant lying obfuscated the fact that the "uranium" fabrication was one among many included in the speech.[38] The allegation that Iraq had attempted to purchase uranium from

Niger had been proven to be based on crudely forged documents almost *one year* before it was included in Bush's speech. Additionally, Bush also trotted out erroneous information about the aforementioned aluminum tubes claiming that "intelligence sources tell us that he (Saddam) has attempted to purchase high-strength aluminum tubes suitable for nuclear weapons production" (State of the Union, Jan. 28, 2003). The statement was altogether false in its implication (that the materials were being used for nuclear purposes) since the International Atomic Energy Agency (IAEA) as well as dozens of leading scientists declared that the tubes were unsuitable for nuclear weapons months before. For the most part, the media gave Bush a free pass and instead emphasized his steely resolve and determination.

After the speech, CNN's Judy Woodruff opined that Bush was "determined" as evidenced by his "set jaw" and "the look in his face." She added that "we heard him say if Saddam Hussein doesn't fully disarm for the safety of our people and the peace of the world, we will lead a coalition to disarm him. He left no doubt as to where this country is headed." Such remarks, which were typical of the media coverage of the speech, speak volumes. First and foremost, they focused mainly on Bush's *performance* and tone rather than on the substance of the speech. They also lent credence to the administration claim that Iraq and Saddam Hussein posed a threat to the American population and world peace. Lou Dobbs, CNN's resident financial expert also weighed in on Bush's performance:

> I think what we witnessed tonight was…a president determined, one with a 'different look' in his eyes…This was President Bush speaking from the heart, absolutely resolute…He conveyed determination…And every constituency watching…I don't think could miss this signal that this president is determined that it will be his policy carried out…The means by which he does so will be his choice entirely.[39]

Dobbs' observations are also telling for they tended to equate Bush's bullying displays of ostentatious bravado with leadership. The very idea that a preemptive war and unilateral military action by the United States would constitute a flagrant violation of international law was simply not on the media's radar screen. Additionally, the fact that Dobbs was, in the words of Susan Douglas,[40] a "pugnacious," "right-wing" ideologue and not a "national affairs journalist" qualified to comment on war and related issues was apparently not a concern for CNN.[41]

The following morning, the aforementioned William Schneider (see above) appeared on CNN Live at Daybreak and offered the following analysis of the speech in response to a question about Bush's case for war: "I think he was very effective in one crucial respect. He supplied an important missing link for many Americans" about the connection "between Saddam Hussein and al Qaeda." "He said there are links between Saddam Hussein and terrorist organizations. The weapons of mass destruction that we know that he possesses can be used to threaten every American man, woman and child. That's what Americans were wondering about. They wondered, if we go to war with him, will we be doing it to protect our interests? And the president made a passionate, grim, but powerful case that Saddam Hussein threatens the United States."[42] Although this segment on CNN was referred to as analysis, Schneider provided nothing of the sort. Rather, his comments served to reinforce the then tenuous administration (and now, discredited) assertion that Hussein was somehow connected to al Qaeda. However, as several reports from the State Department, the CIA and other intelligence agencies had clearly demonstrated, there was no "credible proof of any links between the Islamist al Qaeda movement and the secular Iraqi government."[43] In fact, Osama bin Laden had denounced the Iraqi dictator as an infidel and a traitor to Islam. The desperate attempt to link September 11th to Saddam Hussein was, at best, disingenuous. Yet, Schneider like so many other media pundits and reporters merely presented this fallacy as though it were fact. Bush's statements were not scrutinized in the least and the vast majority of media coverage of the speech simply confirmed the aforementioned tendency of the media 'going soft' on Bush. Furthermore, as Jones has noted, the "trend of positive coverage" only increased in the time frame "leading up to and during the war against Iraq" with some news outlets taking a "direct role in promoting the president's positions."[44]

A report from *Fairness & Accuracy in Reporting (FAIR)* issued just before Colin Powell took to the world stage, noted that while teams of UN experts had not found hidden caches of chemical, biological or nuclear weapons, the media's coverage repeatedly "glided from reporting the allegation that Iraq" was "hiding banned weapons materials to repeating it as a statement of fact."[45] In example after example, the findings of the report demonstrated how the mainstream media helped to build up the case for war. The report concluded by stating that "through constant repetition of phrases like 'the search for Iraq's weapons of mass destruction,'" the media conveyed to the public the impression that the alleged banned weapons on which the Bush administration had rested its case for war were known to exist and that the question was simply whether inspectors were skillful enough to find them. In fact, at the time, the question of whether or not Iraq possessed banned weapons was very much an open one.[46] Perry has noted that the repetitious nature of such reporting is conducive to promulgating propaganda: "It's far cheaper to lard the schedule with talking heads who earn their keep finding ways to restate what official sources have already said. The format is a great boon to the White House. It serves to do the heavy lifting required of any serious propaganda campaign, which is sheer numbing repetition."[47] Such repetition was also on display after the final push to secure public support for an Iraqi invasion came in the form of Colin Powell's presentation to the UN Security Council on February 5, 2003. Bush had alluded to it in his speech and it was expected by many to provide "definitive" proof of Iraq's "evil" machinations. The media coverage of Powell's 'case' is particularly telling and therefore requires further analysis.

No Smoking Gun: Powell's 'Case' Against Iraq

> My colleagues, every statement I make today is backed up by sources,
> solid sources. These are not assertions. What we are giving you are facts
> and conclusions based on solid intelligence. —Colin Powell, Feb. 5, 2003

Prior to Powell's presentation, a number of media outlets were pointing out that Powell himself had admitted that he would not provide a "smoking gun" but would nonetheless provide a compelling case.[48] Subsequent to the Secretary of State's presentation on Iraq at the UN Security Council, many mainstream media outlets treated the various allegations made by Powell as irrefutable facts, rather than attempting to explore or examine the veracity of the claims made. On CNN, William Schneider claimed that Powell had marshaled an "overwhelming array of evidence" that demonstrated Iraq's failure to comply with the UN Resolution. He further suggested that Powell's performance shifted the burden of proof to Iraq and added that "no one disputes the findings Powell presented at the UN."[49] In prefacing an interview with Colin Powell for 60 Minutes II, Dan Rather crossed the fine line from reporting on accusation made by Powell in his Security Council presentation to describing them as facts when he suggested that Powell had "showed" mobile laboratories to be actually operating. In the interview itself, Rather made reference to remarks made by an Iraqi official spokesman who had described Powell's presentation as "a collection of stunts, special effects, and unnamed sources" and asked for Powell's reaction. Powell claimed that he had spent "most of the last four days going after every sentence in my statement, and making sure...we could support those statements. There were no doctored tapes. There were no doctored photos. What you see is the truth, and it is reality, and we are very, very confident in what we presented today." Dan Rather did not push the issue further, seemingly content to take Powell at his word and allowing Powell to subsequently suggest that much of the information presented to the Security Council was "fresh."[50]

In a similar vein, Paula Zahn seemed determined to defend Powell's honor without question while casting any potential detractors as miscreants. In an interview with Jamie Rubin, the former assistant secretary of state in the Clinton administration, Zahn prefaced her question to Rubin about the Iraqi reaction to Powell's presentation as follows: "I wanted to ask your opinion of your reaction to what you heard from Mohammed Aldouri" who we just heard "refute Secretary of State Powell's speech, basically phrase by phrase. You've got to understand that most Americans watching this were either probably laughing out loud or got sick to their stomach. Which was it for you?"[51] In framing the issue this way, Zahn fell into the predictable pattern of criticizing "other" officials while giving a free pass to Powell. Indeed, Zahn's comments served to reinforce the notion (however dubious) that Powell's credentials and the information he presented were indisputable. It also reinscribed the "us versus them" mentality that had been propagated by Bush—i.e., either you believe Powell or you make our stomachs turn.[52] For the most part, the bulk of television coverage after Powell's presentation concerned itself not with the authenticity of the claims made but rather with questions of whether Powell had been *convincing* in his *performance*.

The mainstream press also exhibited the same type of unqualified acceptance of Powell's presentation. A *New York Times* editorial published the day after Powell's appearance before the UN Security Council suggested that he had presented the "most powerful case to date that Saddam Hussein" was defying international law by failing to disarm. A piece by Jennifer Harper in the *Washington Times* chimed in by approvingly citing numerous columnists, political pundits and editorials which suggested that Powell had made his case. For example, Harper referred to the *Los Angeles Times* which claimed that Powell's speech "methodically demonstrated why Iraqi dictator Saddam Hussein remains dangerous to his own people, Iraq's neighbors and potentially, the Western world." A *New York Daily News* editorial declaring the "Powell proved beyond any doubt that Iraq still possesses and continues to develop illegal weapons of mass destruction" was also quoted as was *Washington Post* columnist Richard Cohen who called the speech "a winning hand for Powell" and who sarcastically added that "only a fool—or a Frenchman" would doubt that Iraq retains its weapons. The *Washing-*

ton Times ran a front-page headline that screamed "Classified Data Make Case; Communications Intercepts, Satellite Photos Disclosed." In the story, Bill Gertz asserted that U.S. intelligence intercepts demonstrated "Iraq's efforts to hide banned weapons from the United Nations" and claimed that Powell, "in an extraordinary public display of intelligence data" had shown "Iraq's support for al Qaeda terrorists." The rest of the article, typical of most mainstream media reportage of Powell's presentation, read as if it had been penned by the White House itself.

In three separate articles on the matter, *USA Today* basically validated Powell's and the administrations position. In an article entitled "Powell shares new evidence; Tells UN that Iraq is building bombs, harboring al-Qaeda," Bill Nichols claimed that Powell "forcefully laid out newly declassified evidence of Iraq's efforts to develop and conceal chemical, biological and nuclear weapons, as well as new signs that an al-Queda terrorist cell was set up in Baghdad last year." Nichols went on to refer to Powell's presentation as "dramatic," "comprehensive" and bristling with "new evidence." In an editorial, the paper suggested that Powell's UN address gave "reluctant countries sound reasons to ally with U.S." and suggested that Powell had "delivered" in providing the world with "compelling evidence" and "then some." It was suggested that Powell's "80-minute address was the kind of presentation much of the world has wanted to hear to quell widespread fears that the U.S. will start an unjustified war." Yet a third article, by Barbara Slavin and John Diamond, "Case is stronger when 'biggest dove' makes it; Powell tells UN he's convinced—so the world should be too" maintained that Powell's presentation was "detailed and relentless." The underlying theme was that if a "reluctant warrior" like Powell was convinced of Iraq's misdeeds, then so should everyone. In presenting Powell as a moderate or a "dove" (which isn't saying much given the hard-right makeup of the Bush administration), the media failed to contextualize Powell's actual position. For example, in December 1968 while serving as an Army major assigned to the Americal Division headquarters in Vietnam, Powell received orders to investigate a letter sent by a soldier that claimed U.S. troops were shooting Vietnamese civilians recklessly and indiscriminately as well as torturing prisoners. Powell responded by penning a dismissive memo claiming that relations between the Vietnamese people and American soldiers were "excellent." By then, of course, the Americal Division had been responsible for some of the most odious atrocities of the Vietnam war, including the My Lai massacre.[53] It was also Powell who (at a press briefing shortly after the conclusion of the 1991 Gulf War) when asked his assessment of the number of Iraqi soldiers and civilians killed, responded as follows: "It's really not a number I'm terribly interested in." As Norman Solomon[54] has aptly noted, Powell "owes much of his touted credibility to the fact that he's functioning inside a media bubble that protects him from direct challenge" and that a "tacit erasure of inconvenient history—including his own—is integral to the warm relationship between Powell and the U.S. news media."[55]

Of course, it goes well beyond this since much of what Powell presented to the UN Security Council was based on flawed intelligence reports, misleading evidence, a plagiarized British government document, and in some cases, outright fabrications.[56] In retrospect, Powell's presentation and the subsequent hysteria incited by various administration representatives about Iraq's imminent threat provide an instructive parable about how so-called intelligence reports could be contorted and spun to fulfill a particular political agenda.[57] But none of that seemed to matter to the media lapdogs who breathlessly propped Powell up as the beacon of truth and integrity and who continued to beat the war drum. In what epitomizes the proverbial "too little, too late" a recent article (published after the 'official' conclusion of war) in *Editor & Publisher* asked "Was Press Asleep on Pre-War WMD Issue?"[58] By contrast, alternative media watchdogs had already come to the conclusion that the mainstream media were sleepwalking through a pre-war daze and marching in step with the administration's drive to war. In a two-week study which examined media coverage from January 30, 2003 to February 12, 2003 (basically one week before and after Powell made his 'case' to the UN), *FAIR* found that a whopping 76% of the guests featured on ABC, CBS, NBC, and PBS[59] were either current or former government or military officials who fully supported the war effort.[60] According to the same report, anti-war voices accounted for less than one percent of the views included. At a time when a substantive, meaningful debate on the potential for war was needed, nothing of the kind was offered on the news shows of the major networks.

In the days following Powell's appearance before the UN, polls showed opposition to a pre-emptive war was dissolving. At that juncture, seventy percent of Americans believed that Iraq had chemical and biological weapons and sixty percent thought that Hussein was developing nuclear weapons. Other polls suggested that more than half of Americans actually believed Saddam Hussein had a hand in the 9/11 terror attacks. The public was being prepared for war—truth be damned—and the media were dutifully serving as stenographers for the Bush team's propaganda machine.

Shocking and Awful War Coverage

The lack of attention accorded to questionable intelligence presented by Powell was astonishing but not necessarily surprising since the media seemed anxious to 'get the war on.' After Powell's presentation, the media clock began ticking as various pundits and commentators speculated about how long it would be before the official declaration of war was announced. That only intensified after Mr. Bush declared—just a day after Powell's presentation—that the "game was over." In a televised statement from the White House, Bush echoed many of the charges made by Powell linking Iraq to terrorist groups and suggesting that Hussein possessed weapons of mass destruction. The fact that such claims were bogus didn't seem to bother the mainstream media which obediently and repeatedly reported them as facts. On February 8, in his weekly radio address, Bush stated that "We have sources that tell us that Saddam Hussein recently authorized Iraqi field commanders to use chemical weapons—the very weapons the dictator tells us he does not have." His remarks headlined many media reports and were not subject to much scrutiny. In his final prewar ultimatum on March 17, 2003, Bush declared the following: "Intelligence gathered by this and other governments leaves no doubt that the Iraq regime continues to possess and conceal some of the most lethal weapons ever devised." "No doubt"—Bush's choice of words, implied that there was no ambiguity about the matter. Of course, it has since been revealed that there was considerable doubt—but again, the media were not inclined to investigate the allegations at the time for they had been consumed with when the war would likely start.

In the days following Bush's ultimatum, the networks were awash with current and former military personnel discussing military strategy, weapons and technology—merely the latest example of the expert-on-retainer trend in television news. According to one critical observer, these "military experts—and the TV networks that hire them—see their jobs as providing specialized knowledge about strategy, weapons and tactics that most journalists don't have."[61] Nonetheless, what these sources inevitably contributed to was grossly skewed and biased coverage—coverage that was predominantly enthralled with military prowess and unthinking patriotic claptrap. Major news networks—particularly cable networks—hewed closely to the Pentagon party line, providing a seemingly endless array of gung-ho retired generals and "official" spokespersons who readily adopted the official mantra. As Rendell and Broughel revealed in their three-week study of media coverage (from March 20, 2003 to April 9, 2003), "official voices"

—namely U.S. government and military, past and present—dominated TV news-casts and effectively 'squelched dissent.'[62] The authors of the study concluded that democracy was poorly served by the war coverage.[63]

Of course, the main event—shock and awe—was hotly anticipated. For days, media pundits waited with baited breath and wagging tongues for the onset of the bombing campaign which American Defense Secretary Donald Rumsfeld had promised would be of a force and a scope and a scale that went beyond anything human beings had witnessed before. And the military made sure that the public would get "good" coverage through the use of "embedded" (or what some have mockingly called "in bed") reporters and high-tech equipment. Of course, "Opera-tion Iraqi Freedom" was not the first war orchestrated for television; that distinc-tion belongs, arguably, to the first Persian Gulf War. Yet the latest military forays (including those in Afghanistan) reveal the increasing media savvy of government administrations who have learned to make "ideological warfare as important to its operations as military and economic warfare."[64] Their preferred site for such ideo-logical warfare is undoubtedly television, and more specifically cable television which generally served as an echo chamber for "official" views and which then as-sumed a stance of patriotic cheerleading once the bombs started to fall in Iraq.[65]

The "embed" strategy itself was developed by Assistant Defense Secretary Victoria Clarke[66] and heralded as a new era of military openness. What it actually represented was quite the opposite—ultimate control over media reportage dis-guised as an unprecedented willingness to bring the "true" face of war to the masses. After being confined to press pools with restrictive censorship in the 1991 Gulf War, media organizations seemed positively giddy about the embedded sys-tem and as Andersen points out, "the military did not hide its desire to shape posi-tive coverage, as evidenced by its hiring of a Hollywood set designer to create a media-friendly backdrop for official briefings in Qatar."[67] CNN analyst and retired General Wesley Clark admitted that "restricting the press during the 1991 Gulf War was a 'huge mistake.' "[68] As such, the military well understood the need to enlist media personnel in their efforts to present an acceptable portrait of war to the American public and the mainstream media dutifully obliged. By making journalists part of the military 'team,' military officials were much better able to control the flow of information while concomitantly buttressing their alleged commitment to "transparency."

Reporters, photographers and camera crews were hand-picked, trained in military discipline and then assigned to front-line units. However, in order to be on the front-lines, journalists were required to sign a contract with the military agreeing to a 50-point program about what they could and could not report on. In short, they were instructed to follow 'guidelines' that would virtually eliminate coverage damaging to the war effort. Embedded reporters were required to follow "rules"—for example, the reporters could not travel independently which would make it almost impossible to report independently. All interviews had to be on the record and officers were empowered to censor copy and temporarily restrict electronic transmissions for "operational security" purposes. Official censorship of the media was, of course, not limited to the Iraqi battlefield. Once the reports were sent to the U.S., there were additional filters they had to go through. For example, on January 27, 2003, CNN released a document entitled, "Reminder of Script Approval Policy" which required that reporters send copies of their material to official corporate media editors to ensure that they were suitably "balanced" before "approval" and "authorization" would be granted. No indication of what constituted balance was presumably given; nor was any explanation given as to who would grant approval and authorization. Given that CNN admitted after the 1991 Gulf War that it had allowed Pentagon 'trainees' into the Atlanta news facilities, one has to wonder.[69] CNN was not alone in dictating such draconian restrictions on reporting as most all television networks and print media outlets were on-board and in bed with the Pentagon spin.

In the first two days of wall-to-wall television coverage, some U.S. reporters seemed more hawkish than the generals who were serving as "expert" sources in their anticipation of "shock and awe" and once the show began some on-air reporters "appeared jubilant—as if they were watching a fireworks display and not weapons that kill people."[70] Indeed, once the bombs started falling, television broadcasts were highly dramatic and riveting. On CNN, loud explosions and spectacular displays resembling high-tech fireworks exhibitions were interspersed with audible "oohs" and "aahs" and excited gasps. The images that flashed across the screen "merged cinematic references with reality-style camera perspectives."[71] In some regards, the coverage served to sate the public love affair with reality television. As Richard Goldstein aptly noted, the media-military complex actually helped to create a new genre with its war coverage: hyper-reality TV.

> There's more to the collusion between the networks and the Pentagon than ideology. Both parties have an interest in creating a drama, one that draws viewers into a web of associations, producing thrills, chills, and secret delight. These feelings are heightened by the belief that they con-

vey the real meaning of actual events...Hyper-reality is a fiction that presents itself as fact.[72]

Television also presented "Operation Iraqi Freedom" as entertainment, complete with dramatic titles, graphics, and theme music. The mainstream media also tended to use the Manichean codes of popular culture in presenting the 'battle' as one between good and evil—hence echoing the puerile language deployed by Bush and the administration in the run-up to war. Jensen argues that in adopting the phrase "Operation Iraqi Freedom," the media lent credence to Administration claims about the motives for war.[73] Anchors, correspondents, so-called experts and embedded reporters coded the drama of the war in ways that were sympathetic to the Bush administration and the Pentagon. Editorial voice-overs legitimated the carnage wrought as a regrettable but necessary price of 'freedom' and 'liberation.' The television 'hosts' of the Shock and Awe show assured their audiences that the strikes were 'strategic' as they reveled in the technological marvels they were witnessing. They further guaranteed the public that "collateral damage" (i.e., dead bodies) would likely be minimal —once again parroting the official White House talking points. In short, "shock and awe" was depicted in sanitary terms by military and media pundits who claimed that the accuracy of laser-guided "smart bombs" would make it possible to "decapitate" the Iraqi regime and military while leaving the country's infrastructure largely intact and limiting the number of civilian casualties.[74] Audiences were being directed to worship the Pentagon's proficiency, its war machines and its tactical maneuvers. And on some networks, namely Fox and MSNBC, a sycophantic patriotism was clearly on display.[75] Goldsborough has suggested that many Americans supported the Iraq war because they didn't know what was really going on.

> For the most part, U.S news organization gave Americans the war they thought Americans wanted to see. Fake war. Thomas Kinkade war, prettified, romanticized, glorified war. Americans love blood and guts in their movies, but can't stomach the real stuff in their living rooms. Foreign viewers get reality. For squeamish Americans, television self-censors.[76]

In the subsequent weeks of combat most of the reports from embedded journalists were human interest narratives about the troops, stories about the technology that was being used by the embedded reporters themselves, boosterish descriptions of the military weaponry and advances. Given the close quarters and the fact that the embedded reporters were eating, sleeping and traveling with the troops (not to mention that they were wearing essentially the same equipment which made them almost indistinguishable from the soldiers they accompanied) on a scale unprecedented in the annals of battlefield coverage, it is not surprising that the reporters started to bond with the troops as evidenced by their invocation of "we" as though the reporters and the troops were "one." One of the most strik-ing examples of this tendency came from CNN reporter Walter Rodgers who had been attached to the U.S. Army's Seventh Cavalry. In a dialogue with veteran cor-respondent Christiane Amanpour, Rogers excitedly reported that he was moving inside "a huge wave of steel." He added that the experience was akin to "galloping inside the belly of a dragon," and he approvingly quoted the commander of the brigade who had told him, "If we meet Iraqis along the way, we'll simply kill them, we'll find the enemy and grab him by the nose." Rodgers reporting was typical of the embedded journalists who, far from supplying 'objective' accounts, spun their narratives from the vantage point of the U.S. troops—which of course, had been the Pentagon's intent all along. It should come as no surprise then that military officials articulated their pleasure[77] with the reportage provided by the embedded journalists for as Jensen maintains, "the embedded system served the Pentagon well as propaganda. It conveyed the Pentagon's message, it touted the technological prowess of the U.S. military, and it fed the home audience a con-stant diet of U.S. bravery."[78]

Weapons of Mass Deception, or, the Military Goes 'Hollywood'

In a prescient column penned on the eve of war, Robert Fisk speculated on what the content of war coverage would likely entail. He suggested that journalists would likely dress up in military costumes for their theatrical performances on television; that the media would depict that U.S. and British troops as liberators and offer images that buttressed such claims; that the media would likely focus on torture chambers used during Saddam's brutal reign; that dramatic displays of heroism and "victory" would be offered and that in the hunt for weapons of mass destruction, "any old rocket" would suffice to make headlines. He further claimed that while Bush and Blair were boasting to the world about the great lib-eration, the real story would begin to emerge—anarchy, chaos and a real resis-tance to Western occupation— which would be presented as though it had not been predicted. Remarkably, but not surprisingly, the stenographic media fol-lowed the anticipated script.[79]

As previously mentioned, journalists were barely indistinguishable from the soldiers clad as they were in camouflage, masks and other military paraphernalia. The Jessica Lynch "rescue" and the so-called "fall of Baghdad" provided the heroic tales and imagery of bravery and triumph while President Bush's May 1st *Top Gun*-esque landing on the USS was one of the slickest propaganda productions ever executed. As is well known now, the saga of "Saving Private Lynch" was a well-choreographed "rescue" operation that was carefully crafted by the U.S. military propaganda machinery. Initial reports had suggested that Lynch's convoy was ambushed in the southern Iraqi city of Nasiriya and that Lynch had been shot and stabbed while fighting off Iraqi forces. According to the official, approved narrative she had also been tied up, taken to a hospital in Nasiriyah and then beaten by an Iraqi officer. A week later U.S. special forces allegedly freed her in a daring, surprise raid. Despite resistance from her guards, they broke into the hospital, rescued Lynch and flew her off to Kuwait. That very evening, in an address from the White House, Bush announced her rescue to the nation. Even before any details of the "rescue" account could be confirmed, the media painted the story in vivid, dramatic hues. Hart notes that the *Washington Post* reported that Lynch was "firing her weapon until she ran out of ammunition" before her capture (a claim that was patently false). *People* magazine cited a "Capital Hill source" who had presumably told the media outlet that "some of her wounds were the result of extensive torture." Other media sources depicted the raid to 'save' Lynch as one carried out in a "blaze of gunfire" that heralded a "triumphant moment for U.S. forces."[80] CNN reported that U.S. forces had made a "forced entry into the hospital." Eight days later, the Pentagon supplied the news media with a video made during the mission—the action scenes had Hollywood written all over them. In fact, the "rescue" was filmed on a night-vision camera by a former assistant of director Ridley Scott, who had worked on the film *Black Hawk Down*. The grainy footage of Lynch being carried out of the Iraqi hospital and onto a waiting Black Hawk helicopter was played over and over again and on Fox News, Lynch was quickly dubbed "America's hero."

Subsequently, the Lynch drama was revealed for what it was—fiction. Lynch's injuries—a fractured arm and leg and a dislocated ankle—were sustained due to an accident in the lorry in which she had traveled and not bullet fire. She was not maltreated at the hospital and her rescuers did not encounter any resistance at the hospital. Rather, the rescue was, according to the BBC "one of the most stunning pieces of news management ever conceived." And yet that did not deter media outlets from the crude Fox News Network to the august *New York Times* and *Washington Post* from giving her "homecoming" in late July of 2003 front-page prominence. Despite the overwhelming evidence about the Pentagon's role in choreographing the Lynch rescue, the *Times* saw fit to report the Pentagon's denial of "embellishing" while claiming that "few people seemed to care about the controversy."[81] Inside America's Matrix the image, rather than the truth, matters; "facts have lost value" and "logic rarely applies."[82]

If the Lynch 'rescue' supplied the grandiose images of America's heroism and patriotism, the downed statue of the despotic Hussein became the emblem of American triumph in Iraq. But the so-called "fall of Baghdad" was merely another form of stage-managed propaganda. On the morning of April 9th, 2003, audiences around the world were witnesses to the stirring image of Saddam's statue being toppled in Baghdad's Firdos Square. At one point, a Marine draped an American flag over the statue's face. The flag, which had been flying over the Pentagon at the time of the September 11 attacks, was presumably given to the Marines by the Defense Department (the Pentagon claimed that was a coincidence!). Symbolically it served to reinforce the administration's 'Big Lie,' namely that Saddam Hussein had somehow been involved in the 9/11 atrocities. Of course, the flag was later replaced by an old (not to mention curious) pre-Gulf War-era Iraqi one. The media literally blared the story all day long, repeatedly showing the falling statue and "jubilant" throngs of Iraqis doubtlessly engaged in a spontaneous outpouring of pro-American, anti-Saddam sentiment. The following day, the same iconic image was captured on the front page of newspapers all over the world. *USA Today* proclaimed that the pictures said something about Americans, their "can-do spirit" and their willingness to lend a hand. The *Washington Post* reported that "Iraqis Celebrate in Baghdad." The headline in the *New York Times* proclaimed "Jubilant Iraqis Swarm the Streets of Capital" while the *Boston Globe* suggested that "It Was Liberation Day in Baghdad." Donald Rumsfeld gushed emotionally to television reporters saying that "Watching them, one cannot help but think of the fall of the Berlin Wall and the collapse of the Iron Curtain." In a similar vein, NBC's Tom Brokaw compared the event to the tumbling statues of Lenin in the former Soviet Union. On Fox News Channel (arguably the most biased pro-war network in existence) the *Washington Post*'s Ceci Connelly also echoed Rumsfeld and pontificated that the images from Baghdad projected "pure emotional expression" and that they were "not choreographed, not stage-managed" but rather were "really breathtaking."[83] The pictures appeared to confirm what Washington and pro-war pundits had been saying for months—that Iraqis would greet troops as liberators.

As it turns out, the pictures were part of a tacky media/photo-op staged "by the U.S. military for the benefit of cameramen staying across the street at Baghdad's Palestine Hotel."[84] First, the tight camera angles used were quite deceiving since they gave the impression that the crowd was massive. It was not. Wide an-gled shots revealed that the crowd was quite sparse (approximately 150 people) and heavily populated with Army and media personnel. Furthermore, the joyous, statue-bashing Iraqis were actually militiamen of the Iraqi National Congress, the anti-Hussein outfit led by convicted criminal Ahmed Chalabi—an exile-émigré whom Donald Rumsfeld had hoped would lead postwar Iraq. Rall further claims that the Iraqi National Congress "was flown into Iraq by the Pentagon over CIA and State Department protests."[85] Norman Solomon aptly labeled the episode "the mother of all photo ops" and suggested that the obsessive focus on the toppling statue provided yet another example of the "tremendously subjective character of the media coverage" of the war. "What was notable," he added, was "how few Iraqis were there."[86] The staged Saddam statue event was not only intended to provide Americans with fuzzy feel-good images of their troops being greeted as liberators, it was also meant to provide the administration fodder for Bush's re-election campaign and "CNN, MSNBC and Fox swallowed it whole."[87]

In yet another egregious example of pure propaganda spectacle reminiscent of Leni Riefenstahl's *Triumph of the Will*, Bush's handlers produced an elaborate backdrop for the President to declare the "official" end of the Iraq war. Dressed in a flight suit, Bush (in his role as co-pilot) made a tailhook landing from a vintage Navy aircraft (painted with Navy One and George W. Bush, Commander-in-Chief 'logos') onto the *USS Abraham Lincoln* on May 1, 2003. Bush emerged from the aircraft, helmet in hand and swaggered across the flight deck, amidst a crowd of cheering officers and sailors who had been lined up like an assembly of tin sol-diers. In front of a colossal banner proclaiming "Mission Accomplished," Bush de-livered a speech asserting that the "battle of Iraq" had been a "victory" in the ongoing "war on terror." It was, without a doubt, a made-for-television moment and an obedient media corps ate it up.[88] While some journalists were quick to point out that the event was carefully staged, U.S. television coverage ran the gamut from respectful to gushing. As Canadian journalist Linda McQuaig noted, "only an administration supremely confident of the media's docility would have risked staging an event like that."[89] Indeed, the Bush administration seemed so se-cure about that control that it dared dress Bush up in a Top Gun outfit and the media dutifully saluted. Virtually every newspaper in the United States ran a front page feature story, accompanied by a photo of Bush doing his best Tom Cruise impersonation. Television news and cable media outlets ran the scenes from the *Lincoln* ad nauseum. The fact that Bush had been AWOL for more than a year of the National Guard service that saved him from being sent to Vietnam, didn't seem to register with most media pundits who repeatedly emphasized his (questionable) heyday as a pilot.[90] CNN heralded the landing as "historic," emphasizing that previous presidents had utilized helicopters. In an exchange with Paula Zahn, CNN Senior White House Correspondent Jim King was practically giddy while announcing that "You see history being made" here. "Mr. Bush landing on a Navy jet. The first president to land on a carrier the hard way...Mr. Bush landing with the tailhook approach."[91] Of course, the jet flight was totally unnecessary. While the White House first claimed that the dramatic jet landing was needed because the ship would be hundreds of miles out to sea and therefore unreachable by helicopter, the USS Abraham Lincoln (which had been at sea for ten months) was within helicopter range but that didn't "offer the exciting visuals of a carrier landing and Bush in a flight suit."[92] As a result, the campaign stunt required that the ship slow its pace and circle idly in the Pacific Ocean to guarantee favorable camera angles of the sea instead of the San Diego coastline which was 30 miles away. On MSNBC's Hardball, Chris Matthews commented on Bush's manliness and macho appearance compared to Democratic presidential candidates, including Vietnam veteran Senator John Kerry who had earned a Silver Star for his service in that war. While media parrots were back-slapping Bush for his rugged manliness, Iraq was being looted and chaos reigned but the Hollywood ethos remained intact in the images beamed to the masses.

When it came to the hunt for the elusive weapons of mass destruction, the media seemed more than willing to feed at the trough of administration propaganda and dutifully report Washington's slant as 'truth.' By the time the war had begun in Iraq mainstream media had already been "conditioned to believe, almost as an article of faith, that Saddam Hussein's Iraq was bulging with chemical and biological weapons."[93] Robert Fisk's aforementioned prediction that any old rocket would do to make headlines in the American media was not only on the mark but understated when one evaluates the media coverage. Ackerman provided a detailed account of how the search for weapons of mass destruction had been reported noting that on several occasions, the simple discovery of a stash of conventional arms was loudly touted as a major finding. Such proclamations were typically accompanied by the predictable triumphalism of the pro-war punditry "only to be deflated inconspicuously, and in a lower tone of voice, until the next false alarm was sounded."[94] Citing several examples derived from both broadcast media and the mainstream press, Ackerman illustrates a pattern of misrepresentation wherein journalists "absorbed their aura of certainty" (about the existence of WMD's) from a battery of "'independent' weapons specialists who repeated the mantra of Iraqi concealment over and over." Journalists, in turn, used these 'experts' as outside sources to evaluate the administration's claims. Yet, often "these sources were simply repeating what they heard from U.S. officials, forming an endless loop of self-reinforcing scare- mongering."[95] Parry also notes that for its part, the "U.S. news media—from Fox News to the *New York Times*—repeatedly trumpeted supposed weapons discoveries, only to play down later stories that the original reports were bogus."[96]

By the beginning of May, 2003 when it was becoming increasingly clear that no weapons of mass destruction were likely to be found, the administration changed course on several levels. First, there was the attempt to foreground evidence of Hussein's brutal regime—the so-called torture chambers and mass graves, etc. Then there was the attempt to suggest that the regime change was based on the administration's desire to rid the world of dictators and bring democracy to the region. While there can be doubt that Hussein was a tyrannical leader, the administration's stance on such issues are quite hypocritical. After all, if there was any real concern for challenging despotism, Saudi Arabia (and indeed several other American 'allies') would certainly have to be a candidate for regime change. Subsequently, the official line emphasized "patience"; that is, that sufficient time would be needed to find the 'cache' of weapons. The administration had, of course, not accorded the luxury of time to UN weapons inspectors. On the other hand, some (including Bush himself) began to refer to evidence of a weapons *program*—a far cry from the imminent threat line propagated by the administration prior to the war. As the weeks and months continued to pass, it became increasingly clear that the media obediently served the White House well in helping to manufacture consent for a war on Iraq based on false pretenses. To better understand why the coverage of the recent Iraq war represents "one of the lowest points in U.S. media history,"[97] it is useful to turn our attention to Herman and Chomsky's "propaganda model."

Revisiting the Propaganda Model

In their preface to *Manufacturing Consent*, Herman and Chomsky do not claim that the media function only to circulate propaganda, but they do state that they believe "the propaganda function to be a very important aspect of their overall service."[98] Contrary to the democratic postulate that "the media are independent and committed to discovering and reporting the truth, and that they do not merely reflect the world as powerful groups wish it to be perceived," the propaganda model reveals how the powerful are able (i) "to fix the premises of discourse," (ii) decide "what the general populace is allowed to see, hear, and think about" and (iii) shape/manage public opinion by regular propaganda campaigns.[99] In their propaganda model, Herman and Chomsky outline the influence of five filters: (i) the size, concentrated ownership and profit orientation of the dominant mass media; (ii) advertising as the primary source of income for the mass media; (iii) the reliance of the media on "experts" and "official" sources; (iv) 'flak' as a means of disciplining the media; and (v) 'anti-communism' as a national religion and control mechanism.

As should be abundantly clear from the many examples examined above as well as the various studies cited, the mainstream media relied overwhelmingly on military and government "officials" and "sources" that were clearly pro-war. While there were instances of 'debate,' such disagreements tended to revolve around questions of military strategy and tactical minutiae. In short, the bounds of the expressible were clearly delineated and dissenting voices were effectively squelched. With respect to the anti-communism filter, Herman and Chomsky have both suggested that given the changed political landscape, the label anti-communism may not be as suitable as it was when they first penned their landmark text. However, Chomsky has recently argued that in the post-Cold War world, anti-communism has been replaced with a dichotomy of "otherness." According to Chomsky, this dichotomy functions to impress upon people that "grave enemies" are lurking about, waiting to attack, and that they should seek shelter under the rubric of domestic power. Such tactics serve to frighten people in order to distract them from what is really happening to them. This fearmongering strategy was clearly deployed by the Bush administration repeatedly. Bush himself (no doubt with help from his handlers) has mastered the art of scaring "the people" into submission. Bush's most frequently used linguistic technique is the "negative framework" which represents a pessimistic image of the world. One observer claims that,

> Bush creates and maintains negative frameworks in his listeners' minds with a number of linguistic techniques borrowed from advertising and hypnosis to instill the image of a dark and evil world around us. Catastrophic words and phrases are repeatedly drilled into the listener's head until...it appears pointless to do anything other than cower.[100]

By instilling such fear in the populace, Bush has been able to advance a regressive domestic and social agenda which most Americans actually disagree with. But with most of the focus on the never-ending "war on terror," the media have failed to adequately explore the draconian measures being put in place and therefore have tacitly assisted the administration in this regard. Bush's domestic agenda, however, is actually a microcosm of what he and his administration are now promoting in Iraq—free market policies, privatization of virtually everything, and corporate rule in general. It is therefore necessary to take into account how the media are aiding and abetting such activities. To this end, the propaganda model's remaining three filters provide some insight.

Since the publication of *Manufacturing Consent*, there has been a marked increase in the degree of concentrated ownership of the media. The U.S. news media, in particular, have lost whatever diversity they could once boast and the ability to present different points of view has been all but stifled by media merger mania.[101] The corporations that dominate the media are, as Herman and Chomsky aptly note, in the business of making profits from selling advertising. This very structure narrows the scope of debate and lends itself to feel-good stories and images that are not intended to upset what Herman and Chomsky refer to as the "buying mood." Disgruntled and disgusted audiences do not make for happy consumers so it is no wonder that stories like the Jessica Lynch "rescue" and the "fall of Baghdad" were foregrounded while images of death and destruction were completely marginalized in the sanitized war coverage. As Eviatar has recently remarked, "good war news" sells better:

> Fox News, which kept an American flag on its screen throughout the war and adopted the military's propagandistic war slogan 'Operation Iraqi Freedom' as its won official news banner, was drawing more viewers…The fact is, Jessica Lynch as war hero sells…Almost thirty years ago Phillip Knightley chronicled in *The First Casualty* how journalists get duped into spreading the government's propaganda. At least during Vietnam, the media eventually grew skeptical. But in today's quick, high-tech wars, there's little time for the seeds of dissent to sprout…It's predictable that the war's architects would prefer that the public associate the war with the image of a valiant American heroine and the soldiers who risked their lives to save her. But it's disturbing that American media encourage it.[102]

Part of the growing uselessness of TV news, which mostly presents info-tainment, derives from economic pressures. As the distinction between informing and entertaining is increasingly blurred and the drive for large audiences and hence profits reigns supreme, gathering the news has become a matter of "getting the best live shots, telling a tidy and gratifying 'human' story, making the heroes look like heroes and the correspondents look like models."[103] Of course, it goes beyond this.

One of the most striking examples of the American media's close ties with the political and military establishment becomes evident if one examines the role of Clear Channel in vigorously boosting the war effort. Clear Channel Worldwide incorporated, which is head-quartered in San Antonio, is the single largest radio station owner in the United States. With over 1,200 stations, their monopoly accounts for 9% of the total market share, over half of the talk show radio-industry share, and 60% of the nation's rock-format stations. They are in 248 of the top 250 radio markets and dominate the audience share in 100 out of 112 major markets broadcasting the shows of far-right personalities like Rush Limbaugh and Dr. Laura. The multi-tentacled corporation also controls hundreds of concert venues.[104] In the wake of the September 11th attacks, Clear Channel issued a list of 150 'questionable' songs to their stations and affiliates with the "not-so-subtle hint that these were songs to be steered cleared of."[105] Many of the songs targeted had a clear pro-peace message.

In the run-up to war in Iraq, the conglomerate took a much more pro-active stance. Led predominantly by conservative Philadelphia talk show host, Glenn Beck, whose program is broadcast nationwide by Clear Channel, a series of pro-war political rallies were sponsored and supported by a number of the corporation's 1,200 local radio stations and openly promoted on the corporate website. While the stations that sponsored the rallies claimed that they were "pro-troops" and "non-political," the rallies served to promote jingoism and boost the Bush administration and its policies. Far from being "local" initiatives, the pro-war rallies were part of the agenda of Clear Channel's top executives, who just happen to have close ties to the Bush administration. Clear Channel's CEO, L. Lowry Mays, is a Texan and a generous donor to Republicans and especially George W. Bush. Lowry's sons Randall and Mark, as well as his wife Peggy are also prominent financial supporters of the Bush and the Republicans. The entire Mays clan has significant ties to both the Texas oil industry and the investment banking sector. Tom Hicks, who purchased the Texas Rangers from Bush in 1998 (netting the then-governor $15 million), serves as the acting vice chair of Clear Channel. After

Dixie Chick's lead singer Natalie Maines made a mild disparaging remark about George W. Bush to a London audience, Clear Channel stations played a pivotal role in demonizing the group (and removing their songs from play lists) in a McCarthyite witch-hunt. Landau argues that Clear Channel has sought to use its dominance of the radio airwaves to promote right-wing political ideology and the initiatives of the current Bush administration.

This tendency is, of course, part of a larger pattern/trend that has tilted most American media outlets even further to the right of the political spectrum. This has been enabled, in part, through various policies, most notably the Telecommunications Act of 1996 which allowed for greater concentration of media ownership. Indeed, prior to 1996, a media corporation could not own more that 40 stations. Since then, companies like Clear Channel have taken advantage of such deregulation to broaden the scope of their ideological influence. In addition, the right-wing "flak" machine has also played a considerable role in these developments. For years, dating back to the early 1970s, conservative thank tanks have promulgated the notion that the mainstream media are "liberal." This mantra, while far from reflecting media reality, has proven to be quite successful in its effect.[106] The pro-business right well understood that changing media discourse was a crucial part of "mainstreaming" right-wing ideas and through a well-organized, well-financed and fervent conservative coterie of activists they succeeded in doing so.[107] McChesney and Foster note that the ability of the right-wing campaign in "popularizing the view that the news media have a liberal bias has been accomplished to some extent by constant repetition without any significant countervailing position."[108] Additionally, the conservative campaign has meshed "comfortably with the commercial and political aspirations of media corporations."[109] Such developments have clearly influenced the behavior of the mainstream media in recent years and have generally contributed to the uber patriotism exhibited by some media outlets—Fox springs to mind.[110] However, what is far more insidious and disturbing is not necessarily *what* the media reported or *how* they reported events in the build-up to, and subsequent, war in Iraq but rather that which was virtually rendered invisible by the coverage. It is at this level where Herman and Chomsky's model is particularly insightful.

Herman and Chomsky note that the media tend to line up with the government on fundamental matters not because of any conspiracy or backroom deals —although such deals may be made as the aforementioned Clear Channel incident seems to suggest—but largely because the media themselves are huge corporations that share the same economic and fundamental interests with the corporate elite that essentially controls the U.S. government. As Herman and Chomsky have long contended, media corporations share members of the board of directors with a variety of other large corporations including banks, investment companies, technology companies and oil companies.[111] It is also imperative to note that the global media are, in many respects, the "new missionaries of corporate capitalism" since the commercial media system (dominated mainly by U.S. based transnational corporations) works to advance the cause of the global market and promote commercial values. The multibillion dollar media conglomerates are global in scope and reach. In order to secure profits and new markets, they often rely on the governments of their own countries to protect their interests domestically and internationally. Many of those companies have a stake in the "new Iraq" for as Chatterjee has recently noted, Iraq is a "corporate gold mine."[112] With the occupation of Iraq, U.S.-based media and telecommunications corporations are better positioned to dominate Middle East markets. Already, the Pentagon has awarded MCI, formerly known as WorldCom, a $45 million contract to build a wireless phone network in Iraq—this despite the fact that WorldCom perpetrated one of the biggest accounting frauds in American business history and that it has never previously built such a network. While both the Democratic and Republican parties have been the benefactors of Worldcom's financial largesse, its donations to Republican causes over the years have been massive.[113] Worldcom had been lobbying policymakers for an edge in the lucrative high-speed Internet market right up until its corporate scandal was made public. In June 2002, the company donated $100,000 to a Republican fundraiser featuring George W. Bush. Motorola, Inc., the world's second largest mobile telephone maker also received a contract worth as much as $25 million to set up a radio communications network for Iraqi security and coalition forces in Baghdad.

Other major benefactors of the war in Iraq include firms with close ties to the Bush administration.

Bechtel, one of the world's largest construction firms, was awarded a $680 million dollar reconstruction deal by the U.S. Agency for International Development (USAID) on April 17, 2003. According to the Center for Responsive Politics, Bechtel gave Republican candidates, including Bush, approximately $765,000 in PAC, soft money and individual campaign contributions between 1999 and 2002.[114] The Kellogg Brown & Root unit of Halliburton,[115] the oil services and construction firm headed by Dick Cheney from 1995 to 2000 before his bid for the vice-presidency, was hired to rebuild Iraq's infrastructure in a project worth at least $680 million but one that actually has a overall ceiling of $7 billion.[116] The secret deal was allegedly struck as early as November 2002—at a time when the administration was vehemently insisting that no decision to invade Iraq had been made.[117]

In a resolution (1483) adopted by the UN Security Council in May 2003, the United States secured corporate control over Iraqi resources (including and especially its oil) until at least 2007. Additionally, the resolution ended sanctions against Iraq and paved the way for the creation of a Development Fund for Iraq. Control over the fund rests in the hands of Paul Bremmer (whom some have referred to as the viceroy of Iraq) and will be overseen by a board of accountants including UN, World Bank and IMF representatives. Such developments lend credibility to Naomi Klein's assertion that what the "coalition" forces essentially did was "bomb" Iraq "into a blank slate" so that it could then be rebuilt "in the image that is exactly prescribed by the so-called Washington consensus and the International Monetary Fund and the World bank, where all of the state industries, including oil, are going to privatized."[118] Echoing Klein, Kretzman and Vallette maintain that the implementation of the Development Fund for Iraq has the "fingerprints of the global economic structural adjustment" program written all over it.[119] Of course, such 'programs' have been at the centre of worldwide protests carried out by "anti-corporate" globalization movement activists.

When such activists took to the streets chanting "no blood for oil" in global anti-war protests, they were generally dismissed. President Bush referred to tens of millions of people who took the streets on February 15, 2003 as a "focus group." The very notion that the war could have something to do with American oil and corporate interests was scoffed at. Before the war, Donald Rumsfeld repeatedly stated that any intervention in Iraq had "nothing to do with oil, literally nothing to do with oil."[120] And, of course, the entire administration from Bush, Powell, Cheney, Rice, and Rumsfeld on down all invoked the weapons of mass destruction and Iraq links with Al Qaeda. Given the present-day corporate looting taking place in Iraq, it would appear as though the protesters were right. Yet, what now appear to be the real reasons for going to war—Iraqi oil and the quest for American global corporate hegemony— rarely registered a blip on the mainstream media's radar screen in their build-up to, and coverage of, the war.

Prior to the war, however, many alternative media publications including the *Nation*, the *Progressive*, *In These Times*, *Z Magazine* (and countless articles on Znet), *Mother Jones* and numerous others were in fact carrying out in-depth reporting that clearly demonstrated that the motivation for war with Iraq had precious little to do with weapons of mass destruction and much more to do with control over oil and furthering the aims of American empire. Remarkably, their pre-war suspicions have been confirmed as none other than super-hawk Paul Wolfowitz has recently admitted that the war was fought predominantly for oil and that the decision to go to war with Iraq had virtually been made just days after the September 11, 2001 attacks. In early June, Wolfowitz was asked why there was such a discrepancy between the administration's treatment of Iraq and North Korea. Wolfowitz, who was addressing delegates at an Asian security summit in Singapore, responded as follows: "Let's look at it simply. The most important difference between North Korea and Iraq is that economically, we just had no choice in Iraq. The country swims on a sea of oil." Prior to that, a June 2nd report filed on ZNet pointed out that Wolfowitz had admitted that the Iraq war was planned just two days after 9/11.[121]

Before the war, however, there was little if no discussion about these "reasons" for a pre-emptive attack to be found in the mainstream media. The media provided no context for understanding the issues involved. There was almost nothing in the mainstream media about the nature of U.S. interests in oil production, the political economy of oil, the Bush family and their friends' interest in the oil resources of the region, the relations between U.S. oil companies and the governments of the region, and the fact that American corporations stood to make billions in the rebuilding of Iraq after the military bombed it to smithereens. There was also no discussion of the imperial ambitions of the Bush administration which has wholeheartedly put into practice the dictates of the 'Project For a New American Century' (see above).

This situation directly coincides with one of the most central presuppositions of the PM—namely that the elite, agenda-setting western media fulfill a propaganda function by adhering to an imperialist ideology and by legitimizing U.S. interventionist forays, thereby protecting the fifth freedom which, as Chomsky comments, is generally the freedom of capitalist corporations to rob, exploit, and rape the natural resources and people of the developing world. In the case of the war on Iraq, the media dutifully served as puppets in disseminating the carefully planned propaganda stunts of the Pentagon and the official talking points of the White House. But more important and far more egregious was the role they played in completing obfuscating from view the imperialist escapades of the current administration and the terror which has been unleashed on the Iraqi people under the guise of the "war on terror."

In a democracy the media should, ideally, serve the interests of the people, providing them with the information needed to participate meaningfully in decision making. As Chomsky has noted, "where there is even a pretense of democracy, communications are at its heart." In the current media climate, dominated as it is, by a few huge transnational corporations which stand to benefit from the increased spread of corporate globalization—by imperial means if necessary—democracy is ill served. Until the people "take back the media" from the iron grip of corporations, we would do well to heed Chomsky's advice—namely that citizens of democratic capitalist societies must undertake a course of intellectual self-defence in order to protect themselves from manipulation and mind control. At a time when corporate media mergers are thriving, when journalists are self-censoring themselves in the name of patriotism, and when the United States government seems determined to continue its imperial quest for global corporate hegemony, Herman and Chomsky's PM remains a powerful weapon in our arsenal as we struggle for the establishment of genuinely democratic institutions both at home and abroad.

NOTES

1. See Chomsky's *Necessary Illusions: Thought Control in Democratic Societies*, 1989.
2. See Herman (1998) and Klaehn (2002).
3. Herman, 1998, p. 194.
4. It is imperative to note that analyzing the massive media coverage of the war is a timely and overwhelming task and cannot be done adequately in the confines of a short article or chapter. Indeed, volumes will likely be written about the media's coverage of "Operation Iraqi Freedom" in the years to come. As such, I have been selective in what I have examined for the purposes of this chapter and have limited my analysis to some key events and issues.
5. For a more in-depth examination of the so-called transfer to full sovereignty, see Schwartz, 2004.
6. Scheer, 2003, p. 1
7. Wicker, 2003, p.1
8. As Hedges (2003:16) notes: "In wartime the press is always part of the problem...When the nation goes to war, the press goes to war with it. The blather on CNN or Fox or MSNBC is part of a long and sad tradition."
9. Douglas Kellner's (2001) *Grand Theft 2000: Media Spectacle and a Stolen Election* provides an excellent overview of the pro-Bush media bias that began to manifest itself during the presidential campaign. Others, including Susan Douglas (2000), have argued that the media essentially worked on a daily basis as a fifth column legitimizing Bush's candidacy. Large research studies including one conducted by the Pew Research Center and the Project for Excellence in Journalism found that media coverage during the race for the White House was heavily skewed, favorably, towards Bush while Gore received the worst of negative media coverage. See also Cohen, 2001 and Hart & Naureckas, 2001. In addition, the mainstream media dutifully side-stepped Bush family financial scandals, George W. Bush's disastrous and reprehensible business career, his dubious service in the military and his obvious lack of qualifications for the presidency (cf. Ivins, 2000; Kellner, 2003; Miller, 2002).
10. Additionally, Bush was unscathed by the historical corporate scandals that emerged around Enron and other companies with 'fuzzy' accounting practices despite the fact that Bush, Cheney and other members of his administration had close ties to the corporate scandals. For more discussion on the shameless coddling of Bush by the mainstream media on these and related issues, see Kellner 2003.

11. See Coen, 2001.

12. See also Hart and Ackerman, 2001; Rendell, 2001.

13. See Schechter, 2003, p.1.

14. See Parry, 2003, p.3.

15. According to Bleifuss (2003: 12) citing reports in the *Asia Times*, members of the Bush administration have been meeting with the Taliban in Pakistan in an effort to bring them back into the fold of the Afghan government. This is largely because Afghanistan is increasingly becoming ungovernable beyond Kabul where a U.S.-backed regime is in power. There is also concern about the large number of former Afghan Communists who have returned 'home' since the fall of the Taliban. Apparently, the wicked 'Taliban' so denounced and decried by Bush and his minions (and most Americans) is looking attractive now. So much for liberating the Afghanis!

16. Of the three nations named in the 'axis of evil,' Iraq was, of course, the weakest and hence easiest target. Years of sanctions and bombings had decimated the region and the Iraqi 'military' had been further emasculated (even though it never posed much of a 'challenge' in 1991). But a decisive victory was viewed as central by the Bush administration. To this end and in order to elevate what most knew would be an easy 'military' victory in Iraq to dramatic proportions, the Bush administration constructed a huge propaganda offensive designed to 1) portray Iraq as an imminent threat (which it never was); 2) celebrate U.S. military might as though victory itself had been in doubt presumably because of those (yet unearthed) biological and chemical weapons; and 3) valorize the president as a courageous leader who acted with "resolve" and "determination" to keep the "homeland" safe. As one can clearly see now that the war has "officially" ended, the propaganda script was followed to the letter. What was not predicted by the insolent war-mongers of the Bush administration was what would happen after the predictable 'military' victory and show of force in Iraq. With that region in chaos and troops serving as target practice, the administration seems intent on diverting attention to another region of the world just as they did after Afghanistan. Undoubtedly, the media will follow their lead.

17. See (www.newamericancentury.org)

18. It should also be noted that Mark Gerson—the aforementioned Bush speechwriter—is also listed on the website as one of PNAC's project directors.

19. Most of the strategy delineated in the report was echoed in Bush's September 2002 National Security Strategy document—otherwise known as the Bush Doctrine.

20. See Gowans, 2003, p.1.

21. The statement on Iraq read as follows: We agree with Secretary of State Powell's recent statement that Saddam Hussein "is one of the leading terrorists on the face of the Earth..." It may be that the Iraqi government provided assistance in some form to the recent attack on the United States. But even if evidence does not link Iraq directly to the attack, any strategy aiming the eradication of terrorism and its sponsors must include a determined effort to remove Saddam Hussein from power in Iraq. Failure to undertake such an effort will constitute an early and perhaps decisive surrender in the war on international terrorism. The United States must therefore provide full military and financial support to the Iraqi opposition. American military force should be used to provide a 'safe zone' in Iraq from which the opposition can operate. And American forces must be prepared to back up our commitment to the Iraqi opposition by all necessary means (http://www.newamericancentury.org/Bushletter.htm).

22. Dan Rather stated the following on the David Letterman show on September 18, 2001: "George Bush is the president, he makes the decisions, and, you know, as just one American, whenever he wants me to line up, just tell me where."

23. For an analysis of the AEI, see Scatamburlo, 1998.

24. CNN Live Event/Special, Jan. 29, 2002 transcript, http://www.cnn.com/TRANSCRIPTS/0201/29/se.03.html.

25. Included in the list of investors in Arbusto—George W. Bush's initial company that went bust—were members of the bin Laden family. Additionally, as has been widely reported (but

certainly not in the mainstream media) the bin Laden family had been an investor in the Carlyle investment group—in which both James Baker and George Sr. are major partners. See for example, the documents assembled at www.bushwatch.com and Shorrock, 2002 for a revealing expose of Carlyle. Of course, the Bush-bin Laden family connections have not been substantively explored by the media.

26. For an exhaustive accounting of Bush's real 'character,' see Kellner, 2003.

27. See Kellner, 2003, p.210.

28. The IAEA did issue a report, in 1998, but the report made no such assertion. In fact, the IAEA clearly stated that it found no indication of Iraq having achieved its program goal of producing nuclear weapons. The report did say that Iraq had been six to twenty-four months away from nuclear capability before the 1991 Gulf War.

29. MacArthur, 2003.

30. Eleven months after this chapter was written, the *New York Times* (on May 26, 2004) reassessed its pre-Iraq war coverage, particularly its coverage of weapons of mass destruction. In an "Editor's Note," the influential newspaper admitted a lack of rigor in its reporting on WMD claims.

31. The exchange went something like this: Russert: "Aluminum tubes." Cheney: "Specifically aluminum tubes." "There's a story in *The New York Times* this morning and I want to attribute the *Times*."

32. Miller has recently come under heavy criticism for her many bogus reports based on unsupported and undocumented assertions. In fact, the aforementioned "story" was leaked by Dick Cheney's office. In addition, Miller's source for many of her front page exclusives was none other than disgraced Iraqi National Congress Leader Ahmad Chalabi. See Alterman, 2003, Baker, 2003 and MacArthur, 2003 for more discussion of Miller's role in promulgating the Bush administration's propaganda.

33. This is cited directly from the transcript of the interview which appeared on PBS. See "Rice On Iraq, War and Politics," September 25, 2002.

34. See "President Bush, Colombia President Uribe Discuss Terrorism," September, 25, 2002.

35. See Judis & Ackerman, 2003.

36. In an October 2002 opinion poll conducted by the Pew Research Center for People and the Press, 66% of Americans said they believed Hussein was involved in the 9/11 attacks on the U.S. Seventy-nine percent believed that Iraq already possessed, or was close to possessing, nuclear weapons.

37. Indeed, many of the top leaders of the current administration, particularly Donald Rumsfeld and Dick Cheney, embraced Hussein's dictatorship in the 1980s when Iraq was the enemy of Iran. From 1980-1988, the Reagan-Bush administration greatly assisted Iraq in its war against Iran. Klare (2003) notes that under Reagan, Iraq was actually removed from the list of countries that presumably supported terrorism and was provided with billions of dollars worth of assistance. And it was Rumsfeld who delivered the good news to Saddam Hussein when he traveled to Baghdad in December, 1983 as a special representative of then-President Ronald Reagan. Additionally, the Department of Defense—then headed by Dick Cheney—never spoke out even after it was informed that the Iraqis were using chemical weapons, on an almost daily basis, against Iranians. Such actions were essentially condoned by the United States. See also Chomsky, 2003.

38. For a thorough, point-by-point analysis debunking many of the claims made in his State of the Union address, see www.accuracy.org/2003/

39. "CNN Coverage of the State of the Union Address."

40. See Douglas, 2003, p. 13.

41. While CNN did not openly embrace Fox News' uber patriotism and jingoism, it did follow Fox's lead in "giving short shrift to any hint of dissent or disorder concerning Bush administration affairs" (Perry, 2003:9). And, it is difficult to disagree with Douglas's (2003:8) observation that the CNN coverage of the latest Iraq war has made "CNN, its credibility and dignity, a huge casualty."

42. "State of Union Speech Analysis" CNN Live at Daybreak, January 29, 2003.

43. See http://www.accuracy.org/2003.

44. See Jones, 2003, p.1.

45. See *FAIR*, Feb. 4, 2003, p.1.

46. The criticism of the media's behavior in the build-up to war on the issue of WMD's seems all the more telling. More than a year after the war began, WMDs have yet to be unearthed.

47. See Perry, 2003, p.8.

48. It has since been reported that Powell resisted White House and Pentagon pressures to present the dubious material. Ramonet (2003:1) suggests that in his "UN Security Council speech of 5 February 2003 Powell was obliged to read a draft prepared by Lewis Libby, chief of staff to vice president Dick Cheney. It contained such tenuous information that Powell was said to have become angry, thrown the sheets in the air and refused to read it. Finally Powell asked to have the head of the CIA, George Tenet, sit in view behind him to share responsibility for what was being read."

49. See "Many Believe Burden of Proof Has Shifted," February 2, 2003.

50. See "Powell-Rather Interview Transcript," February 5, 2003.

51. See "Iraqi Scientific Advisor Responds to Powell," February 5, 2003.

52. Michael Massing, an editor for The Columbia Journalism Review, has recently suggested that during the coverage of the Iraq war, "Paula Zahn looked and talked like a cheerleader for the U.S. forces" (2003:4).

53. See Solomon & Cohen, 1997, p.127.

54. See Solomon, 2003, pp. 1-2.

55. See also, Solomon & Cohen, 1997 and Solomon & Erlich, 2003.

56. Powell's presentation to the UN Security Council was based, in no small part, upon an intelligence dossier prepared by the British government entitled "Iraq—Its Infrastructure of Concealment, Deception and Intimidation." It was later revealed, by Channel 4 News in Britain, that the report plagiarized large portions of an essay written by a graduate student from California named Ibrahim al-Marashi. For further discussion of this see Nichols, 2003. For overall critiques of Powell's presentation in terms of its misrepresentations, distortions, and obfuscations see Cockburn, 2003; Fisk, 2003; Hans, 2003; Tomchick, 2003.

57. See Judis & Ackerman, 2003.

58. It took almost six months after Powell's presentation and three months after the war was officially declared "over" for the mainstream media to run stories about the doubts that were mounting regarding Powell's "evidence" presented to the UN.

59. The *FAIR* study examined 393 on-camera sources who appeared in nightly news reports about Iraq on ABC World News Tonight, NBC Nightly News, CBS Evening News, and PBS's NewsHour with Jim Lehrer.

60. See *FAIR*, March 18, 2003.

61. See Tugend, 2003, p.1.

62. See Rendell & Broughel, 2003, pp. 12-14.

63. The study looked at 1, 617 on-camera sources appearing in stories about Iraq on the evening newscasts of six television networks and news channels. The programs studies were ABC World News Tonight, CBS Evening News, NBC Nightly News, CNN's Wolf Blitzer Reports, Fox's Special Report with Brit Hume and PBS's NewsHour With Jim Lehrer.

64. See McChesney & Foster, 2003, p.1.

65. This of course does not underestimate the role of influential newspapers in beating the drum for war. It is important to note, however, that most of the American populace depended on television for news about the war. This also explains why television "was widely considered to be the most influential of the news media that covered the conflict. The pervasiveness of the medium was another. Businesses around the country had TV sets tuned to cable news networks day and night" (Sharkey, 2003:2).

66. Prior to holding this position, Clarke was associated with Hill and Knowlton, the public relations firm infamous for promoting the bogus baby-incubator story during the first Gulf War. For a revealing look at this hoax and the manner in which it was used to mobilize support for U.S. military action, see Kellner, 1992.

67. See Andersen, 2003, p.6.

68. *Ibid.*

69. See Fisk, 2003, p.2.

70. See Jensen, 2003, p.24.

71. See Andersen, 2003, p.7.

72. See Goldstein, 2003, pp. 1-2.

73. See Jensen, 2003, p. 25.

74. Similar claims had been made during the Persian Gulf war—many of which were later found to be grossly exaggerated.

75. See, for example, Sharkey, 2003.

76. Goldsborough, 2003, p.1.

77. Should anyone doubt the military establishment's approval of the performance of the embedded reporters, one need only consider the following remarks made by Lt. Col. John Robinson (who oversaw the embedding program from U.S. Central Command in Tampa, Florida) in relation to the possibility of sending embedded reporters into Liberia: "It is very likely that we will want to embed if there are troops that actually go into Liberia . . . It has proven to be successful. We have been able to provide our perspective to the story" (cited in Strupp, 2003:1).

78. See Jensen, 2003, p.23.

79. See Fisk, "How the News Will Be Censored in This War."

80. See Hart, 2003, p.8.

81. Cited in Pilger, 2003, p.2.

82. See Parry, 2003, p.1.

83. Cited in Andersen, 2003, p.9.

84. See Rall, 2003, p. 1.

85. *Ibid.*

86. Solomon, cited in Gilbert & Ryan, 2003.

87. MacArthur sited in Morgan, 2003, p.1.

88. Bush's "communications people just so happened to have scheduled his Lincoln speech for the time slot usually inhabited by CSI on CBS and Will & Grace on NBC." The week before those two shows had garnered a combined "43 million viewers" (Corn, 2003:3).

89. See McQuaig, 2003, p.1.

90. See Corn, 2003 and Zorn, 2003.

91. See "Bush Lands on..."

92. See Parry, 2003, p.3.

93. See Ackerman, 2003, p.10.

94. See Ackerman, 2003, p.11.

95. *Ibid.*, p. 12.

96. See Parry, 2003, p.1.

97. See Douglas, 2003, p.9.

98. See Herman & Chomsky, 1988, p. xi.

99. *Ibid.*

100. See Brooks, 2003, p.21.

101. See for example, Chomsky, 1997; Herman & McChesney, 1997; McChesney & Foster, 2003. Even Ted Turner, founder of CNN, recently admitted that the media coverage of Iraq was decidedly pro-war in its bias. In comments made to the Commonwealth Club in San Francisco on April 24, 2003, Turner—himself a billionaire and the largest shareholder in the world's

largest media company, AOL Time Warner—said that the American media was far too concentrated: "There's really five companies that control 90 percent of what we read, see and hear. It's not healthy."

102. See Eviatar, 2003, pp. 18–20.

103. See Perry, 2003, p. 8.

104. See Frank, 2003 and Morello, 2001.

105. See Morello, 2001, p.10.

106. See Alterman, 2003; Croteau, 1998; Husseini and Solomon, 1998; McChesney and Foster, 2003; Parry 1998; and Scatamburlo, 1998.

107. The nexus of conservative think tanks and organizations that have helped to fuel the myth of the liberal media is examined in detail in Scatamburlo, 1998.

108. See McChesney & Foster, 2003, pp. 12–13.

109. *Ibid.*, pp. 14–15.

110. See Alper, 2003 and Crowther, 2003.

111. See http://www.mediachannel.org/ownership/chart.shtml for a breakdown of the Big Six media companies and http://www.fair.org/media-woes/interlocking-directorates.html for a telling list of the interlocking directorships of media and other major corporations.

112. See Chatterjee, 2003.

113. See Conason, 2002.

114. See Rall, 2003[b].

115. According to a recent report in the Financial Times, Halliburton claimed that work in Iraq had "boosted its revenue as it swung from a loss to record second-quarter income" (McNulty, 2003:1).

116. See Shorrock, 2003 and Renner, 2003.

117. See Leopold, 2003.

118. See Harris and Klein, 2003, p.1.

119. See Kretzman & Vallette, 2003.

120. Cited in Cohn, 2003, p.1.

121. See Leopold, 2003 and Wright, 2003.

REFERENCES

Ackerman, Seth. "The Great WMD Hunt." Extra, July/August 2003, pp. 10–15.

Alper, Rogel. "Foxa Americana." http://www.globalpolicy.org/security/issues/iraq/media/2003/0409foxa.htm (2 pages)

Alterman, Eric. "When It Raines..." *The Nation*, June 30, 2003, pp. 10, 23.

Alterman, Eric. "Your Show of Shows." *The Nation*, August 21/28, 2000, pp. 13–14.

Andersen, Robin. "That's Militainment!: The Pentagon's Media-Friendly 'Reality' War." *Extra*, May/June 2003, vol. 16, no.3, pp. 6–9.

Arnove, Anthony. "Pro-War Propaganda Machine: Media Becomes Branch of War Effort." *Z Net*, March 19, 2003. http://www.zmag.org (5 pages).

Baker, Russ. "'Scoops' and Truth at the *Times*." *The Nation*, June 23, 2003, pp.18, 20–21.

Bleifuss, Joel. "The First Stone." *In These Times*, July 21, 2003, pp.12–13.

Brooks, Renana. "A Nation of Victims." *The Nation*, June 30, 2003, pp. 20–22.

Chatterjee, Pratap. "Iraq: A Corporate Gold Mine." *Alternet.org*, May 22, 2003. http://www.alternet.org (4 pages).

Chomsky, Noam. *Necessary Illusions: Thought Control in Democratic Societies*. Toronto, Ontario: Anansi, 1989.

Chomsky, Noam. *Media Control: The Spectacular Achievements of Propaganda*. New York: Seven Stories Press, 1997.

Chomsky, Noam. "Confronting the Empire." *Z Magazine*, March 2003, pp. 24-31.

CNN.com. "Bush to U.N.: We Will Not Wait," February 6, 2003. http://cnn.usnews

Cockburn, Alexander. "The Great 'Intelligence' Fraud." *The Nation*, March 3, 2003, p.8.

Coen, Rachel. "Are You a Terrorist?: Media Passivity Enables Rollback of Civil Liberties." *Extra*, November/December, 2001, pp. 21-22.

Cohen, Jeff. "Pitching Softballs: Why Are Journalists Going Easy on Bush?" *FAIR*, March 25, 2001, retrieved on-line from www.fair.org/articles/softball.html .

Cohn, Marjorie. "Why Iraq and Afghanistan? Cheney Tellas All: It's About the Oil." http://www.counterpunch.org/cohn07302003.html (2 pages).

Corn, David. "Bush's Top Gun Photo-Op." *The Nation*, May 2, 2003. http://www.alternet.org/print.html?StoryID=15806. (3 pages).

Coussin, Orna. 'It's More Than Exciting, Christiane." *Ha'aretz*, May 24, 2003 . http://www.globalpolicy.org/security/issues/iraq/media/2003/0324exciting.htm (4 pages).

Croteau, David. "Challenging the 'Liberal Media' Claim." *Extra!*, July/August, 1998, pp. 4-9.

Crowther, Hal. "Weapons of Mass Stupidity: Fox News Hits a New Lowest Common Denominator." *Creative Loafing Charlotte*, June 4, 2003. http://charlotte.creativeloafing.com/newsstand/2003-06-04/news_cover.html (5 pages).

Douglas, Susan. "Bush's Fifth Column." *In These Times*, Dec 25, 2000, pp. 61-62.

Douglas, Susan. "CNN—War Casualty." *The Nation*, April 14, 2003, p. 8, 24.

Douglas, Susan. "Fighting Awful War Coverage." *In These Times*, May 5, 2003, p. 13.

Douglas, Susan. "Nose Loops: A Media Accessory." *In These Times*, July 21, 2003, pp. 9.

Eviatar, Daphne. "The Press and Private Lynch." *The Nation*, July 7, 2003, pp. 18-20.

Fairness & Accuracy in Reporting. "Iraq's Hidden Weapons: From Allegation to Fact," Feb. 4, 2003. http://www.globalpolicy.org/security/issues/iraq/media/2003/0204fair.htm (2 pages).

Fairness & Accuracy in Reporting. "Media Advisory: A Failure of Skepticism in Powell Coverage, Disproof of Previous Claims Underlines Need For Scrutiny," February 10, 2003. http://www.fair.org/press-releases/un-powell-iraq.html (3 pages).

Fairness & Accuracy in Reporting. "In Iraq Crisis, Networks Are Megaphones for Official Views," March 18, 2003. http://www.fair.org/reports/iraq-sources.html (4 pages).

Fisk, Robert. "Powell Presentation: It Was Like Something Out of Beckett." *The Independent(UK)*, February 6, 2003. Http://www.zmag.org/content/Iraq/FiskPowell.cfm (4 pages).

Fisk, Robert. "How the News Will Be Censored in This War." *The Independent(UK)*, February 25, 2003. http://www.globalpolicy.org/security/issues/iraq/media/2003/0225howthe.htm.

Fisk, Robert. "The War of Misinformation Has Begun." *The Independent (UK)*, March 16, 2003. http://www.globalpolicy.org/security/issues/iraq/media/2003/0316warof.htm (3 pages).

Frank, Joshua. "Manufacturing News and Promoting War: Texas Style." *ZNet*, April 3, 2003. http://www.zmag.org (2 pages).

Gertz, Bill. "Classified Date Make Case; Communications Intercepts, Satellite Photos Disclosed." *The Washington Times*, February 6, 2003, AO1.

Gilbert, Matthew and Ryan, Suzanne. "Did Iconic Images from Baghdad Reveal More About the Media than Iraq?" http://naw.ijaq.net/saddam_statue.htm

Goldsborough, James O. "TV Hid Reality of Iraq War." *DailyBreeze.com*, July 1, 2003. http://www.signonla.com/content/opinion/nmgolds05.html (3 pages).

Goldstein, Richard. "The Shock and Awe Show." *The Village Voice*, March 26-April 1, 2003. http://www.villagevoice.com/issues/o313/goldstein.php (4 pages).

Gowans, Stephen. "Ex-Bush Speechwriter: I Was to Provide a Justification for War." *What's Left*, January 8, 2003. http://www.globalpolicy.org/security/issues/iraq/attack/2003/0108 speechwriter.htm (4 pages).

Hans, Dennis. "The Disinformation Age: How George W. Bush and Saint Colin of Powell Are Lying America Into An Unncessary War—and What Honest Journalists Can Do About It." *Scoop*, March 4, 2003. http://www.scoop.co.nz (13 pages).

Harper, Jennifer. "Powell Address Sways Some Skeptics of War." *The Washington Times*, February 7, 2003, A13.

Harris, Scott and Klein, Naomi. "Bomb Before You Buy: An Interview with Naomi Klein." *ZNet*, July 15, 2003. http://www.zmag.org (2 pages).

Hart, Peter and Ackerman, Seth. "Patriotism & Censorship." *Extra!*, November/December, 2001, pp. 6-9.

Hart, Peter; Naureckas, Jim. "Serial Exaggerators." *Extra!*, January/February, 2001.

Hart, Peter. "Salvaging Private Lynch: Shoring Up a Wartime Tale that 'Buoyed the Nation.'" *Extra*, July/August, 2003, pp. 8-9.

Hedges, Chris. "The Press and the Myths of War." *The Nation*, April 21, 2003, pp. 16-18.

Herman, Edward S. and Chomsky, Noam. *Manufacturing Consent: The Political Economy of the Mass Media*. New York: Pantheon Books, 1988.

Herman, Edward S. "The Propaganda Model Revisited" in *Capitalism and the Information Age: The Political Economy of the Global Communication Revolution*. Eds. Robert McChesney, Ellen Meiksons Wood and John Bellamy Foster. New York: Monthly Review Press, 1998, pp. 191-206.

Herman, Edward and McChesney, Robert. *The Global Media: The New Missionaries of Corporate Capitalism*. London & Washington: Cassell, 1997.

Husseini, Sam and Solomon, Norman. "The Right-Leaning Rolodex." *Extra!* July/Aug 1998, p. 13.

Ivins, Molly. *Shrub: The Short But Happy Political Life of George W. Bush*. New York: Vintage Books, 2000.

Jensen, Robert. "The Military's Media." *The Progressive*, May 2003, pp. 22-25.

Jones, Mary Lynn F. "No News Is Good News." *The American Prospect*, May 1, 2003. http://www.globalpolicy.org/security/isues/iraq/media/2003/0501nonews.htm (4 pages).

Judis, John & Ackerman, Spencer. "The Selling of the Iraq War." *The New Republic Online*, June 19, 2003. http://www.tnr.com (14 pages).

Kellner, Douglas. *The Persian Gulf TV War*. Boulder, Colorado: Westview Press, 1992.

Kellner, Douglas. *Grand Theft 2000: Media Spectacle and a Stolen Election*. Lanham, Maryland: Rowman & Littefield, 2001.

Kellner, Douglas. *From 9/11 to Terror War: The Dangers of the Bush Legacy*. Lanham, Maryland: Rowman & Littlefield, 2003.

Klaehn, Jeffery. "A Critical Review and Assessment of Herman and Chomsky's 'Propaganda Model.'" *European Journal of Communication*, 2002, vol. 17, no.2, pp. 147-182.

Klare, Michael. "Bogus Reasons for War on Iraq." *Alternet.org*, January 30, 2003. http://www.alternet.org/story.html?StoryID=15069

Kovach, Bill and Rosenstiel, Tom. "Campaign Lite: Why Reporters Won't Tell Us What We Need To Know." *Washington Monthly*, Jan., 2001, retrieved on-line from www.journalism.org/resources/publications/articles/campaignlite.asp (7 pages).

Kretzmann, Steve and Vallette, Jim. "Operation Oily Immunity." *CommonDreams.org*, July 23, 2003. http://www.commondreams.org/views03/0723-06.htm (2 pages).

Leopold, Jason. "Defense Dept. Secretly Tapped Halliburton Unit to Operate Iraq's Oil Industry." *ZNet*, May 13, 2003.

Leopold, Jason. "Wolfowitz Admits Iraq War Was Planned Two Days After 9/11." *ZNet*, June 2, 2003. http://zmag.org (3 pages)

MacArthur, John. "All the News That's Fudged to Print: If You Think Jayson Blair was Loose with the Facts, Look at How the Times Covered Iraq." *Globe and Mail*, June 6, 2003[a]. http://www.globalpolicy.org/security/issues/iraq/media/2003/0606fudged.htm (3 pages).

MacArthur, John. "The Lies We Bought: The Unchallenged 'Evidence' For War." *Columbia Journalism Review*, May/June 2003[b]. http://www.cjr.org/year/03/3/macarthur.asp (5 pages).

Massing, Michael. "The Unseen War." *The New York Review of Books*, May 29, 2003, vol. 50, no. 9. http://www.nybooks.com/articles/16293 (8 pages).

McChesney, Robert W. and Foster, John Bellamy. "The Commercial Tidal Wave." *Monthly Review*, March 2003, pp. 1-16.

McChesney, Robert and Foster, John Bellamy. "The 'Left-Wing' Media?" *Monthly Review*, June 2003, pp. 1-16.

McNulty, Sheila. "Work in Iraq Benefits Halliburton." *Financial Times*, August 1, 2003. http://financialtimes.com (2 pages).

McQuaig, Linda. "Bush Unchallenged by Media." *Toronto Star*, May 25, 2003. http://www.commondreams.org/views03/0525-02.htm (2 pages).

Miller, Mark Crispin. *The Bush Dyslexicon: Observations on a National Disorder*. New York: W.W. Norton & Company, 2002.

Morello, Tom. "The New Blacklist." *Extra!*, November/December, 2001, p. 10.

Morgan, David. "U.S.: Critic Accuses Media of Aiding U.S. War Propaganda." *World Revolution News*, May 1, 2003. http://www.worldrevolution.org (4 pages).

Naureckas, Jim and Rendall, Steve. "A Failure of Skepticism in Powell Coverage." *Extra*, April 2003, vol. 10, no. 2, pp. 6-8.

New York Times. "The Case Against Iraq," February 6, 2003.

Nichols, Bill. "Powell Shares New Evidence; Tells U.N. That Iraq is Building Bombs, Harboring Al-Qaeda." *USA TODAY*, February 6, 2003, A01. http://pqasb.pqarchiver.com/USAToday

Nichols, John. "Dubious Dossier." *The Nation Online*, February 6, 2003. http://www.thenation.com/thebeat (2 pages).

Parry, Robert. "In Search of the Liberal Media." *Extra!* July/August, 1998, p. 11-12.

Parry, Robert. "America's Matrix." *Consortium News*, June 2, 2003, retrieved on-line from www.consortiumnews.com .

Perry, Steve. "All the President's Lies, Part I: Better Late Than Never." *City Pages*, July 30, 2003. http://babelogue.citypages.com (11 pages).

Pilger, John. "The War on Truth." *ZNet*, July 31, 2003. http://www.zmag.org (4 pages).

Rall, Ted. "How We Lost the Victory." *Alternet.org*, April 15, 2003. http://www.alternet.org (3 pages).

Rall, Ted. "Say It Slowly: It Was About Oil." *Alternet.org*, April 25, 2003. http://www.alternet.org (3 pages).

Ramonet, Ignacio. "State-Sponsored Lies." *Le Monde Diplomatique*, July 15, 2003. http://www.zmag.org (6 pages).

Rendall, Steve. "The Op-Ed Echo Chamber." *Extra!*, November/December 2001, pp. 14-15.

Rendall, Steve and Broughel, Tara. "Amplifying Officials, Squelching Dissent." *Extra: The Magazine of FAIR*, June 2003, vol. 16, no. 3, pp. 12-14.

Renner, Michael. "The Other Looting." *Foreing Policy in Focus Special Report*, July 2003. http://www.foreignpolicy-infocus.org/papers/looting2003_body.html (8 pages).

Scatamburlo, Valerie. *Soldiers of Misfortune: The New Right's Culture War and the Politics of Political Correctness*. New York: Peter Lang, 1998.

Schechter, Danny. "The Link Between the Media, The War, and Our Right to Know." *Mediachannel.org*, May 1, 2003. Http://www.mediachannel.org/views/dissector/moveon.shtml (4 pages).

Scheer, Christopher. "10 Appalling Lies We Were Told About Iraq." *Alternet.org*, June 27, 2003. http://www.alternet.org/story.html?StoryID=16274 (5 pages).

Schwartz, Michael. "Who's Sovereign Now?" *ZNet*, June 17, 2004. http://www.zmag.org

Sharkey, Jacqueline E. "The Television War." *American Journalism Review*, May 2003. http://www.ajr.org (9 pages).

Shorrock, Tim. "Selling (Off) Iraq: How To "Privatize" a Country and Make Millions." *The Nation*, June 23, 2003, pp. 11-14, 16.

Shorrock, Tim. "Crony Capitalism Goes Global." *The Nation*, April 1, 2002, pp. 11-16.

Slavin, Barbara and Diamond, John. "Case Is Stronger When 'Biggest Dove' Makes It; Powell Tells U.N. He's Convinced—So the World Should Be, Too." *USA TODAY*, February 6, 2003, A10. http://pqasb.pqarchiver.com/USAToday

Solomon, Norman. "Colin Powell Is Flawless—Inside A Media Bubble." *Z Magazine*, February 7, 2003. http://www.zmag.org/content/Iraq/solomonpow.cfm (3 pages).

Solomon, Norman and Erlich, Reese. *Target Iraq: What the News Media Didn't Tell You*. New York: Context Books, 2003.

Strupp, Joe. "Was Press Asleep on Pre-War WMD Issue?" *Editor & Publisher*, June 12, 2003. http://editorandpublisher.com (2 pages).

Strupp, Joe. "Only 23 Embedded Reporters Left in Iraq." *Editor & Publisher*, July 9, 2003. http://editorandpublisher.com (2 pages).

Tomchick, Maria. "Powell's Flimsy Evidence." *ZNet*, February 9, 2003. http://www.zmag.org/content/ForeignPolicy/tomchick_powellevidence.cfm (5 pages).

Tugend, Alina. "Pundits for Hire." *American Journalism Review*, May 2003. http://www.ajr.org (7 pages).

USA TODAY. "Powell Lays Out Convincing Evidence of Iraq's Defiance," February 6, 2003, A12. http://pqasb.pqarchiver.com/USAToday

Wicker, Tom. "Press Isn't Asking Right Questions About Iraq." *Common Dreams*, March 11, 2003. http://www.commondreams.org/views03/0311-11.htm (1 page).

Wright, George. "Wolfowitz: Iraq War Was About Oil." *Guardian Unlimited*, June 4, 2003. http://www.guardian.co.uk/Iraq/Story/0,2763,970331,00.html

Zorn, Eric. "Media AWOL in Noting Irony of Bush's Flight." *Independent Media TV*, May 6, 2003. http://www.independent-media.tv (3 pages).

Television Transcripts:

"CNN Live Event Special," January 29, 2002. http://www.cnn.com/TRANSCRIPTS/0201/29/se.03.html

"Rice on Iraq, War and Politics," September 25, 2002. http://www.pbs.org/newshour/bb/international

"CNN Coverage of the State of the Union Address," January 28, 2003, CNN Live Event/ Special. http://www.cnn.com/TRANSCRIPTS/0301/28/se.00.html

"State of Union Speech Analysis." January 29, 2003, CNN Live at Daybreak. http://www.cnn.com/TRANSCRIPTS/0301/29/lad.14.html

"Iraqi Scientific Adviser Responds to Powell," February 5, 2003, CNN Live Event/Special. http://www.cnn.com/TRANSCRIPTS/0302/05/se.05.html

"Powell-Rather Interview Transcript," February 5, 2003, CBSNEWS.com. http://www.cbsnews.com/stories/2003/02/05/60II/printable539564.shtml

"Did Mr. Powell Take Case Against Iraq to New, Convincing Level?" February 6, 2003, CNN American Morning with Paula Zahn. http://www.cnn.com/TRANSCRIPTS/0302/06/ltm.11.html

"Many Believe Burden of Proof Has Shifted." February 6, 2003. http://www.cnn.com/TRANSCRIPTS/0303/06/lt.06.html

"President Bush Set to Announce End of Combat in Iraq..." CNN Inside Politics, May 1, 2003. http://www.cnn.com/TRANSCRIPTS/0305/01.ip.00.html

"Bush lands on USS Abraham Lincoln to Deliver Speech Declaring End to Fighting in Iraq." CNN Special Events, May 1, 2003. http://www.cnn.com/TRANSCRIPTS/0305/01/se.00.html

Government Documents:

Bush, George W. "State of the Union," January 29, 2002.
http://www.whitehouse.gov/news/releases/2002/01/20020129-11.html

Bush, George W. "State of the Union," January 28, 2003. http://www.whitehouse.gov/news/releases/2003/01/20030128-19.html

Chapter Three
Israel Asper And Israeli Propaganda
Robert Everton

ISRAEL ASPER, OWNER OF MEDIA EMPIRE, CANWEST Global,[1] publicly complained on October 30, 2002 at a gala reception of 400 Israeli supporters in Montreal promoting Israeli Bonds, about 'biased' international news coverage given to the Israeli-Palestinian conflict. He then ran a lengthy opinion piece, with much the same content, in all the CanWest Global newspapers on November 2, 2002, entitled 'End Media Bias against Israel.' In his opinion piece, unhampered by any alternative views or balanced opinion, Asper wrote, 'Too many of the journalists are lazy, sloppy or stupid. They are ignorant of the history of the subject on which they are writing...The result is that the biggest casualties of the Palestinian-Israeli war are truth and the integrity of the media.' (*Canadian Jewish News*, Nov. 7, 2002 or any CanWest Global newspaper, Nov. 2) 'Much of the world media have abandoned the fundamental precepts of honest reporting,' Asper was quoted in the Canadian Press Newswire (31 Oct. 02). The report began, 'CanWest Global founder Israel Asper said Wednesday pervasive anti-Israel bias in the international media is a cancer that is destroying much of the media's credibility.' The report later continued, 'Asper challenged his audience to be more aggressive and vigilant in acting against media bias by protesting, cancelling subscriptions and boycotting advertisers of media guilty of dishonest reporting.'[2]

These are very serious allegations. Israel (or 'Izzy') Asper is well known for his uncritical support for the state of Israel.[3] Critics of Asper, including numerous CanWest Global journalists, claim Asper imposes strict 'guidelines,' even censorship on CanWest Global's coverage of Israel.[4] Yet here Asper and his media are presenting the claim that the media are biased *against* Israel!

Is there any truth to this claim? A minimal requirement for mass media, that becomes critical if that media empire dominates a national market in a particular medium, in any society that calls itself a democracy, is that it not be biased in its news coverage. If a marginalized outlet carries partisan views because they were excluded from the mainstream, then let such outlets acknowledge their partisan nature. Never should we tolerate media being dishonest in their reporting. Media analysts have a responsibility to inform the public of partisanship or bias whenever this is the case. Everyone has a responsibility to denounce dishonesty in any media. Intentionally reporting false information to mold public opinion should never be tolerated in any society seeking to be democratic. When it is tolerated, that society would then have adopted a critical element of a totalitarian society.

Let us analyze if there is any discernible bias in the Canadian media by analyzing the coverage of the next event of major significance to be reported on regarding Palestine or Israel following Asper's speech. This event was an attack on November 15, 2002 by Palestinians on Israelis in the West Bank city of Hebron.

The Case Study

This chapter examines the coverage of the November 15 attack and any references to this event in subsequent news reports until the end of 2002. The study begins by focusing on the reporting of CanWest Global newspapers (newspapers owned and/or controlled by CanWest). These dailies are: St. John's *Telegram*; Charlottetown *Guardian*; Halifax *Daily News*; Ottawa *Citizen*; Montreal *Gazette*; *Edmonton Journal*; *Calgary Herald*; Victoria *Times-Colonist*; Vancouver *Province*; *Vancouver Sun*; and the *National Post*. Except for the *National Post*, they all once formed a part of the relatively prestigious Southam chain (by Canadian standards). By the beginning of 2002, all were owned by CanWest Global. The three dailies from the Maritimes were sold in mid-2002,[5] but their sale included a provision that they would, for a cost, continue to receive their feed of news and editorial content from CanWest News Service (Canada NewsWire, Feb. 14, 2003).

CanWest Global reporting of this incident is then compared, first to the coverage offered by the Canadian newspaper of record, the *Globe and Mail*, over the same period and secondly to the CTV and CBC television news coverage. Finally all this is compared to coverage by the U.S. newspaper of record, the *New York Times*. National 'journals of record' are critical in terms of historical claims because, unless contradicted by more convincing accounts, they serve in North America as legitimate and authoritative sources for historical accounts being cited as 'historical facts.'

This case study should allow us to assess the degree of accuracy of Canadian reporting regarding Israel and Palestine, including that of CanWest Global. Since the initial government information provided was shown within 24 hours to be false, we can also get a glimpse at the degree to which Canadian media are prepared to hold accountable sources shown to have provided false information.

Four distinct periods can be mapped out in analyzing these reports. The first is the period, of one to two days, depending on the media outlet,[6] in which the original false version of the attack was disseminated. This may be referred to as the 'initial period.' The second is the period of the following eight days in which most reports clarified the inaccuracy of the initial claims. It may be called the 'clarification period.' The third period is from immediately following the clarification period until a month after the events. The fourth and final period would be any report printed more than a month after the event. This last period may be considered the 'institutional memory' of this event. The CanWest Global reporting differed in each of these periods, as will be seen below.

The November 15 Attack in Hebron, Palestine

On November 15, 2002, Palestinian militants, apparently from the Palestinian group, Islamic Jihad, attacked and killed twelve (wounding fifteen other) Israeli soldiers, border police and security forces stationed in Hebron. Hebron is a Palestinian city in the West Bank, populated by 130,000 Palestinians with Israeli enclaves, home to approximately 450 'settlers.' Israeli military at the time of writing this article occupied the city, as they did the entire country of Palestine. Two Palestinian militant groups, Islamic Jihad[7] and Hamas[8] claimed responsibility for the attack. It seems probable that members from both groups may have participated in the military conflict, although without having coordinated their involvement with the other. Only one report[9] claimed there to have been more than two[10] or three[11] combatants from either group. One explanation may be that when fighting broke out, as a product of planned action from the one group, nearby militants from the other may have spontaneously joined in the attack.

Millions of potential news stories occur each day, yet only a few are selected as 'newsworthy' or deemed 'worthy' of being included in the news. This attack was indeed newsworthy, but not only for the death toll involved. The initial story was arguably even more newsworthy for at least two other reasons. First, the attack resulted in the death of the Commander of Israeli forces in Hebron, Colonel Dror Weinberg, the highest-ranking Israeli officer killed by Palestinians in years. This single death, in itself, is extremely newsworthy.[12]

Secondly, the attack was also important for it signaled a *change in tactics* for at least some of the Palestinian groups, from one that was seemingly of random violence against all Israelis with suicide bombers, to a select violence that targeted Israeli military and security personnel. This was the greatest loss of life of Israeli military forces in one incident since the Palestinian *intifada* began in 2000. Killed, besides the colonel, were a Lieutenant, a Chief Superintendent (of border police), 2 Staff Sergeants, 3 Sergeants and a Corporal.[13] No unarmed civilian worshippers were killed, wounded nor even attacked during the event. All 'settlers,' other than those serving as military or security personnel, had returned to their armed enclave fifteen minutes before the attack began.[14]

The original reports in Canada of the November 15th attack presented only the official Israeli government version of events. Some versions acknowledged their sources; others did not bother. The reports claimed that Palestinian 'terrorists' had attacked Israelis settlers on their way home from prayer at the Tomb of the Patriarchs. Some of the reports mentioned the loss of life of Israeli soldiers, but it was claimed that this was the result of their intervention to save the civilians.

The next day the official version from the Israeli Army clarified that there had actually been no attack on civilians returning from prayer, but instead it had been an armed attack on 'Israeli soldiers and security forces.' The Israeli daily newspaper, *Ha'aretz*, posted in its article 'Hebron Brigade Commander among 12 Killed': 'According to an initial investigation by the army, in contrast to a version of events given by the foreign ministry, the *Islamic Jihad* fire was not directed at worshippers but at security forces...' (Haaretzdaily.com, Nov. 16, 2002).[15]

The story then became newsworthy for yet another, possibly even more newsworthy, reason: Israeli deception of the international media. In their role as 'watchdog,' the international media would be expected to reveal such deception, if for no other reason than to reduce the likelihood of such intentional media deception happening in the future. As well, one would expect any legitimate media to inform their readership of misinformation that the media themselves had previously circulated, as well as to notify readers that this source is not a reliable one for future information of this nature. But this scrutiny only exists when there is a spirit of or a demand for accountability.

So why then would the Israeli government and military spokespersons intentionally claim that settlers had been attacked on their way home from prayer, when necessarily they would be required to retract those claims later? Would this not result in a loss of credibility for the Israeli authorities, thereby undermining their credibility regarding any of their claims, previous or future?

Why the Initial Deception?

By circulating a version of an armed attack against settlers returning from prayer, the Israeli government avoided prominent news coverage of two major stories. First, they lessened the focus on Palestinian militants being able to kill the Israeli troop commander of the region. Secondly, they avoided widespread international debate over the adoption of new tactics by some Palestinian groups that have begun to specifically target the Israeli military, as opposed to detonating explosives against a seemingly random Israeli civilian population. This latter characterization is pivotal for an Israeli portrayal of Palestinians as 'terrorists.'

Instead, by misinforming the international media, Israeli authorities generated, at least momentarily, a widespread sympathetic attitude towards Israelis as seemingly innocent 'victims' of Palestinian terrorism. These are significant achievements in themselves for the Israeli authorities, although we must yet take into account the degree of damage to Israeli credibility caused by having initially provided misinformation. But first, there is even more that may have motivated the initial false version.

The November 21, 2002 edition of the *Canadian Jewish News* reprinted an article from the Israeli daily, *Ha'aretz*, which suggest an additional possible motive for the misinformation campaign. The article begins 'Prime Minister Ariel Sharon said Sunday, that a *window of opportunity* existed in the coming *48 hours* to establish a 'compact' zone of Jewish territorial contiguity between Kiryat Arba and the Jewish enclave in the heart of Hebron, including the Tomb of the Patriarchs' (emphasis added). The article continues, 'Sharon told leaders of the defense establishment...that it should reassess his 1996 proposal for 'territorial contiguity'.' The carved-out area would then be protected by the construction of a massive wall.

Near the end of the article, it explained, 'At Sunday's meeting, Sharon pushed for his territorial contiguity plan, saying that for `operational and political' reasons, Israel must move quickly. An opportunity has been created and facts have to be created in the coming 48 hours, he said.'[16] One assumes that Sharon's reference to 'facts must be created' was a reference to establishing a greater Israeli presence in a more extensive area in Hebron as a *fait accompli*.

Thus Ariel Sharon seems to have been predisposed to use the opportunity to promote a plan which, when Sharon was a military officer six years earlier, had been ridiculed. But now that he was Prime Minister, he expected his plan to be treated seriously. He seems totally clear about the need to act quickly since only a 'window of opportunity' existed for Israel to take advantage of the confusion sown by the dissemination of a false version of events. This false information, clearly disseminated with intent for partisan political gain, seems to meet all the necessary requirements for the traditional label of 'propaganda.'

There are three issues of the weekly *Canadian Jewish News* in 2002 that mention the November 15 attack. The other two articles were in December (5 and 12). Both referred to the November attack as killing 12 Israelis, without specifying that the dead and wounded were all military or security forces. This is a highly suspect move given the initial confusion created from the dissemination of false information, not to mention that it had occurred less than a month earlier. Both instances also labeled the assault as 'terrorist,' which carries the clear implication that an attack was directed against civilian forces in a random manner, rather than against military troops.

The second reference was worded 'Palestinian terrorists killed 12 Israelis on November 15 on their way back from praying at the Tomb' (Dec. 12). Here the misinformation is not merely one of omission, but of presenting false information in an effort to maintain alive the false version of events—the overt propaganda. Instead of acknowledgment that Palestinian militants now employ new and more effective tactics against selected military targets, the myth is maintained that this was a terrorist attack against unarmed and innocent civilians (among those who from a distance are uninformed enough to believe that the Israeli 'settlers' in Palestine may actually be either unarmed or innocent in their relations with Palestinians).[17]

For the Israeli government to have spread a false version of events with impunity suggests that they knew in advance that they could do so without the international media exposing the move for what it was: propaganda. They would have been able to depend on the international media to be cooperative. If this is true, then this would be complicity in disseminating propaganda and the major news now would become the overlooking of the international media complicity in disseminating Israeli propaganda.

Ultimately, one is not too terribly surprised to find a partisan portrayal of events in a partisan publication, say the *Canadian Jewish News* or perhaps an Arab publication. What may be more surprising to many Canadians would be that the major, privately owned, national media of this country are disseminating accounts that qualify for what traditionally has been known as propaganda.

What then *was* the daily Canadian newspaper coverage of this issue actually like? Let's begin with the CanWest Global newspapers.

CanWest Global Newspaper Reporting

In the eleven CanWest Global daily newspapers examined, there were 106 articles in total, published between November 15, 2002 and the end of the year, which were identified by employing both the keywords 'Hebron' and 'killed' in a Boolean search with these two terms. Fifty-eight of these articles, when examined, mentioned the attack of November 15th. Two of these stories are from the same newspaper (*Ottawa Citizen*) on the same day with identical content, since both early and late editions of reports were filed. The only difference between them is the title.[18] Therefore, the stories will only be counted once. This leaves a total of fifty-seven stories that mention the events of Nov. 15. Two other stories from the same newspaper and date were considered in both their versions, given their content was significantly different.[19]

These fifty-seven stories were published in the following numbers per newspaper: St. John's *Telegram* (9); Charlottetown *Guardian* (5); Halifax *Daily News* (2); *Ottawa Citizen* (6); Montreal *Gazette* (7); *Edmonton Journal* (3); Vancouver *Province* (1); *Vancouver Sun* (9); *Calgary Herald* (5); Victoria *Times-Colonist* (4); and the *National Post* (6). Eleven of these fifty-seven stories belong to the initial period. All 11 presented the initial claim that the attack was against Israeli settlers, not military and/or security forces. Equally all 11 articles, except one, cited only Israeli sources. Presumably this source too was Israeli, given its claims, but it was merely cited as 'sources.' The remaining sources were identified as: 'army sources,' 'Israeli security sources,' 'a soldier named Anik on Israeli Army Radio,' 'Foreign Ministry officials,' 'the military' and in one case, 'Israeli military and witnesses.'

All presented the official version as *fact*. None implied any doubt over the veracity of the account provided by so much as even qualifying the statements through referring to the allegations as 'claims.' Much of the information given is not attributed to any source at all. Ten of the eleven stories that ran the initial false version of attacking and killing settlers were accompanied by a photograph, obviously having a greater impact than does text alone. Of the photographs used, two were with captions accurately identifying a 'wounded soldier' (*Calgary Herald* and *Telegram*). Three other photographs were of Israeli-Palestinian conflict other than the attack itself. Two versions of articles ran in the *Vancouver Sun* were accompanied by a graphic with a caption describing a 'settler removes blood-stained stretcher.' Graphics appeared three times on November 16 with a caption that claimed the picture above was of a 'wounded settler.' Given these graphics appeared in both CanWest's national daily newspaper (*National Post*) and their daily in the country's second largest city (Montreal *Gazette*, pages 1 and 29) the false impressions created are not minor issues. They would seem to require meticulous efforts at clarification for any serious newspaper that cared about honest reporting and its own credibility.

Two of these stories were published in the Montreal *Gazette*, on Nov. 16, 2002, with both versions using a photograph of an Israeli said to be an 'injured Jewish settler' on his 'way from Sabbath eve prayers.' The second lengthier version from the Late Edition, was moved to the front page from page 29; this modified version had added five paragraphs at the beginning, presenting the propaganda version of the Israeli ministry. The source of the information is not given in this article. The first reference to a source was an unidentified 'the sources said.' The story's lead paragraph included the statement that 'stiff Israeli military action' was likely. But no sources are cited. Israeli government propaganda was given a privileged position.

CanWest Global's Clarification Period

Having earlier run a story in which the nature of the event was misrepresented as a result of being fed inaccurate information, one would expect all media which reported the initial false claims to explicitly clarify the situation in any follow-up stories on Hebron, by at least explicitly stating that the Israelis attacked were soldiers and security forces. It would, of course, be gross negligence to not make this clarification.

Yet not all the CanWest Global stories did so.

Furthermore, one would expect any honest newspaper with a modicum of integrity to investigate and publish what had *actually* occurred once it learned that it had seemingly intentionally been deceived by propaganda from a government, *any* government (especially one which explicitly refused to explain why it had earlier given the media this false information). To fail to do so would suggest possible media complicity in disseminating propaganda. This will be examined in the following section.

In the clarification period of the following eight days (from November 17 to 25 inclusive) there were a total of 24 articles that mentioned the events. Twenty of these clarified that the Israelis who were killed or wounded were all military or security forces. Only four stories of the fifty-seven mentioned that the attack had occurred fifteen minutes after the settlers had safely returned to their fortressed enclaves.[20]

Four other articles failed to clarify the basic misinformation. Of these four, the Montreal *Gazette* and the St. John's *Telegram* (Nov. 17) acknowledged that all the dead were members of the 'Israeli security forces,' but both still claimed that the attack occurred when Jewish worshippers were still walking back to their houses. The Vancouver *Province*, for its part, on Nov. 17, continued to maintain that the attack resulted in the death of 'settlers and soldiers.'

The *National Post* in its November 18 edition, ran two articles on the events. In the dominant story, highlighted on the front page, the first reference to the target of the attack is unspecified, 'Friday's attack killed 12.' But this was later followed by the claim 'The operation started with an attack on Jewish worshippers making their way on foot from the Tomb of the Patriarchs.' Note that this misinformation was printed, not on the 17th as were the misrepresentations in the three other articles, but yet another day later, on November 18, while the clarification itself, by the Israeli military, had been made public on the 16th. Thus two days after the official clarification, the *National Post* chose, for its part, in its most prominent coverage, to continue to print the key elements of the Israeli 'propaganda' version.

This is all that much more problematic since this was a front-page story accompanied by a graphic photograph, while the account in the same edition that was much more accurate was buried inside the newspaper on page 9. That other, less visible, account explained 'Initial reports of Friday's attack said it was aimed at worshippers returning from Friday evening prayers. But the army now says the dead were members of the security services and the worshippers had all returned to their homes before the shooting broke out' (*National Post*, Nov. 18, A9). Elsewhere, newspapers from the same CanWest Global chain, the *Ottawa Citizen*, *Edmonton Journal*, *Vancouver Sun* and *Calgary Herald* had all, on the *previous day*, written, 'The worshippers had returned to the settlement about 15 minutes before the Palestinian gunmen armed with M-16 rifles launched simultaneous attacks on an armoured jeep carrying military reservists and a military foot patrol.' Even another story in the same edition explained the misinformation. But it appears the *National Post* editors were unconcerned enough over accuracy to even check.

CanWest Global Accountability and Integrity in Reporting

So how did the newspapers respond to learning that they had been lied to by the Israeli Ministry of Foreign Affairs? The CanWest Global daily newspapers failed abysmally to investigate nor even acknowledge that they had published false information. Instead they seem to have largely simply ignored the awkward situation.

There is little doubt that if the Palestinian authority was caught having offered an inaccurate version of events, Canadian newspapers would focus on such deception, probably repeatedly and with great effect. It is indeed the duty of the press to do so; it is the most immediate means by which to hold sources accountable for what they present as fact. Are they a credible source for future information?

How then was the Israeli government taken to task and made accountable for having initially misrepresented the nature of the attack by claiming it was Jewish civilians returning from prayer who were the targets of the attack? Of the twenty articles in the newspapers examined that did acknowledge during the clarification period that the attack was on the Israeli military, not civilians, only four stories even raised the issue of the Israeli government being asked to explain its reason for having previously issued the earlier false version. All of these were reprints of a lone article from the *Washington Post* by Molly Moore (Nov. 17).

Three articles did this by mentioning that the Israeli government 'declined' to explain why (*Edmonton Journal, Calgary Herald* and *Vancouver Sun*). One story (*Ottawa Citizen*) worded it as the government 'refused' to explain why. And that was the end of it!

Of the twenty stories during the clarification period which did now describe the attack against the Israeli military and security forces, only five of them even acknowledged in any manner that this was a change from their previous reporting on this same story.[21] That makes five stories of out the twenty-four printed during this clarification period (or five out of the total fifty-seven stories). Approximately eighty percent of the stories in the clarification period, then, did not even refer to any change in the official story at all! This is an astounding level of irresponsibility in terms of seeking accountability from sources for the information they supply. The overwhelming majority of the stories did *not even mention* that the Israeli authorities, who had been the exclusive sources for their stories of Nov. 15 and 16, had made a massive reformulation of their story. These Israeli sources are clearly privileged by CanWest Global news outlets. They were allowed to deceive with impunity. It is difficult to avoid wondering whether this was the result of a conscious effort to falsely report the news for partisan reasons.

These five stories (four reprints of a single *Washington Post* article, plus the *National Post* article of Nov. 18 buried on page 9) were the only CanWest articles to explicitly recognize that their earlier version of events had been incorrect, although even these articles fell short of acknowledging that this was the result of Israeli government disinformation. Two of these stories (*Edmonton Journal* and the *Ottawa Citizen*) even acknowledged the deception in their initial titles. Interestingly enough, in the case of the *Ottawa Citizen*, the Nov. 17 title was *changed* from 'Israel admits Victims of Friday attack were military, not worshippers' (Early Edition) to 'Military Takes control of city in Retaliation for Sabbath Massacre,' (Final Edition) although the rest of the story was identical. This, of course, served to conceal the deception—not to clarify it.

The use of the term 'Sabbath Massacre' was promoted by the Israeli Ministry of Foreign Affairs (*Edmonton Journal* and *Ottawa Citizen*, Nov. 17) and described in the Nov. 17 *Province* as 'what is being dubbed the 'Sabbath Massacre.' Only the Nov. 18 *National Post* articles offered an alternative framing to this characterization, quoting former Israeli general, Matan Vilnai as saying, 'It wasn't a massacre, it was a battle.'[22] It is revealing that the change of title in the *Ottawa Citizen* coverage, from its early to its late edition on Nov. 17, consisted only of changing the title from one which acknowledged the Israeli government had misrepresented the attack to a title that referred to the so-called Sabbath Massacre.

It is interesting that Izzy Asper in his diatribe against the quality of reporting referred to the Jenin 'massacre *myth*' by claiming that *only* 54 Palestinians had been killed in Israel's assault on Jenin according to a UN Commission, as if a claim by someone that the tolls were higher would dismisses the fact that 54 Palestinians had been massacred. Yet his newspapers had no difficulty in calling the death of 12 Israelis a 'massacre.' In the case of Jenin, we have at least 54 Palestinians being killed by the Israeli state. In the case of Nov. 15, we have 12 military and security forces being subjected to an armed attacked as an occupying foreign army in Palestine. Which is actually the 'massacre myth'?

Does Asper believe that it is only Israeli deaths that can be labeled a massacre? Only two of the CanWest Global newspapers even mentioned the only previous massacre of worshippers in Hebron in the last fifty years. In fact it was not merely a previous one, but actually the only one in the last half century, since this recent one was merely a fabricated claim that worshippers had been killed. But there is another significant difference between the two attacks. The largely unmentioned massacre of eight years earlier occurred when an armed Jew attacked hundreds of unarmed Palestinian civilians at prayer. Neither of the two passing references to this massacre even labeled the event as a 'massacre,' yet six of the CanWest newspapers used the term in reference to the 12 Israelis killed.

With regard to why the initial deception occurred, how many articles among the entire body of fifty-seven stories in which the Nov. 15 attack is mentioned, cited another source, besides the Israeli officials, who for their part were already exposed as unreliable? None. Not even one. Only the Israeli government was asked for comment on why the Israeli government had lied. Their refusal to offer an explanation simply resulted in the matter being dropped—never to be mentioned again! What a privileged position. This is, of course, not what one would expect from any news publication with integrity that attempted to report the news accurately.

If one expects a newspaper with integrity to investigate and publish what had *actually* occurred once it learned that it had seemingly been intentionally deceived by propaganda from a government, then what would failure to do so suggest? It would seem to imply complicity of that outlet in disseminating propaganda. CanWest Global newspapers not only failed miserably to publish any explanation of what had occurred, their newspapers typically did not even acknowledge that their readers had been roundly deceived by Israeli propaganda. For the majority of newspapers controlled by CanWest Global, it was a cover-up by omission.

That the Israeli media may respond in this manner to the Israeli government would be one matter (although I don't believe they typically do),[23] but for the international media to respond with such apparent collusion is a totally different matter. It would suggest that the media which reported in the manner that the CanWest Global newspapers did, are complicit in intentionally spreading Israeli disinformation and propaganda.

Canwest Global: Contextualized Information?

The St. John's *Telegram* on Nov. 17 acknowledged through a quote from the new Israeli Army Commander in Hebron, Col. Noam Tibon, that 'there was concern that Jewish settlers from Hebron and the nearby settlement of Kiryat Arba would go on a rampage...' while the 130,000 Palestinians were confined under curfew to remaining indoors. The article, unlike any of the reporting in the CanWest-owned papers under review, continued by acknowledging what is widely documented elsewhere, 'settlers in Hebron and Kiryat Arba have a history of vigilante action against Palestinians.'[24]

Only three other articles among these fifty-seven that discuss the events of Nov. 15 come close to acknowledging the nature of the Israeli occupation and this fanatical quality of the Israeli 'settlers' in occupied Palestine. The *Province* on Nov. 17, quoted Mustafa Al Natche, the Palestinian mayor of Hebron, as saying, 'The people are very frightened because they know the settlers here are fanatics...We can only hope the Israeli Army will try to keep order.' Other reports point out that the Israeli military does not have a history of protecting the Palestinians.[25] The only other indication that suggested feared potential Israeli viligante action was a quote that appeared in both the Montreal *Gazette* and the Halifax *Daily*, 'About 1,000 settlers attended a rally after the end of the Sabbath, some chanting 'revenge' and 'death to Arabs.' Army commanders urged settler leaders to prevent vigilante action.'[26]

There are also currently campaigns, heavily promoted by the extreme right-wing Israeli parties, to displace Palestinians even further, ultimately expelling them from what little remains of Palestine, to surrounding Arab countries. Although this deportation, forced migration or expulsion is widely discussed in Israel, it is done so in different terms—'transfer' is the dominant euphemism. Others consider it simply a form of ethnic cleansing.[27] The issue of Palestinian expulsion and the occupied nature of Palestine are beyond the scope of this paper, but they should not be ignored as important elements in contextualizing the situation. Neither was ever mentioned in any of the CanWest Global newspapers as background information to the existing situation. Never was it explicitly acknowledged in these CanWest Global reports that Palestine was militarily occupied by Israel.

One *National Post* report did note that the Israeli settlers were frequent targets, but failed to offer any reasonable context of why this may be the case.[28] One is left to assume it must be the result of some inexplicable violent nature of Palestinians. Neither did any of the CanWest coverage acknowledge that the November 15 military attack was a blow to the Israeli Army, as did other international reports. How could this not be a devastating loss for the Israeli Army, at least in Hebron?

Canwest Global's Third or Interim Period

There were fourteen stories printed between November 27 and a month after the attack (December 15) in this third or interim period. That leaves a final eight stories printed after December 15 before the end of the year in the fourth period of institutional memory. Each of these categories will be reviewed in turn.

Of the fourteen stories in the third period, eight of them clearly acknowledge the attack to have been against the Israeli military and security forces and that these were the lone Israeli victims. But there are also six other reports—one shy of half—in this interim period which refer to the victims merely as unspecified 'Israelis.' While this would not be a serious matter in most situations, in this one it is highly problematic since there had been confusion sown, seemingly intentionally by the Israeli Foreign Ministry and military, surrounding whom exactly was killed. This then becomes a very serious omission. In not specifying the victims, the Israeli propaganda campaign is rewarded for its efforts at attempted propaganda, even though exposed, rather than being sanctioned. This is a highly partisan and totally unacceptable message to send to those who seek to use the national media for ideological purposes and disinformation initiatives, instead of as channels for news.

CanWest Global's Institutional Memory

The fourth and final period is one that begins a month after the event and includes all subsequent reporting on the issue. This refers to how the event is remembered. It reflects what may be considered to be the industry's institutional memory. Variations in institutional memory from one media outlet to another may indicate hidden relations and influences. Surprises in the institutional memory around any event may be significantly revealing of influences from less apparent factors.

Once a story has been filed, whether it was a single story of an event or involved some degree of follow-up, it becomes part of the history of that event or theme. Newspapers have traditionally clipped their stories and filed them for future reference. When a journalist begins to cover a story she is expected to look through the file for that particular topic or issue. This is a fundamental practice of journalism, even though today the files may be digital instead of newspaper clippings. The files simply supplement the human memory. One assumes that significant events will be remembered and, when relevant, referred to in subsequent stories on this theme. Story files work simply to ensure that important information is not lost. They provide the memory banks for an institutional memory. If the contents of a story are acknowledged in future media accounts, this information becomes part of the institutional memory. This often occurs, but not always. When it does not, it is critical to determine why.

Thus there are two distinct categories into which reports in this period may be classified: those reports that are 'incorporated' into the dominant logic and those that are 'ignored.' The information that is incorporated into the dominant worldview works to shape our understanding of an issue and ultimately of the world around us. Publicly declared information that is subsequently ignored in the institutional memory becomes concealed from readers. The importance of maintaining this misinformation would seem to be considerable for any media institution, if it were prepared to risk its credibility as a publication by continuing to perpetuate misinformation even once it had been exposed as false.

Eight stories form part of the institutional memory, being reported between Dec. 15 and Dec. 31. Only three of the eight stories (37.5%) even mentioned that the Israelis killed were either military or security forces. In two of these three accounts, however, the first instance of referring to the casualties mentions only 'Israeli' deaths, although later in the articles the nature of the deaths is clarified. If the articles had not later clarified the nature of the deaths, they would have qualified for the 'ignored' category as well.

In one of the remaining accounts (*Telegram*, Dec. 22), the story claimed that 'settlers' had been the target of the attack. This information is incorrect, ignoring the clarification made in earlier coverage.

In yet three others (*Citizen*, Dec. 19; *Gazette*, *Telegram*, Dec. 20) it was claimed once again that both soldiers and settlers were killed. In the case of the *Gazette*, the false claim of settler deaths was made in the caption beneath a photo that accompanied an article. This is particularly disturbing since often readers will limit their reading of a story to merely the title, the lead or, when there is one, a caption under a picture. Over a month after the event, in spite of these very same newspapers having clarified that this was false, they once again make this claim of settlers being targeted and killed in the attack! These three accounts, as well, were distorted and ignored their own earlier clarifications.

As if to add insult to injury, there is even one instance, in a summary of the year's events, which claimed that only 'settlers were killed' (*Guardian*, Dec. 31). This is no longer a CanWest Global-owned newspaper, but it receives its feed from CanWest Global. This was in an entry in the 'Year in Review.' One assumes that those who compile, circulate or edit such a summary would have enough integrity to be trusted to accurately portray at least the general elements of what took place. The entire entry on this matter reads, 'Palestinians attack Israeli settlers in West Bank town of Hebron, killing at least 12.' This is, incidentally, the first instance in reporting owned or controlled by CanWest Global (beyond the reports from the first day) that questioned whether there may have been more than 12 Israelis killed. This story, too, is distorted and belongs in the 'ignored' category within the period of institutional memory.

Why would four of the eight newspaper reports continue to claim that settlers were killed, while yet a fifth article continued to assert that settlers had been targeted in the attack? Only Asper and/or his editors can explain why they chose to resurrect what was exposed as Israeli propaganda and to present it once again to their readers as though it were fact. Asper's impassioned positions on Israel alone would suggest that CanWest Global's coverage was not merely handled sloppily because the editors at CanWest Global simply did not care about the particular issue.

These five stories are not merely 'distorted,' but given the history of the story, they are highly damaging and revealing. Five of the eight newspaper articles in the remarkably short period of the 'institutional memory' already had reverted to advancing the claims made in the crass propaganda attempt. Over half of the CanWest Global stories (62.5%) appearing in this period re-asserted barefaced Israeli propaganda *as fact*. This occurred after this very same false information had been widely exposed to be false, including in CanWest Global newspapers (although never followed up nor seemingly even investigated, no matter how superficially).

Thus, of the eight articles from this period of institutional memory, three are in the 'incorporated' category, while an astounding five stories fall into the 'ignored' category because of the distorted information they convey. This means that over half of the CanWest Global stories in the period of institutional memory ended up reverting to spreading a false, propaganda version of events, in spite of these claims having been previously revealed to be false in these very newspapers.

In his opinion piece carried in the CanWest Global newspapers on Nov. 2, 2002, Israel Asper claimed of journalists who had not covered events as he would like to see them covered, 'They didn't even ask the fundamental question: Is this true?' In the CanWest Global reporting on follow-up to the November 15 attack, it is clear that had the journalists involved asked the fundamental question of whether this is true, they would have concluded that it is not. But whether the journalists had concluded the stories were false would be irrelevant if their editors were intent on printing false versions. If the responsibility for this sloppy and/or deceitful reporting did not lay with the editors rather than the reporters, then alternatively they could have been over-ridden, directly or indirectly by their papers' owners, the Aspers. But no matter who within the organization was responsible, the newspapers as news organizations have to assume responsibility for preventing exactly what Asper most denounced—dishonest reporting.

Was there ever any clarification of these gross inaccuracies in the CanWest Global reporting? Not in any of the CanWest Global papers has there yet been any such clarification, much less an apology. It would seem that the CanWest Global newspapers are grossly partisan in their coverage of Israel and, to date, have demonstrated no intention of setting the record straight. Of course, this would not likely be a surprise to most observers who have followed the events of Southam newspapers following their purchase by Asper's CanWest Global.[29] Journalists have frequently complained of extreme partisanship by Southam's new owners in regard to the coverage of Israel. This would seem to be an example of precisely that. Journalists at CanWest's Southam knew what line was expected from them in their reporting: a biased pro-Israeli slant.[30]

The Globe and Mail

Some aspects of the coverage of the November 15 attack in the *Globe and Mail* contrasted starkly with that of the CanWest Global newspapers. First, there was a significant difference in the number of articles between November 15 and the year's end that even mentioned the event. There were only two articles in the *Globe*, one on November 16 and the other on November 18. Secondly, although the coverage of the event was equally poor, there was a significant difference in the contextualized information offered. Even with so few stories, the *Globe and Mail* provided greater background information to help readers understand the event. There were no follow up stories that later referred to the November 15 attack.

The first article offered the same false version based on the misinformation supplied by the Israeli government. However, the article, written by Paul Knox, did not even attribute any of this misinformation to *any* source. Instead it simply presented the initial official Israeli version as fact! This is extremely presumptuous for a journalist who was not on location, but using, at a minimum, third hand information. Furthermore *all* the dead and wounded were described as settlers returning from prayer or as worshippers. Strangely not a single soldier or border guard was acknowledged to be among the dead or wounded.

The sources cited were much less forthcoming. Two witnesses were invoked, one identified only by his first name (Anik) and the second unidentified, to offer such comments as, 'There was shooting everywhere.' Approximately halfway through the article the Israeli media were cited as the next source, in the eleventh paragraph (of a total of eighteen). No Israeli official is ever acknowledged as the source of any of the information presented!

The second article, printed on November 18, was filed by Paul Adams from Tel Aviv. It acknowledged the true nature of those attacked and killed, but failed to address the issue of Israeli government deception at all.

By Paul Knox failing to acknowledge who the original sources were and by the follow-up article failing to identify the intentional effort at deception by the Israeli government, the *Globe and Mail's* sloppy coverage can indeed also be seen to have been careless and guilty of significant omissions of basic relevant facts, thereby misrepresenting the overall situation. The Israeli initial efforts at disinformation were not taken to task in the slightest; indeed the presenting of false information was not even mentioned.

On the other hand, both *Globe* articles did provide information that allowed the event to be better contextualized than did most CanWest Global articles. For example, even the initial article acknowledged, 'Jewish fanatic Baruch Goldstein massacred 29 Arabs in 1994 at the mosque on the site of the same Tomb.'

The Toronto Star

Although the *Toronto Star* coverage is not analyzed in this study, for lack of access to their stories, a general comment on their coverage: it reveals an entirely different attitude towards informing their readers.

The *Toronto Star* on-line stories on the Israeli-Palestinian conflict offer a box immediately beside the news, with links to other sources of information. These are, in order, Amnesty International Report (2002), Human Rights Watch Report (2002), *Jerusalem Post*, *Ha-artez* On-line (English), Bitter Lemons (think tank), Mideast Web for Peace and Education, *PeaceWatch*, the *Palestine Report*, and the *Washington Post*. This offers an impressive nine links to other sources for relevant information on the topic under discussion; these are sources that represent some degree of diversity of opinion.

These links may somewhat favour one side (two Israeli dailies, but only one moderate Palestinian publication), but at least there are links to viewpoints from more than one perspective. There is a respect, independent of whether this may be fudged somewhat to favour one side, for some degree of diversity, if not balance around some point of centrality, unlike the CanWest Global reporting.

Canadian Television Coverage

The same issues were reviewed in the television news coverage of CTV and CBC from November 15, 2002 to the year's end. The transcripts are available in the same files as the Asper's *National Post*.[31] This is the same news filing service as used by those dailies that were Southam newspapers. It is strange that the transcripts of the Global television newscasts are not also made available here. But they are not. Unfortunately only the text of CTV and CBC television coverage was available for review. Their coverage, however, is significant.

One would not expect the coverage to be more than a re-transmission of some U.S. feed, as even a casual observer of Global Television would know. This is not surprising given Izzy Asper's assertion that 'TV stations are gigantic advertising machines, there to be filled with product.'[32]

The CTV November 15 national story attributed its sources for the information presented to the Israeli military, while CBC attributed the information merely to 'Israel,' implying the Israeli government. Both CTV and CBC stories were filed from Hebron. CTV told the tale of the attack on settlers returning from prayer, with soldier casualties as well. Both used the same quote of the Israeli Foreign Ministry, coining the term 'Sabbath Massacre.' Both used part of the same quote from a *Hamas* spokesperson.

None of the stories on either network mentioned that among the dead was a colonel or that the Israeli commanding officer in the region had been killed in combat.

There the similarities ended. The CTV account cautioned the event was 'likely to *provoke* Israel to respond with force…' and acknowledged the numeric inequality between the settlers and the Palestinians at the end of the account. If presented at the beginning of a story, it may tend to encourage a viewer to ask herself how do the 'settlers' manage to impose themselves in such a situation being such a small minority of the total population? This suggests that extreme violence may well be their approach. When this information is presented at the end, it works more instead to contribute to a sense of empathy for the outnumbered Israelis.

CBC, on the other hand, gave the numbers up front, allowing viewers to frame the situation accordingly. The CBC account made reference to the Jewish settler, without naming him, who attacked hundreds of Palestinians at prayer in 1994, killing 29. It presented this example as reflective of the nature of the relations in Hebron—based on tension and animosity. CTV mentioned the 1994 massacre also, but not until the following day in the second of its three reports mentioning the attack.

The CBC story also gave the reason for the attack as stated by the group to first claim responsibility, *Islamic Jihad*—in retaliation for the assassination of one of their leaders in Jenin the week before, as had many of the daily newspapers. CBC reported two deaths by Israeli military in retaliation that evening. It explained that there had been talks with these very same groups of curtailing attacks on Israelis in Israel. It stated though that in occupied Palestine, 'Palestinian militants of all stripes consider Israelis settlers and Israeli soldiers to be legitimate targets.'

Further it contextualizes the attack by saying, in spite of some negotiations, 'attacks like the one tonight are actually on the rise again.' The report ended referring to expected Israeli retaliation from military and settlers alike.

In spite of being almost the same length, the CBC report provided a wealth of greater information, allowing for events to be more appropriately contextualized, even with the misinformation that they too had presented in the lead.

In the clarification period, CTV acknowledged that all killed were military or security guards. But CTV also continued to report that settlers had not only been attacked but wounded. They offered no quotes from anyone, only the reporter.

The CBC report, for its part, said, 'The army is now saying it appears last night's ambush was directed, not against worshippers as originally reported, but against soldiers who were escorting them and security forces from a nearby settlement. Israel blamed it on the Palestinian Authority which regards soldiers and settlers in the occupied territories as legitimate targets.' The CBC used clips from three different sources: the Israeli Foreign Minister, the Palestinian Authority spokesperson and a spokesperson from the *Islamic Jihad*.

The only other English-language story from either network in 2002 that mentioned the attack is a CTV story on November 17, the third evening in a row to refer to the event. Here the report merely referred to '12 Israelis killed...by Palestinian gunmen two days' earlier. This is seemingly neutral in its account, except that CTV never did clarify to its viewers that the previous claims that settlers were being attacked and wounded were false, so its lack of clarification and reference to '12 Israelis killed' is actually a serious issue of misrepresentation through omission.

Thus, of the television coverage reviewed, CBC provided accounts that were significantly better than the rest. CTV, for its part, provided accounts that were sloppy and which ended up leaving their viewers with a false view of the world, in part owing to Israeli government propaganda that was not clarified once it was exposed. Neither, however, reverted to explicitly presenting false claims in their period of institutional memory.

International Media Coverage

What about international media? As the scope of this project was merely to review the major Canadian newspaper coverage, only one U.S. daily was examined: the *New York Times*. This is probably the most significant U.S. daily, for like Canada's *Globe and Mail*, the *New York Times* is the U.S. newspaper of record.

Thus the *New York Times* coverage of the November 15 event will be briefly reviewed, specifically to determine the nature of their coverage regarding the strengths and weaknesses already identified in the Canadian coverage.

The New York Times

The *New York Times* printed a total of twelve stories between November 15, 2002 and the year's end that employed the terms 'Hebron' and 'killed.' Eight of these stories mentioned the November 15 attack. These are numbers similar to the coverage in some of the CanWest Global newspapers (*Gazette*, 7; *Vancouver Sun*, 9; *Telegram*, 9). One article is in the initial period; three are in the clarification period. Two are in the interim period; two are in the period of institutional memory.

Regarding sources, the Israeli officials are acknowledged as the source of the initial reporting, in the lead paragraph of the first story. In the clarification period, the three stories slowly provide greater information to clarify the initial misinformation.

The Nov. 17 article acknowledged that no worshippers were killed, but continued to maintain they had been attacked. It took until Nov. 18 before the *New York Times* printed, 'The Israeli army initially said the attack was on Jewish worshippers, but it appears to have been directed at security forces that guard settlers.' The next report to mention Hebron, three days later, appropriately continued to seek answers on the issue:

> The Israeli Foreign Ministry at first said that gunmen had killed worshippers on the way home from prayers, but that account was inaccurate. The army spokeswoman said that the army was investigating the incident and planned to publish an account of it.

In the clarification period, over the three articles, the *New York Times* gradually acknowledged what had happened, although it was slow in doing so. It was the only article reviewed to claim that the Israeli Army committed itself to publishing the results of an inquiry later that would explain why the initial accounts were falsified. The *New York Times*, however, never did follow up on this claim in their future reporting.

In the remaining four stories the newspaper was consistent in acknowledging that those attacked and killed were either soldiers, the dreaded border police or security forces. In the 'interim period' both stories mentioned the incident; both were explicit in naming the military and security forces as only those who were attacked and killed. The same was true of both stories in the period of its institutional memory. All four stories acknowledged the nature of the event; none 'slipped' in their characterization. Although the *New York Times* was slow to clarify the true nature of events, once it did, it stuck with the version it had acknowledged. It did not resort to resurrecting claims that already been discredited as did the CanWest Global papers, for whatever possible reason.

New York Times' Contextualization

The *New York Times*, like the *Globe and Mail*, included reference in its very first account of the incident, to the 1994 massacre of 29 Palestinians at prayer. Importantly it did also mention that 150 other Palestinians at prayer were also wounded. But on the other hand, it failed to characterize the mass killing as a 'massacre' in spite of referring to the November 15 attack in the preceding paragraph as the 'Sabbath Massacre.' Unlike the *Globe*, the *New York Times* also failed to refer to the Israeli killer as a 'fanatic,' but instead mentioned he was originally from Brooklyn, identifying him as a 'doctor.'

Unlike any of the other accounts reviewed, the *New York Times* admitted that the Israeli killer 'remains something of a underground hero' to the settlers. Only two CanWest Global papers (*National Post* and *Calgary Herald*), for their part, even acknowledged the 1994 incident of Goldstein massacring praying Palestinians, in spite of it being an apparent parallel to the alleged version reported in the first two days. The *National Post* version however claimed 'a Jewish militant shot dead 29 Arabs at a mosque *near* the Tomb of the Patriarchs,' instead of praying in the very holy Tomb itself, mistakenly cultivating the illusion that each religion could have its own separate holy site. Neither of the two brief CanWest references to the 1994 massacre mentioned that 150 worshipping Palestinians were also wounded before the unarmed worshippers could overpower the Zionist fanatic.

In stark contrast to the CanWest Global reports, the *New York Times* included such key information as the following, which allows readers to make a little more sense of what is taking place. This information, from a Palestinian perspective, was not found in any of the CanWest Global coverage:

- Even Palestinians who oppose attacks in pre–1967 Israel overwhelmingly support attacks on settlers and soldiers in the West Bank, regarding such violence as lawful resistance to occupation.
- Israel does not recognize such distinctions between its citizens on either side of the 1967 boundaries, and officially neither do either the *Islamic Jihad* nor *Hamas*, which consider all of Israel as occupied territory.

These two sentences alone provide a wealth of information that might well be precisely what is missing for many readers to make some sense of what is taking place. It is the perspective, first, of Palestinians; and secondly, of the Palestinian militant organizations, seeking, in their minds, national liberation.

Alternatively the readings from the CanWest Global papers would tend to have generated an emotional response of outrage and anger towards Palestinians, who were cast as displaying a disrespect of human life and religious tolerance.

The November 17 article, which acknowledged that all the dead were soldiers or security forces, was the only coverage reviewed which claimed, 'The ambush was a devastating blow to the Israeli Army...' In summary, the *New York Times* offered much greater contextualization for the story than any of the CanWest Global papers and included significant information to allow for an assessment of the situation beyond simply villanizing Palestinians.

Izzy Asper's notion of balance appears to be so far to the right that, in his rant against bias, published in the CanWest Global newspapers, he accused the CBC and the *New York Times* of both being not only biased, but 'left-wing'! This study shows clearly that CBC and the *New York Times* had the best and most accurate reporting of those outlets reviewed. In fact, in comparison to the shoddy propaganda presented through Asper's CanWest Global newspapers, both the CBC and the *New York Times* stood out as examples of 'quality' reporting.

The Propaganda Model

This study shows that Canadian media coverage of the first major event in Israel or Palestine following Izzy Asper's claim of media bias revealed that indeed the Canadian media does seem highly partisan in their coverage of Palestinian-Israeli conflict. It would in fact qualify to be considered propaganda, by any meaningful definition of the word. However Asper's claim that the nature of the propaganda is pro-Palestinian has been shown to be a gross mischaracterization, indeed the exact opposite of what actually occurred. No indication of Palestinian propaganda was visible. Instead the propaganda discovered in Asper's own CanWest Global newspapers is undeniably pro-Israel. Both the Israeli state and Asper's newspapers have abused their respective positions by choosing to disseminate propaganda, instead of offering information through honest reporting. The credibility of both is seriously damaged; but Canadian mainstream media silence on this issue has prevented the public from knowing this.

The communication theory of news that most accurately seems to capture the nature of the North American mainstream media today would seem to be the Propaganda Model advanced by Edward S. Herman and Noam Chomsky in 1988, initially amid dismissive mutterings of derision for alleged over-simplification. The Propaganda Model, however, has shown itself to be more credible than first appeared, while the North American media have shown themselves, in recent years, to be less credible and more subservient to dominant interests in their journalism than many had thought.

Typically this has occurred through structural means without routine, direct, overt imposition of content by media owners. In this case, however, the Aspers have gone to an extreme. This extremism works in the case of CanWest Global to convert Canadian national mainstream media from sources of news, no matter how skewed, into mouthpieces for crass foreign government propaganda. This extremism also would serve to encourage CanWest Global journalists to engage in self-censorship merely to preserve their jobs.

Corporate ownership
Ownership of the CanWest Global media empire seems to have directly influenced the content of its editorial and news coverage.

In late 2000, Asper's CanWest Global purchased the Southam newspapers and eventually the *National Post* from Conrad Black's Hollinger Corporation.[33] Since the beginning of 2002,[34] CanWest Global sought to reverse Southam's long-standing policy of editorial independence, by imposing three national editorials each week on all Southam dailies. In response to national outrage, the Aspers, for now at least, reduced this proposal to once a week. No local editorials could disagree with the positions advanced in the head office. Moreover, journalists claimed, no journalist or columnist was to print comments in disagreement with the centrally determined policies. More than seventy CanWest Global journalists openly signed a letter criticizing CanWest Global's top-down, national editorial policy. Then CanWest Global management issued an internal memo that attempted to limit the journalists' right to express their opinions even around the water cooler or over coffee. The stated consequences were suspension or firing.[35]

Key ex-Southam publishers and editors have been replaced once CanWest Global took over the Southam newspapers. The Montreal *Gazette* publisher, Michael Goldbloom, left his job over Asper's centralized approach and 'different perspectives' (i.e. coverage that includes even minor criticism of Israel).[36] The *Gazette* was one of the Southam papers where most conflict emerged over Asper's centralizing efforts to undermine editorial independence and integrity in reporting, while claiming to do exactly the opposite.[37] Opposition at the *Gazette* to the new management values and practices of hierarchical centralization led to a protest group of prominent journalists, editors and publishers being formed, *Diversity of Voices*. This group included several prominent former Southam editors, publishers, directors and even a former president and CEO.[38]

Besides *Gazette* publisher Goldbloom, there was *Halifax Daily News* editor, Bill Turpin, who resigned when ordered by head office to not publish a column criticizing corporate policy. Then there was Russell Mills, publisher of CanWest Global's *Ottawa Citizen*, who lost his job in June, 2002 seemingly for running an editorial calling for the resignation of Asper's fellow-Liberal, Prime Minister Jean Chretien.[39]

CanWest Global's ownership seems to have clearly played a decisive role in the news content, replacing editors and publishers of its major dailies,[40] not to mention getting rid of columnists who present views different from their own.[41]

Advertising

CanWest Global seems to be more ideologically driven than mainstream media would typically be, according the Herman and Chomsky model where advertising plays a decisive role in shaping corporate policies around content. For Asper to call for a boycott of advertisers in newspapers that show bias is not a typical position for media owners. It is extreme. Advertisers would obviously not be pleased with such positions, above all if they thought they themselves may be targeted.

Even the value of CanWest Global shares seems to have been negatively affected by Asper's political agenda. The firing of *Ottawa Citizen* publisher, Russell Mills, led to the cancellation of subscriptions. Opposition to Asper's top-down imposition of views through his newspapers has led to widespread outrage.[42]

This is not typical of corporate media behavior. It reflects a situation where one person has built a personal corporate media empire. Typically one could expect a corporation to devise policy based on seeking to maximize profit. This case study points towards Izzy Asper's CanWest Global as being complicit in promoting Israeli propaganda. This then would seem to be an instance of political and/or ideological motivation of a media baron overriding basic economic interests.

Sources

As for the sources employed by CanWest Global newspapers in their initial coverage, many were unidentified. But there were 139 references to sources employed in the fifty-seven articles that directly referred to the events of November 15, 2002 in Hebron: 110 of these were from the Israeli government (28), Israeli political opposition (4), Israeli military (50), Israeli media (13), Israeli settlers (6) or Israeli witnesses (9). No Palestinian residents of the houses that lined the combat zone were interviewed or cited.

Four times a hospital worker or medic was cited. Three sources were unspecified residents, witnesses or 'sources,' although two seem clearly to be Israeli.

There were no Palestinian witnesses cited. None of the CanWest Global coverage cited the opinion of an expert in the affairs of that region.

That leaves twenty-two other references to sources from a total of 139. Ten of these are brief references to *Islamic Jihad* claiming responsibility for the attack. One other is *Hamas* doing the same. Six are either the Palestinian Authority or 'local officials' reporting on the Israeli military retaliation. Two are Palestinian victims of Israeli retaliatory attacks. The last three quote a Palestinian protester celebrating in the refugee camp of *Shati* in the Gaza Strip. None of these 22 Palestinian sources is used to comment on the specifics of what occurred on November 15.

Thus, all identified 110 sources who were cited in offering specific information as to what allegedly occurred during the November 15 attack were Israeli. This occurred in a city which is 97% Palestinian!

Flak

As for the Propaganda Model's element of flak, this can be seen in Asper's attack on the CBC for its reporting on Israel and Palestine. CBC, whose reporting has been shown in this case study to be exemplary, was attacked by Izzy Asper, whose news reporting on this very issue has been shown instead to be exceptionally unprofessional and simply unacceptable for newspapers in a society seeking to be democratic. This is presumably an instance of name-calling in order to divert attention away from Asper's newspapers' own distorted coverage and severe misinformation.

Anti-Communism

'Anti-communism,' indeed continues to be carted out on rare occasions, but since September 11, 2001, this element of the Propaganda Model has largely been replaced in North America by 'anti-terrorism.' The attempts to maintain that the Palestinian attack was directed against Israeli civilians suggest an effort to cultivate and preserve an image of Palestinian 'terrorism' when actually the targets of the Palestinian gunmen were all Israeli military and security personnel.

In conclusion, the Asper management of the Southam newspapers and the *National Post* has placed CanWest Global newspapers' credibility on the line in order to promote Israeli propaganda.

Conclusions

The political cost that Israel experienced in the CanWest Global media as a result of being caught spreading disinformation seems to have been nil. Israeli officials were allowed to act with impunity in spreading propaganda without any loss of credibility, even after being publicly caught and exposed doing so. The disinformation, besides generating a mood of sympathy for Israel, allowed the Israelis to avoid a lead in stories which otherwise would likely have profiled the killing of the Israeli commanding officer in the region and acknowledged the effectiveness of the Palestinian attack militarily. As noted above, this disinformation instead allowed a preservation of the image of Palestinian 'terrorism.'

Absolutely none of the media reviewed followed up on the Israeli disinformation that was initially spread to frame the story when it first broke. But there are even greater elements of dishonest reporting that allowed the Israeli government to reap benefits from their propaganda efforts. The CanWest Global newspapers (and those receiving the CanWest feed) stand out in their sloppiness and/or dishonesty by reverting to presenting as fact, disinformation that had already been exposed in their own newspapers as false and which clearly appears to be an effort of Israeli propaganda. Since the propaganda was largely successful, even though it was exposed, makes one wonder how many other previous and subsequent stories about Israel or Palestine are simply propaganda creations that have yet to be publicly exposed.

If one were to apply Asper's criteria of boycotting a newspaper for its dishonest coverage of Israeli-Palestinian relations, then that boycott would clearly be leveled against the CanWest Global newspapers above all other mainstream media. The CanWest Global newspapers to offer the most distorted reporting seem to be the Montreal *Gazette* and the *National Post*. The least distorted and most honest of the CanWest Global coverage is provided by the *Calgary Herald*. The greatest use of shameless propaganda by reasserting claims that had already been widely revealed, even by CanWest Global newspapers, to have been false falls to the Montreal *Gazette* and two newspapers to which CanWest Global supplies feed, the *Telegram* and the *Guardian*.

So, as posed in the beginning, why is it that the Israeli government and military spokespersons would intentionally claim that settlers had been attacked on their way home from prayer, when necessarily they would be required to retract those claims later? Would this not result in a loss of credibility for the Israeli authorities, thereby undermining their credibility for their previous and future claims?

It seems the international media did not extract any accountability at all from the Israeli government for their intentional deception. This would make them complicit in maintaining deception around events in Palestine. Seemingly the Israeli government knew this, and therefore could act with impunity in lying, without great concern for the consequences of doing so. If this is true, it suggests a very sad state of affairs: one that should outrage Canadians and democrats everywhere; one that deserves to be investigated by an impartial committee.

All this occurred in a context where a poll of Canadians found two-thirds of those consulted to already consider media concentration a serious problem that needs to be addressed. Seventy-one percent of those polled thought media owners should not limit what journalists could comment on.[43] This poll was conducted between June 27 and July 4, 2002, by Strategic Communication Inc., weeks *before* CanWest Global fired their Ottawa publisher, Russell Mills.

The conclusions seem obvious: i) following Asper's own advice, boycott CanWest Global media (and, following Asper's advice, any who advertise in them as well); ii) call for federal reforms to end media monopoly; iii) publicize widely any false reporting in an effort to hold media accountable for the accuracy of their reporting; and iv) establish an independent committee to review CanWest Global reporting. If the federal government does not or cannot establish a respectable, independent and impartial review committee, then civil society must do so.

There is indeed a 'cancer' affecting Canadian newspaper reporting today. No democracy can be possible in a climate of media deception, impunity and institutionalized abuse of power.

Postscript

With the passing away of Izzy Asper in the fall of 2003, has CanWest Global's policy regarding Middle East coverage changed since that time? Those who were not observing firsthand a continuation of the policy soon found their answer through the media themselves. The policy has actually gotten worse. On 17 September 2004, CBC broke a story of CanWest altering Reuters stories on the Israeli-Palestinian conflict and the war in Iraq sufficiently to 'thereby chang(e) the meaning of those stories' (CBC, 17 Sept 04).[44] Three days later the *New York Times* also ran a version of the same story.[45]

The CanWest Global practice consists of CanWest editors strategically inserting one critical, emotional and inflammatory word into stories they receive from international wire services. The word is 'terrorist'—a keyword today within the propaganda model. It is routinely used to apply to those who resist either U.S. occupation of Iraq or Israeli occupation of Palestine.

The practice was not limited to Reuters' stories. A week earlier an AP story, by Hamza Hendawi, carried by the *Ottawa Citizen* on U.S. troops bombing Fallujah, described those resisting the U.S. bombardment as 'terrorists' by inserting that

word seven times throughout the article, including the lead ('U.S. jets pounded terrorist positions in Fallujah...') and even the title.[46] When readers took exception to
the claim through letters to the editor, the editor was obliged to retract the claim
that these were actually 'terrorists.' (Arguably they are no more terrorists than
would be U.S. citizens taking up arms against an invasion by a foreign power.)

Ottawa Citizen editor Scott Anderson defended CanWest Global's practice of
inserting the word 'terrorist' at his discretion, acknowledging that the term was
typically only applied to Arab organizations or individuals. Anderson was quoted
as claiming he did not believe he had a responsibility to inform his readers that
CanWest was making such changes in content. He dismissed the issue by claiming
that CanWest was merely 'editing for style' (CBC, 17 Sept 04).

Reuters' global managing editor, David Schlesinger, disagrees. He was cited by
CBC as claiming CanWest to have 'crossed a line from editing for style to editing the
substance and slant of news from the Middle East' (CBC 17 Sept 04; direct quote of
CBC, not Schlesinger). There can be no reasonable disagreement with this.

The number of ethical issues this raises is enormous. But none are acknowledged by CanWest. Schlesinger, for example, seemingly had no problem with
CanWest activities other than where it compromised Reuters. 'If they want to put
their own judgment into it, they're free to do that, but then they shouldn't say
that it's by a Reuters's reporter.' This is not a minor issue, but it far from the only
one. Foreign journalists in Iraq are as vulnerable to attack and kidnapping as
other non-Iraqis, if not more. They become even more targeted when they are reported to have made volatile statements indiscriminately labeling Iraqi national-
ists and sovereignists as 'terrorists.' Had Canadian journalist captured by Iraqi
insurgents in 2004, Scott Taylor, worked for CanWest or had his stories reported
in a CanWest newspaper, he may not have been released, but would likely have
been executed instead.

But what does this practice of turning journalism into propaganda mean to
the general reader? What does this do to the responsibility of journalism to provide an informed public, vital to any democracy? What does this do to the public
sphere that journalism has an historic responsibility to create in any society seeking or claiming to be a democracy?

CanWest Global clearly sells us all out. It sells out its historic responsibility to
journalism and to democracy, in exchange for making a buck and promoting propaganda. Both are actions in the service of the private interests of the owners, as if
to say, 'The public be screwed.' Am I ever going to buy another CanWest newspa-

per? Certainly not! Who wants to spend money on propaganda, especially if one's intent is to purchase news? A boycott of CanWest seems most rational, until there is a return to some degree of very minimal integrity in journalism, instead of the outrageous agenda of mere crass propaganda. Unfortunately, this is not a change that one can reasonably expect to occur under the current ownership.

NOTES

1. CanWest Global owns Canada's largest daily newspaper chain, while also being the country's second largest private broadcaster, in addition to its broadcast holdings in Australia, Ireland, the UK and New Zealand (Dene Moore, 'Izzy Asper, founder and chairman of CanWest Global Communications Corp., defended the company's contentious editorial policy before its Shareholders,' *Canadian Press Newswire*, January 30, 2002).

2. The italicized words within the quotations were in quotation marks in the original. *Canadian Press Newswire*, October 2, 2002.

3. See Stephen Kimber, 'The Last Spike' in *Media*, 8 (4), Winter 2002, 30. Kimber has been a career journalist and today is Director of the School of Journalism, at the University of King's College, Toronto.

4. The Aspers '...have clamped down on news, criticism or commentary that is anything but 100-per-cent pro-Israel.' See the article by anonymous *Gazette* workers 'The *Gazette* Intifada' in *Media*, 8 (4) Winter, 2002, 6-7. Also Kevin Michael Grace, 'See no Evil! Or else!' *Report Newsmagazine*, 29 (13) June 24, 2002 14.

5. These three newspapers were among 12 newspapers and 32 other publications CanWest Global sold to the Transcontinental Group in July, 2002 for $255 million (*CP Newswire*, 2 October, 2002; *Canadian Printer*, July/August, 2002, 6) .

6. Typically this resulted in television offering its initial coverage on the same day, but newspapers not filing a report until the following day. This is a result of production schedules determined by the nature of the medium.

7. As reported on November 16, 2002: Montreal *Gazette*, A1; *Ottawa Citizen*, A1; *Vancouver Sun*, A14; *Victoria Times-Colonist*, A3; *Calgary Herald*, A10.

8. John Daniszewski '*Hamas* won't Relent in its Attacks on Israel,' *Calgary Herald*, Nov. 19, 2002, A17.

9. Adrian Humphreys, 'Canadian Seen as Planner of Hebron Attack,' *National Post*, Nov. 18, 2002, A1.

10. 'Jews Ambushed Walking Home From Prayer Service,' *Edmonton Journal*, Nov, 16, 2002, A4.

11. Alan Philps, 'Sharon Backs New Outpost in Hebron,' *National Post*, Nov. 18, 2002, A9.

12. Alan Philps, 'Sharon Backs New Outpost in Hebron,' *National Post*, Nov. 18, 2002, A9.

13. *Canadian Jewish News*, v.32 (46) Nov. 21, 2002

14. Molly Moore, 'Israeli Forces Take Control of Hebron: 40 Palestinians Arrested after Ambush,' *Calgary Herald*, Nov. 17, 2002, A5.

15. In Ran HaCohen, 'Looking Behind *Ha'aretz*'s Liberal Image,' *Letter From Israel*, Oct. 2, 2002 at www.antiwar.com/hacohen/h100202.html, RaCohen reveals the intentional shift in the information *Ha'aretz* daily prints in Hebrew each day and the English version of selected news items. 'It often omits certain items, certain columns, that *Ha'aretz* does not find 'suitable' for foreign eyes...'. An example, RaCohen offers is a 'translation' as follows for when Israeli military uses Palestinian neighbours as human shields, from the Hebrew original: 'If nobody answers, we have to tell the neighbour that he will be killed if no one comes out,' to the English version: 'If nobody answers, he comes back and we go to work.'

16. Emphasis added. *Canadian Jewish News*, Nov. 21, 2002.

17. 'The Jewish settlers of Hebron are fanatic extremists even by Israeli standards. They regularly ransack Palestinian shops, cut electricity lines and water pipes, wreck cars, and attack school-children.' Ran Hacohen, 'Hebron, City of Terror,' *Letter from Israel*, February 19, 2003; www.antiwar.com/hacohen/h-col.html.

18. 'Israel Admits Victims of Friday Attack were Military, Not Worshippers,' became 'Military Take Control of City in Retaliation for Sabbath Massacre,' *Ottawa Citizen*, Nov. 17, 2002, A7.

19. One of these was the 'Palestinian Ambush Kills 12 Israelis: 15 Others were wounded by Gun-fire and Grenades as they Left Prayers Shrine in Hebron,' *Vancouver Sun*, Final Edition, Nov. 16, 2002, A14, with a photograph; two reports, with entirely different content were curiously listed under this same title. The second of these were the Early and Late Editions of the Montreal *Gazette*, Nov. 16, 2002, with both versions using a photograph of an 'injured Jewish settler' on his 'way from Sabbath eve prayers.' From the early to the lengthier, late edition, the story moved from page 29 to the front page, with the Final Edition having added five paragraphs at the beginning, presenting the propaganda version of the Israeli ministry. The source of the information is not given, however - merely an unidentified 'the sources said.' The lead paragraph included the statement that 'stiff Israeli military action' was likely.

20. These were the *Ottawa Citizen*, *Edmonton Journal*, *Vancouver Sun* and *Calgary Herald*, all on Nov. 17, 2002.

21. As well as the four reprints of Molly Moore's story, there was mention of this in a story in the *National Post*, Nov. 18.

22. Alan Philps, 'Sharon Backs New Outpost in Hebron,' *National Post*, Nov. 18, 2002, A9 and Adrian Humphreys, 'Canadian Seen as Planner of Hebron Attack,' *National Post*, Nov. 18, 2002, A1.

23. A cursory glance at the Israeli media suggests the opposite - that Israeli mainstream outlets are more diverse than their counter-parts in Canada or the United States. It was, after all, Conrad Black, then a Canadian, who purchased the *Jerusalem Post* and turned it from a progressive, social democratic newspaper to a narrow conservative one.

24. Jason Keyser, 'Israeli Troops Seize West Bank City,' St. John's *Telegram*, Nov. 17, 2002, A14.

25. 'The 450 Hebron settlers are supported by about 4,000 Israeli troops, who are there for the settlers, not for the Palestinians. Since mid-November, following a clash with Islamic Jihad activists in which 12 Israeli combatants were killed, the Army has been holding the city under continuous curfew, lifted only for a few hours in more than two months (!) to allow for shopping. When Palestinians do venture out on these rare occasions, they are often harassed by settlers, who stage violent processions whenever they have a pretext.' Ran Hacohen, 'Hebron, City of Terror,' *Letter from Israel*, February 19, 2003. www.antiwar.com/hacohen/h-col.html

26. The articles were 'Retaliation for Hebron ambush begins,' Montreal *Gazette*, Nov. 17, 2002, A9 and 'Israelis retake Hebron,' *Halifax Daily*, Nov. 17, 2002, 10.

27. Ran Hacohen 'Ethnic Cleansing: Past, Present and Future' *Letter from Israel*, December 30, 2002 at www.antiwar.com/hacohen/h123002.html.

28. Alan Philps, 'Sharon Backs New Outpost in Hebron,' *National Post*, Nov. 18, A9.

29. Mike Gasher, 'Does CanWest know what all the Fuss is about?' *Media* 8 (4) Winter 2002, 8-9. Also 'An Editorial from the *Kitchener-Waterloo Record*, June 22,' *Canadian Press Newswire*, June 24, 2002.

30. Anonymous Canwest Global journalists, 'The *Gazette* Intifada,' *Media* 8 (4) Winter 2002, 6-7.

31. This can be found on NewsDisc 2002 #4.

32. Quote from Allan Levine's *From Winnipeg to the World: The CanWest Global Story* (CanWest Global Communications Corp.) as quoted in 'The Story of Izzy,' *Marketing Magazine*, 107 (47) Nov. 25, 2002.

33. 'Hollinger International Cuts Quarterly Dividend to Lower Debt,' *Canadian Press Newswire*, Sept. 11, 2002.

34. Barbara Shecter 'Editorial policy 'Mischaracterized': Readers deserve National Viewpoint, CanWest Head says,' *National Post*, January 31, 2002, FP5.

35. Anonymous CanWest journalists, *Media* 8 (4), Winter 2002, 6-7.

36. Mike Gasher 'Does CanWest Know What all the Fuss is about? The Aspers have Inadvertently given new Life to Criticisms of Corporate Concentration,' *Media*, 8 (4) Winter, 2002, 8-9.

37. 'CanWest Sends 'editorial values' Memo to Staff as Media Debate Continues,' *Victoria Times-Colonist*, June 21, 2002.

38. Kevin Michael Grace, 'See No Evil! Or Else!' *Report Newsmagazine* 29 (13) June 24, 2002, 14.

39. 'Editorial from the *Kitchener-Waterloo Record*, June 22, 2002' *Canadian Press Newswire*, June 24, 2002.

40. These are the Montreal *Gazette, Ottawa Citizen*, Halifax *Daily News* and *Regina Leader-Post*.

41. For example, Lawrence Martin—see Kevin Michael Grace, *Report Newsmagazine* 29 (13), June 24, 2002, 14. Or veteran columnist Peter Worthington—see Joanne Byfield, 'Izzy's Way or the Highway: Asper Makes it Clear Who's the Boss and What His Newspapers Think,' *Report Newsmagazine*, 29 (8) April 15, 2002, 50-51.

42. Gillian Livingston, 'CanWest Global Communication Shares Brushed six-year lows Wednesday as Worries over the Sale of TV Stations in New Zealand and Criticism of Editorial Actions in Canada Continued to Drag Down the Multimedia Company's Stock,' *Canadian Press Wirenews*, June 19, 2002. From a high of $22 a share in early 2000, CanWest Global shares dropped to $11 in the first half of 2002, driven down largely by generalized market trends (John Gray, 'Communications and Media [Outlook 2002]' Canadian Business, v.75 (1) January 7/21, 2002, 38). In August, 2002, shares dropped to $6 and projected a drop to $4 per share (Roman Franko 'CanWest Global Communications,' *National Post*, August 15, 2002, IN3). In November, 2002, CanWest Global had its credit ratings cut by Standard and Poor's Rating Service, making borrowing to finance its $4 billion debt more expensive ('S&P Lowers Credit Rating on Media Company CanWest Global Communications,' *Canadian Press Newswire*, November 18, 2002).

43. 'Canadians concerned about Concentration of Media, Suggests New Poll,' Halifax, *Canadian Press Newswire*, July 5, 2002. The survey is reported to be 'accurate to within plus or minus 3.1 percentage points, 19 times out of 20.' It was commissioned by the Communications, Energy and Paperworkers Union.

44. CBC, 'Canwest Papers Accused of misusing word 'Terrorist' 17 September 2004, http:www//cbc.ca/story/canada/national/2004/09/17/canwesterrorist/040917html.

45. Ian Austin, 'Reuters Asks a Chain to Remove its Bylines' C9, *New York Times*, 20 Sept 04.

46. Hamza Hendawi, 'U.S. Attacks Fail to Weaken Terrorists' Grip on Fallujah,' A9 *Ottawa Citizen*, 9 September 2004.

Chapter Four

Propaganda And Its Affordances: El Salvador In The *Globe and Mail* And The Question Of Intellectual Responsibility

Peter Eglin

"Talk about Nicaragua and Cuba," he [Colonel Ponce] hissed, and Mr. Cristiani immediately obliged, raising the spectre of dangerous expansionism on the part of existing Communist states. —Linda Hossie, "El Salvador's Widening Reality Gap"[1]

IN THIS CHAPTER I EXAMINE THE REPRESENTATION of the civil war in El Salvador in selected news reports and editorials in the *Globe and Mail* from 1987 to 1991, focussing on the massacre of the Jesuit intellectuals, their cook and her daughter at the University of Central America (UCA) in San Salvador on 16 November 1989. The analysis is carried out in terms of the propaganda model of Herman and Chomsky in *Manufacturing Consent* (2002 [1988]). Particular attention is accorded the post-massacre, arms-from-Nicaragua story in the context of renewed demands for the cancellation of U.S. and Canadian aid to El Salvador. I use the results of the media inquiry to address the question of the extent of the responsibility of Canadian university-based intellectuals for the human rights abuses visited on Salvadorans by their U.S.-backed government in the period.

In the works of Chomsky and of Herman, singly and jointly, is to be found an uncompromising analysis of the organization and operation of the structure of rule in the world. It is informed by three elementary, if widely unobserved, ethical principles: we are responsible for the anticipatable consequences of our own actions; we should apply the same moral standards to our own actions as we do to those of others; in seeking to defend human rights we should seek to act in relation to those atrocities and abuses where our actions *can* have an effect. To the extent that our own government is democratic and we thereby accrue both a responsibility and a capacity to influence it, then our first responsibility internationally is to defend the human rights of those our own government is oppressing. Accordingly, being U.S. citizens, Herman and Chomsky focus on the United States. There, as more or less everywhere outside of the state socialist countries, rule is founded in the ownership and control of basic resources by a capitalist class. These resources include the elite and mass media of communication, which are themselves either huge corporations or are owned by even larger corporations. According to the standard theory of democracy, in advanced industrial societies that depend for their proper functioning on an informed citizenry, the media are indispensable organs of information, opinion and debate. Thus it is that under state capitalism these essential means by which the public can come to exercise effective political choice reside in largely private hands. For example, the *Globe and Mail*, Canada's self-declared "national" newspaper and acknowledged news "agenda setter,"[2] was and mostly still is owned by the nation's richest man, Ken Thomson (though it is now part of the corporate media empire of Bell Canada Enterprises). Since the major media are largely paid for by corporate advertisers rather than consumers, even "publicly owned" media corporations such as the Public Broadcasting System in the United States or the Canadian Broadcasting Corporation in Canada, tend to resemble their private counterparts in the structure and content of their programming, at least in the domain of news.

According to the propaganda model the media are assigned a function in state capitalist societies such as the United States and Canada:

> It is their function to amuse, entertain, and inform, and to inculcate individuals with the values, beliefs, and codes of behaviour that will integrate them into the institutional structures of the larger society. In a world of concentrated wealth and major conflicts of class interest, to fulfil this role requires systematic propaganda…
>
> …The raw materials of news must pass through successive filters, leaving only the cleansed residue fit to print. They fix the premises of discourse and interpretation, and the definition of what is newsworthy in the first place, and they explain the basis and operations of what amount to propaganda campaigns.[3]

Chomsky explains how the "manufacturing of consent" by the propagation of "necessary illusions" had become, in fact, the operative requirement for the smooth functioning of modern democratic societies ever since the seventeenth-century English revolution let democracy loose among the people and the "rascal multitude" started to become a problem for state managers.[4] Since, thanks to the growth of democracy, there came to be limits on the extent of brute force such states could exercise against their own populations, controlling what people thought became even more important in democratic than in totalitarian societies. State theorists, corporate propagandists and popularizers then provided the necessary theoretical justification for such managed democracy, and university trained intellectuals have been propagating it ever since.[5]

Propaganda and its Affordances

Thanks to the media analyses of Chomsky, Herman and others,[6] it is possible to identify standard propaganda techniques employed by state managers and their obedient media. Just as Canada is generally less hawkish than the United States on Central America so the *Globe and Mail's* reporting tends to give a more truthful picture than that in the *New York Times*. Nevertheless both are elite capitalist papers, and both share some basic assumptions about the necessity of state power residing in the hands of parties serving capital. Much about the pattern of reporting and editorial content follows from this, as Herman and Chomsky have shown in convincing detail for Central America and elsewhere. That Canadian foreign policy and Canadian news reporting are somewhat more humane than their American counterparts also follows from the propaganda model. Though not without influence, the Canadian institutional actors are on the margins of power. In general, their actions and opinions count for less. Therefore the opportunity for some degree of departure from the required norms is greater. Moreover, the El Salvador bloodbath is, in the first instance, a U.S.-backed atrocity, not a Canadian one.

The propaganda techniques designed to handle a possible foreign policy (that is, domestic public relations) crisis such as the massacre of the Jesuits, their cook and her daughter include the following. Since reporting of such an atrocity cannot itself be avoided, there will be attempts to pin the blame on official enemies—the left in one form or another, that is the guerrillas of the Farabundo Marti National Liberation Front (FMLN) in this case—rather than the actual culprits (since the actual culprits are "us" or "our" agents). If such a gambit is implausible, the possibility of it will at least be taken seriously. If responsibility will not stick on the left, blame it on the extreme right, that is the "death squads" in this instance. If it has to be admitted that the death squads are actually made up of the security forces and police, allow that these are elements that are out of control of the government itself. In fact, if necessary blame the government for not reining them in. In any event, avoid as long as possible saying that the government did it, and for whom they are doing it. When you do acknowledge the truth, say ten years later, both as to the identity of the killers and of their chief backers, make it clear that since that time you, or they, or both of you have "changed course." In any event frame the event as a more or less even contest between the left and the right, if not indeed the East and the West, and let coverage reflect this. If necessary play up a "leftist atrocity" to achieve the proper balance. Since the victims are actually ours, or those of our agents or clients, and are therefore by definition "unworthy," do not humanize them. Do not depict them in such a way as to elicit readers' sympathy for them. Do not stir readers to outrage. Do not trace the line of responsibility back and up to where it belongs. Thus, commenting on U.S. treatment of the situation in El Salvador in the Fall of 1989, before the UCA massacre had occurred, Chomsky writes:

> In accord with the usual convention, the escalating violence was attrib-
> uted to "extremists of the left and right," with the reform-minded govern-
> ment standing by in helpless impotence. This is the standard technique by
> which editors, commentators, and congressional doves mask their tacit
> support for death squads and other methods "used to shield the govern-
> ment from accountability for the torture, disappearances and extrajudicial
> executions committed in their name" (Amnesty International, corroborat-
> ing other independent analyses). The source of the terror is adequately
> demonstrated by the impunity with which it is conducted, not to speak of
> ample direct evidence implicating the security forces—truisms emphasized
> by human rights monitors to no avail.[7]

The "usual convention" and "standard techniques" are clearly visible in the stance of the Government of Canada, as Secretary of State for External Affairs, Joe Clark, revealed to the House of Commons when tabling a document on "Peacekeeping in Central America" on 2 December 1987:[8]

> The tradition in the region…has been for crises to be resolved by force
> and military rule…
>
> The region is still torn by extremism—extremism of the right, ex-
> tremism of the left—and it is marked by poverty, injustice and exploita-
> tion…
>
> Moreover, despite their unanimity, there are deep suspicions
> among them—doubts that the civil authorities in El Salvador, Guate-
> mala and, to a lesser degree, Honduras, will in the end be strong enough
> to control the army, to control the police, to end the tradition of repres-

sion. There is also a profound scepticism as to whether the Sandanistas will let real democracy threaten the revolution which their constitution describes as irreversible.

...That is to mention simply the complexities of the region itself which are complicated further by the extension to Central America of the competition between the United States and the Soviet Union...

Obviously, another question in Canada concerns the public position we should take regarding the support by the United States of the Contras, and the support by the Soviet Union and Cuba of the Sandinista Government and of guerrilla activity in El Salvador. We oppose third party intervention in Central America, whatever the source, and have made that position clear to both superpowers...

The real issue in Central America is not Marxism, nor is it death squads, nor even is it the abuse of human rights. Those are symptoms. The root problems are economic and social, and Central America needs peace to resolve them.

A review of the *Globe and Mail's* treatment of El Salvador before and after the massacre shows these practices at work, albeit in a more muted form than in the *New York Times*. Thus, when Herbert Anaya, president of the non-governmental Human Rights Commission, was murdered in October 1987, the *Globe* editorialist wrote:

There is no proof that the government was involved in the killing, but it must take responsibility, nonetheless, since it has done almost nothing to bring to justice the murderers of El Salvador that have tortured and killed thousands of the country's citizens over the years. The men who killed Mr. Anaya may have been members of the armed forces or the police. They may have comprised a freelance death squad, looking to derail the peace process. Whoever they were, they could rest assured that they would get off, as have all but one or two of their kind over the years, scot-free.[9]

The government of El Salvador escapes blame, if not responsibility. In the same editorial the United States and Canada are portrayed as follows:

All Central American countries depend on aid for their economic survival—and they will depend on it even more, if the economic inequalities that threaten regional peace are to be removed. Unfortunately, donor countries are reluctant to tie aid to human rights records. The

United States *has* tied aid, but it ignores human rights violations anyway. Canada and Europe are small donors in the region, but they have
not used what muscle they have to favor human rights compliance.

In this, as in everything favoring the Arias Plan, the United States
is unlikely to take the lead. But an insistence on human rights compliance as a condition of aid from smaller donors would be a significant
factor in U.S. political debate about Central America. It seems a small
beginning but so did the Arias plan before it took off.[10]

While tacitly acknowledging the central role of the United States in all that goes
on in Central America, the writer nevertheless avoids accusing the U.S. government of anything to do with Anaya's murder. The criticism is reserved for actions
at one remove from direct criminal responsibility, namely whether aid is tied to
nations' human rights records. And even when it is acknowledged that in the U.S.
case it makes no difference whether such a policy exists or not, the obvious conclusions are avoided. At least the writer does point out the potential influence the
Canadian government can have on debate in the U.S. Congress about the annual
renewal of aid to El Salvador on which that government depends. This is a matter
to which I will return. Acknowledging the utility of a small, or "middle," power
acting on principle is rare in this forum. That it might act on principle anyway,
utility aside, is a view beyond the pale.

The next four editorials reflect the standard view. For convenience of reference let me label them "A," "B," "C" and "D." "A" occurs on 28 December 1988 in
the run-up to the March 1989 elections ("The Dirty Nine-year War of El Salvador"), "B" on 22 March 1989 following the elections ("Arena for El Salvador"), "C"
on 19 June 1989 in response to another atrocity ("Fear Stalks El Salvador"), and
"D" on 18 November 1989 following the UCA massacre ("The Pain and Violence
in El Salvador").[11] They are notable for the uniformity of their *balanced* representation of the conflict and of the *well-meaning* U.S. role in it.

Thus, on *balanced responsibility* we have:

- "The campaigns of terror waged by Marxist guerrillas, right wing death
  squads and fear crazed soldiers." (A)

- "Both sides ["the U.S. -backed government and the guerrillas"] are willing
  to make their arguments in blood." (A)

- "To undermine the rule of law and illustrate their mastery of the country-
  side, the guerrillas have begun to assassinate mayors and justices of the

peace [no source given]. According to Americas Watch, a New York-based human rights organization, the military killed 52 civilians in the first six months of 1988, nearly the same number as in all 1987. Amnesty International charges that right-wing death squads have abducted, tortured and killed hundreds of judges, human-rights workers and teachers during the last 18 months." (A)

- "The intransigence of the left and the recklessness of the United States in failing to discipline forces it armed…" (A)

- "El Salvador is a mostly agrarian society, dominated by a tiny oligarchy, which controls the nation's coffee and cotton industries. President Cristiani is himself an immensely rich property owner and coffee planter …The nine-year civil war with a determined Marxist guerrilla force has devastated the national economy…Rebel forces have sought to smash the national economy as a means of undermining the government…Their attacks are calculated to have cost the national economy as much as $300-million a year. They have also discouraged virtually all foreign investment and much domestic investment." (B)

- "It was the U.S. hope that President Duarte could build a political consensus of the centre to defeat the left-wing guerrillas and marginalize the right-wing extremists." (C)

- "A United Nations report issued yesterday charges that Mr. Cristiani's government has presided over a 'resurgence of torture' and summary execution of political opponents this year. The report also accuses the… (FMLN), the coalition of left-wing rebel groups, of assassinating civilians it believes collaborate with the death squads." (D)

- "But the real economic reform that is so desperately needed has been blocked by the continued confrontation between the far right and the Marxists." (D)

And on the *well-meaning* role of the United States there are the following formulations:

- "Alarmed at the prospect of yet another Marxist state in the region, the U.S. threw massive support in 1984 behind moderate reformer Jose Napoleon Duarte and his Christian Democratic Party and sponsored an all-out war against the guerrillas." (A)

- "The U.S. administration says all it wants to do is strengthen democracy in El Salvador. But U.S. foreign policy is generally more practical than altruistic. For reasons of domestic security, the U.S. wants to eliminate communism and create co-operative, client states throughout Central America." (A)

- "The United States is looking for vindication of its policy and a demonstration that democracy really is getting stronger in El Salvador." (A)

- "For the last five years, the U.S. has propped up the inept Christian Democratic government of Jose Napoleon Duarte, providing it with as much as $2-million a day—more than the El Salvadoran administration raised in all other revenues combined. By flooding military aid into the deeply impoverished Central American country, the U.S. hoped to contain the Marxist rebel forces long enough for the moderate Duarte government to bring about much needed social and economic reforms." (B)

- "Mr. Duarte and his moderate Christian Democrats received massive support from the United States which feared another Marxist victory in the region." [For continuation, see (6) above.] (C)

- "Despite all the financial and military support it has provided El Salvador, the United States has never succeeded in pressuring the government to pursue the death squad killers...With the collapse of U.S. policy, El Salvador seems doomed to a new era of inhumanity." (C)

- "Since the middle of this decade, the U.S. government has poured more than $1-million a day into El Salvador in an attempt to strengthen democracy there and to begin to bridge the terrible gap between the few very rich landowners and the poverty-stricken peasant majority." [For continuation, see above.] (D)

Whether the result of honest, mistaken belief, rank stupidity or cynical lying these views are indefensible. Despite noting that U.S. aid through the eighties supplied about half the El Salvador state revenue,[12] and despite knowing that the "president's 'main [or major] source of power...is the U.S. embassy',"[13] and despite noting that the overwhelming proportion of civil war deaths were both civilian and caused by the security forces and police,[14] and despite noting that the death squads are made up of the same agents out of uniform,[15] and despite noting the virtually total impunity of the killers, the editorial writers persist in transmitting fantasies about U.S. motives, practices and results. In complete conformity with the line pursued by the U.S. Government, U.S. Congress and U.S. media for the previous ten years, the *Globe and Mail* represents the Government of the United States as: wishing to "strengthen democracy," "support moderates," "reduce inequality," pursue "social and economic reforms," and pressure the El Salvador "government to pursue death squad killers"; concerned about domestic security it is alarmed by and seeks to contain or defeat another possible "Marxist" or "communist" government in the region; it is "reckless"; its policy has collapsed.[16]

In truth, within the parameters of public relations and domestic political management, U.S. motives can be represented as a set of commandments to its client governments. In setting them out in this way I do not seek to be cute or frivolous but, on the contrary, to be deadly serious and to counter obfuscation with forthrightness:

- You shall obey.

- You shall know your place in our system of rule. If you insist on acting independently you shall be made into our enemy and know our wrath. Your crimes, however petty or imaginary, will be unforgivable.

- Your place is to make your resources and markets available to us, for they are ours anyway, whether in your hands or not.

- You shall do whatever is necessary to the people of your society to secure your, that is our, place (as understood above). As long as this is so, democracy as business-elite rule with periodic public ratification is tolerable. Any greater degree of authentic democracy is communism[17] and is to be smashed. We shall provide you with the means of violence, directly or indirectly, or do it ourselves. In pursuit of this end no crime is too egregious, no amount of dictatorship too intolerable, no degree of social inequality impossible not to justify.

Within this motivational framework the correlation of U.S. aid with client state terror, with the deterrence of democracy and with impoverishment of the majority of the people is perfectly intelligible. As long as the necessary goals are realized the reduction to squalor and ruin of the great mass of the people is immaterial; the policy has succeeded.[18]

Being patently monstrous, however, such an account is inexpressible in the mainstream—perhaps, as Chomsky says, unthinkable there. And so fantasies are repeated around the intellectual campfires. The problem is, to recall an old sociological saw, "if men define situations as real, they are real in their consequences" (W.I. Thomas). The consequences of inaction, rejection and delay in responding to the massacre at UCA, including in a remote intellectual backwater like my own university (Wilfrid Laurier University), are not beyond calculation.[19] If the deceitful media accounts I have discussed are a source of usable justification for doing nothing, doing nothing in its turn provides a space in which these and other such accounts and their effects can be reproduced.

Arms from Nicaragua

The case at hand provides an instance of the replay of a classic propaganda technique in the Central American context, what could be called the weapons from official enemies device. What, at the time of the 1984 Nicaraguan elections, was the (fictitious) "Soviet MIGs" story,[20] became throughout the civil war in El Salvador the "arms from Nicaragua" story. That is, to be more precise, it became the "arms from the Sandinistas (the Nicaraguan government)" story. The precision is important since the FMLN got the bulk of their weapons by buying them on the black market from the Nicaraguan contras or the Salvadoran army itself. But since the U.S. doctrinal system required that they be getting them from official enemies in the region (so as to persuade the U.S. Congress to keep the aid flowing), the U.S. media obliged by repeating government claims, without credible evidence, that the Sandinistas (and Cuba) were the source.

The game was played again following the UCA massacre, and it was played in the Canadian press. And, as in the United States, there was the simultaneous question of the possible stopping, suspension or continuation of Canadian aid to El Salvador. It is the inter-relationships among media propaganda, timely campus protest, domestic government decisions about aid, and murder by the client government that I wish to bring out in the following consideration of the post-UCA-massacre "arms from Nicaragua" story.

On 23 November the *Globe and Mail* printed the following story on page A10. Notice first the misleading headline. This was, I believe, the first notification that aid had in fact been interrupted, but notice that *this* story is subordinated to the one about the aid's continuation. Notice second, third and fourth that the "interruption" is not cancellation or suspension, that it is not in response to the UCA massacre, but has been caused by "transportation difficulties" consequent upon the rebel offensive.

Salvador Aid To Continue, Officials Say
by Charlotte Montgomery
The Globe and Mail

The Canadian government's aid program in El Salvador has been brought to a temporary halt by the rebel offensive, but officials say Ottawa does not plan to heed the urgings of churches and other organizations and suspend it.

Since 1986, when government-to-government aid was resumed after a five-year interruption, Canada has put more than $12-million into about 100 projects agreed on by both countries.

A brief halt caused by the latest outbreak in the 10-year-old civil war is unlikely to have any lasting impact on Canada's program, Michael Jay, Central America program officer for the federal Canadian International Development Agency, said yesterday.

Mr. Jay said the interruption of aid was necessary because of transportation difficulties during the fighting that broke out 12 days ago. When the shooting is over, he said, programs should resume.

Labor organizations and churches have repeatedly urged Ottawa to cancel bilateral aid projects in El Salvador. Unions have sponsored visits to Canada by Salvadorean labor representatives who have argued for an end to aid on the grounds that Canada's paying for social services frees Salvadorean government funds for military purposes.

(The Human Rights Commission of El Salvador has estimated that 400 children in the country die each week of illnesses related to malnutrition and that the government's budget for defence and public security is more than triple the amount allocated to health.)

The Canadian Hunger Foundation, an independent agency that administers Canada's bilateral aid in El Salvador, has temporarily stopped approving new project[s], a spokesman said. The foundation administers a fund made up of revenues from the sale of fertilizer provided by CIDA.

Mr. Jay said the fund gives money to local groups for projects to provide shelter, health care or other basic needs for the country's poorest citizens. An evaluation shows that from 1986 to 1988 about 200,000 poor people were assisted, he said.

Notice also that the article reports that "*Salvadorean* labor representatives" (emphasis mine) were calling for an end to aid, as were the usual suspects, "labor organizations and churches." (There is clearly a quandary here for churches and others wanting to provide humanitarian aid. It is caught in the *Globe* story two days later, "Canadian Churches May Send Escort With Aid to El Salvador." Why the escort? "The military had stolen from homes, clinics and relief shelters," and "many of the Salvadorean church and aid workers who would normally carry out programs for their Canadian counterparts have been arrested."[21]) *The chief point here is that, despite the* Globe's *obfuscation, there was clearly an opening in which appropriate action could possibly have an effect on subsequent events.*

Recall the *Globe*'s own editorial advice from 28 October 1987 cited above: "An insistence on human rights compliance as a condition of aid from smaller donors [that is, Canada and others] would be a significant factor in U.S. political debate about Central America. It seems a small beginning but so did the Arias plan before it took off." In fact, this was the position of the opposition Liberal Party in the voice of shadow foreign minister Lloyd Axworthy responding to Joe Clark's statement quoted above specifically on the question of U.S. aid to the Contras:

> When we visited Washington after our trip to Central America, the group that I was with met with a number of Congressmen to talk about what would happen if Canada said no to Contra aid, specifically, clearly, directly, not in vague language of third party intervention, but clearly. They said that right now the issue is in the balance, that Congress must decide within a matter of months one way or the other. It is not the Reagan administration that will decide. Ultimately, it will be the Congress of the United States that will decide. There are people in that Congress fighting desperately to stop that aid on both sides of the House in both Parties. They said that if a country like Canada, with the kind of legitimacy and credibility that we have, seen as a good ally of the U.S., were to take the stand that the peace process is paramount and that the stoppage of aid is the priority, then that message would be heard in the halls of Congress. It might change 10 or 15 votes. I do not know the numbers, but they said it would have an impact and it would make a difference. We would add credibility.
>
> Charges often heard in that kind of political debate about those going against aid to the Contras being soft on communism or something, the kind of rhetoric you hear from the right wing in the U.S., could be

stopped if allies like Canada, the European countries and others took a stand. The American Congressmen told me that if we took a stand, then maybe some of the Europeans would take a stand, and all of a sudden the Americans would see it as the international community saying, "Stop this immoral practice." We could make a difference, Mr. Speaker.[22]

Two years later U.S. political debate about the renewal of aid to El Salvador in the wake of the UCA massacre had already begun and been reported on the front page of the *New York Times* on 18 November 1989. The *NYT* editorial on the same day ("The Suspects in El Salvador") concludes, "Democrats in Congress say they will cut off military aid if El Salvador cannot halt and will not punish death squads. If Mr. Cristiani ignores that warning, the message will soon be bipartisan." In Canada, by contrast, the *Globe and Mail's* editorial of 18 November does *not* raise the question of *Canada's* aid to El Salvador, but points instead at the question of U.S. aid. Its front-page story of that day reports Canadian religious leaders' condemnation of the murders, but has nothing to say about Canada's aid. It had reported the previous day (17 November) the call by a committee of Canadian church leaders and non-government organizations (including Canadian Jesuits), at a meeting with senior External Affairs officials, for Canada to use its influence internationally in support of a ceasefire in the civil war. Then on 21 November, in the penultimate paragraph on the inside page of its front-page story on temporarily jailed Canadian volunteer Karen Ridd, it notes that, "In Ottawa, Monique Landry, minister of state for external relations, said Canada would use its new membership in the Organization of American States to press for a ceasefire and resumption of peace talks in El Salvador." On the same day it replays a part of the 18 November *New York Times* editorial that raises the question of a cut in U.S. aid, while reporting that President "Bush warned Congress yesterday not to cut U.S. aid to El Salvador in response to the murder of six Jesuit priests, their housekeeper and her daughter, saying the Salvadorean government was not to blame, and the House quickly scrapped an aid-cut proposal." On 22 November the *Globe* reports Canadian missionary Brian Rude, who had been arrested, jailed and returned to Canada, saying Canadian aid should be halted as it conferred legitimacy on the government of El Salvador. On 23 November the government of Canada announces it will not be cutting aid, though aid has been "brought to a temporary halt."[23]

The opening for action was made available locally in Kitchener-Waterloo via a press announcement the same day (November 23) of a meeting the following day hosted by the two local Members of Parliament (MPs). And, to be sure, local community groups, students at the neighbouring University of Waterloo, labour organizations and the churches took to the streets in protest.[24] But at the local MPs' meeting, which was largely devoted to the concerns of local Salvadorans about the fate of refugees, there may have been two, at most three, faculty in attendance from the two universities combined.

Into this window of opportunity, then, stepped not Canadian university presidents, faculty associations and learned societies demanding effective action from their government to stop their colleagues being murdered abroad, but the media propaganda machine.[25]

> Powerful sources regularly take advantage of media routines and dependency to "manage" the media, to manipulate them into following a special agenda and framework...Part of this management process consists of inundating the media with stories, which serve sometimes to foist a particular line and frame on the media (e.g., Nicaragua as illicitly supplying arms to the Salvadorean rebels), and at other times to help chase unwanted stories off the front page or out of the media altogether (the alleged delivery of MIGs to Nicaragua during the week of the 1984 Nicaraguan election). This strategy can be traced back at least as far as the Committee on Public Information, established to coordinate propaganda during World War 1, which "discovered in 1917-18 that one of the best means of controlling news was flooding news channels with 'facts,' or what amounted to official information."[26]

On 27 November 1989 the *Globe and Mail* reported on page A8 that "Cristiani Cuts Ties With Managua for Alleged Weapons Smuggling." The story out of San Salvador is credited not to Charlotte Montgomery or Linda Hossie but to the unknown Douglas Grant Mine together with Associated Press (AP) and Reuter News Agency. No sources are given except for "a nationally televised address" by President Cristiani "one day after military authorities discovered two light planes delivering weapons to the rebels," one of which was said to have crashed with "sophisticated weapons, including 25 surface-to-air missiles." The article notes that the missiles are "the first concrete evidence to back up the accusations" made by the United States and "a succession of U.S.-supported governments here" that Nicaragua "provided secret military assistance to the guerrillas in their decade-old war for power." Also included in the article, again with no sources cited, is the story that a " 'large arsenal' of weapons stored for the rebels" has been uncovered at "the house of a U.S. woman...Jennifer Casolo."[27] (A church worker like Brian Rude, and comparable to Karen Ridd, Casolo "spent four years in El Salvador working for the Texas-based Christian Education Seminars as a guide for visiting U.S. congressmen [sic] and religious groups," including 18 days in police detention for this suspicious-looking "discovery."[28])

Buried in between the paragraphs of these two stories is one sentence reporting the news that Americas Watch has released a report saying that "circumstantial evidence made it virtually certain that the Salvadorean armed forces were responsible for the Nov. 16 massacre of the priests." A more graphic version of the same news is presented in the *Kitchener-Waterloo Record* on the same day. In a three-story spread two-thirds of the space is devoted to the arms story (Canadian Press [CP]), most of that given to a photograph of the seized weapons (AP), the other third being divided between the Americas Watch report (Reuter) and a tiny item on the arrival in the United States of Mrs. Barrera Cerna, "the only known witness to the massacre of six Jesuit priests" (AP).[29]

The next day, 28 November, the *Record* divides its coverage more or less evenly between "Salvador 'Carnage'," an Associated Press story reporting Mrs. Barrera's testimony that the killers looked like soldiers, and a Washington-based story by AP-CP, "Bush Will Protest Soviet Allies' Action in Central America."[30] What is otherwise a U.S. presidential trip to Moscow to meet Gorbachev and talk about Eastern Europe becomes a Central American story "after El Salvador reported that a shipment of surface-to-air missiles was sent by Soviet-backed Nicaragua to leftist Salvadoran guerrillas." Although not on the topic of arms shipments the *Record* observes the same "balance" the following day, 29 November. Two Associated Press stories juxtapose the murders by "men in military uniforms" of six men and a boy of 14—"six of them were lined up against a wall...and shot to death"—on 18 November, and the assassination of a "prominent Salvadoran rightist" by "gunmen."[31]

The same day, 29 November, the *Globe and Mail* puts the colourful title, "Pilot Reported Dead by El Salvador Speaks to Press," over a Reuter story from Managua about a pilot said to have been one of those who had died in the crash of the plane carrying the alleged arms shipment. The last paragraph of the article reads: "The FMLN said the Salvadorean government was using Nicaragua's alleged involvement in arms supply as a pretext to divert attention from its 'savage air and artillery attacks against the civilian population'."[32] In the *Globe* article by Linda Hossie of 4 December ("El Salvador's Widening Reality Gap"), which I quoted at the head of this chapter, a reporter's tape recorder at a presidential news conference in San Salvador on 23 November caught Armed Forces Chief of Staff Col. Rene Emilio Ponce telling Mr. Cristiani, " 'Talk about Nicaragua and Cuba'... and Mr. Cristiani obliged." The following paragraph of this article reports that, "The conference was interrupted repeatedly by the sounds of air-force bombing nearby."

A few days later the story is still running as unnamed "diplomats and Sandinista officials" are reported to say that, "Missiles Part of Anti-U.S. Gambit"[33] Then, the following day, 9 December, Charlotte Montgomery reports in the *Globe* that the "Nicaraguan Ambassador [to Canada] Rebuts Arms Shipment Story."[34] As far as I am aware, apart from a lengthy letter to the editor on 23 December devoted to exposing the "White House spin" on these U.S.-sourced stories, the "arms from Nicaragua" story effectively stops here in the *Globe and Mail*.[35]

The point is not in the first place whether the story is true or not. The same questions arise in either case. How does it get to be a story? Why the fuss? It is just a sick joke for Americans and Canadians to fulminate against the FMLN arming themselves from Nicaragua, in the face of U.S. and Canadian practice of arming fascists in El Salvador and in the rest of the world, if necessary in the Canadian case via the United States, or in the U.S. case via third countries such as Honduras, Panama, Israel and Guatemala.[36] The purpose of the story providers is propaganda to fill the media spaces with stuff that will make readers think twice about protesting and calling for such things as aid cancellation and possible armed UN intervention, and to subordinate or remove other stuff that would enrage them to the point of doing just that if those stories were given full and proper play. Throughout this critical post-massacre period the crucially telling story of the brutal FBI treatment and interrogation of Mrs. Barrera, the sole massacre witness, and the course of the U.S.-obstructed murder investigation generally, comes out in dribs and drabs as space is devoted to irrelevant arms from Nicaragua. And when the arms story has run its course new tactics take over as "El Salvador Begins Public-relations Effort":

> The government of El Salvador is dispatching delegations to Canada, the United States, South America and Europe to tell its version of the country's battle against rebel forces...[37]

The article nicely lines up the opposing forces. The "mission to Canada, headed by [a] Salvadorean deputy foreign minister...includes an opposition parliamentarian, the country's central bank president, businessmen and a farmers' union representative." It faces off against "Canadian non-governmental organizations... churches, labor organizations and groups with development projects in El Salvador [who] have repeatedly urged the federal government to end a government-to-government aid program which has cost $12-million since 1986." So it's not in question what is at stake. By their actions the El Salvador government shows it thinks Canada important enough to need persuading. Not for the $12 million, which is peanuts and after all does go mostly to the superfluous poor, but for the influence that the sight of Canadian good guys blessing their country can have in the U.S. Congress where the big aid decisions are made.

The Consequences of Inaction, Particularly for Sociologists

As no one knows for sure what would have happened had universities and their faculty (not to mention the *Globe and Mail* which never editorialized in favour of the Canadian government doing anything) responded as they should have after 16 November, it is of course impossible to say conclusively that what did happen occurred as a consequence of our failure to act. But short of conclusiveness there is much to counsel against complacency. The aftermath was, in short, that Canadian aid continued; that American military aid continued, if somewhat reduced;[38] that it was then cut by 50% ($42.5 million) by the U.S. Congress in October 1990, but maintained by other means in the form of $50 million in "economic aid" from the U.S.-controlled International Monetary Fund that President Cristiani could re-allocate as necessary for "defence purposes";[39] that it was then restored in January 1991;[40] that for at least a year after the UCA massacre a "'gigantic and infamous web of complicity' that blocks the investigation of the massacre, [was] 'entrenched in the desks of the Ministry and Vice-Ministries of Defense and behind the walls of the U.S. Embassy';"[41] that convictions for murder were eventually secured for two of the estimated 30 soldiers involved, but not for anybody occupying a ministry or embassy desk;[42] and that "death squad killings, summary executions and torture have persisted in El Salvador since the massacre of six Jesuit priests by soldiers a year ago, a UN human rights report said Monday."[43] For example, on 15 January 1990 in the last paragraph of a Reuter story out of Washington, "Armed Forces Implicated in Murders of 6 Jesuits," the *Globe and Mail* reported that:

> The bodies of Hector Oqueli Colindres, who is deputy secretary of El Salvador's National Revolutionary Movement, and that of Gilda Flores, a

Guatemalan human rights lawyer, were found near the Salvadorean border on Friday. Both had been shot in the head.[44]

The UN human rights report just referred to was compiled by "Jose Antonio Pastor, a university professor from Spain." He is quoted as saying, "'Thus far in 1990, government action against humanitarian, trade union, peasants and other organizations has continued.'" Moreover:

> Pastor counted 40 politically motivated summary executions of civilians by security forces from January to August of 1990, compared with 51 in the same time span in 1989. He obtained the figures from the Archdiocesan Legal Protection Office.
>
> The office also listed 46 assassinations by death squads in January through August 1990, compared with only 17 such slayings in the same months of 1989. The Salvadoran government's Human Rights Commission counted 42 summary killings by security forces in the first eight months of 1990.[45]

On the weekend of 12/13 January 1991, four days into the "campaign for the first election since the far-right Arena government and the rebels' Farabundo Marti National Liberation Front began negotiations last year to end the 10-year-old civil war...the worst fears of El Salvador's leftist political leaders came true...when a San Salvador radio station broadcast a threat from two of the country's death squads to kill opposition and labour leaders, priests and intellectuals."[46] The broadcast statement is of no little interest, remembering that at least two of the murdered Jesuit faculty at UCA were not only "priests and intellectuals" but, more specifically, social scientists whose sociological analyses of El Salvadorean society were critical to their work for a negotiated settlement to the civil war. The Reverend Michael Czerny, the Toronto sociologist who went out to San Salvador to replace Segundo Montes, said of them,

> "They were not just martyrs for justice and human rights. They were especially martyrs for the truth." He notes that Rev. Ignacio Ellacuria, the rector of the university [the *Globe*'s possibly Christian Marxist], had said that neither the government nor the [FMLN] rebels had the sole right to speak for the people. There was another voice that had to be present at the negotiating table, the "voice of civil society." The government of El Salvador had refused to hear this voice; the rebels had come to admit its importance...Father Czerny has a renewed appreciation of the role of in-

tellectuals in society. "The university is indispensable to social development. Neither the government nor social movements can endure without some give and take with the university."[47]

Against that sociological analysis consider the one contained in the broadcast statement made by the two death squads:

"At this time," the statement reads, "we are going to talk in all frankness about our philosophical basis and the politics of our movement.

"This country's society is divided into three classes: a superior creative class composed essentially of specialists and large landholders; a smaller class that tries to imitate this superior class; and an inferior rustic class that is made up essentially of workers, poor peasants, students and small businessmen.

"Another group exists that we hold in low regard and consider very small—the dangerous intellectual class that tries to contaminate the above-mentioned classes.

"The death squads' message to this intellectual class and opposition leaders is clear.

"The superior capitalist class in our country is naturally the strongest, and its destiny, without question, is to govern and regulate the inferior classes. And what is more, it has a duty to exploit, dispose of, conquer and even exterminate elements of these inferior classes when the benefits of capitalism require such.

"Our adversaries, the subversives and the great inferior mass, must be exterminated, or at least their leaders..."

"Whatever course of action is justified, whatever action, justice is a luxury that we cannot allow."[48]

ARENA won that election. Six months later:

A labour activist who worked with San Salvador's urban poor was found slain yesterday at his organization's headquarters. The body of Martin Ayala, 45, was found bound hand and foot to a pillar at the headquarters of the Council of Marginal Communities. His throat had been cut and a blood-stained machete was left by the corpse. Witnesses said his wife, Maria Leticia Campos, who had been guarding the organization's headquarters with Mr. Ayala overnight, was taken to hospital with serious knife wounds.[49]

Conclusion

So, finally, what exactly am I saying? I have two conclusions, one about the *Globe and Mail*, the other about Canadian academics. During 1989 the news reports of Linda Hossie on the civil war itself (from San Salvador in July and November) and on efforts at peace talks (from Mexico City in September and San José in October), and those of Charlotte Montgomery on the story in Canada, provided reliable, revealing, professionally defensible coverage of the main events both abroad and at home. In contrast to the news coverage, the paper's editorial line comprised the tropes of balanced responsibility between the two sides for the war and its atrocities, and a well-meaning but ineffective United States. While the demands made by the war's opponents for Canada to cut its aid were reported, the *Globe* itself took no position. Instead it ran a succession of pieces on the story of arms from Nicaragua. Through propaganda, and by failing to take advantage of the opening provided, paradoxically, by the UCA massacre to press the Canadian government to cut its aid programme, the *Globe* contributed to the probability of further atrocities, subsequently realized. The last point may also be applied to us academics.

If we professors at Wilfrid Laurier University had felt strongly enough our human, academic kinship with the murdered faculty, their cook and her daughter at the University of Central America in San Salvador, we would have raised such a *collective* stink of outrage at their killing that, perhaps, our academic brothers and sisters down the street at the University of Waterloo would have done the same, followed, who knows, by extended family members at the universities in the neighbouring towns of Guelph, London and Hamilton, yea, even unto the University of Toronto, and then in the country as a whole, and that in so doing we would *together* have found common cause with our students, with trade unions (remembering that many of us are unionized ourselves), with churches (to which many of us belong) and with non-governmental organizations (to which many of us contribute time and money), that is with the kin of those other categories of death squad targets, so that the Government of Canada would have had to listen and, perhaps, have cancelled our bilateral aid program with El Salvador in keeping with the wishes of representatives of the Salvadoran recipients, which would have influenced other "small donors" to do the same which, then, as the *Globe and Mail* and Lloyd Axworthy in opposition had suggested two years earlier (but *not* in the immediate aftermath of the massacre), would have given pause for thought in the Democrat-dominated Congress of the United States of America, perhaps, who knows, leading to outright cancellation of their military aid to El Salvador which, you never know, could have stopped the killing and torture of people just like us by philosophers and sociologists of the sort just quoted.

NOTES

1. This occurred "during a presidential news conference on Nov. 23 when a reporter's tape recorder clearly picked up Armed Forces Chief of Staff Col. Rene Emilio Ponce telling Mr. Cristiani what to say." Linda Hossie, "El Salvador's Widening Reality Gap," *Globe and Mail*, 4 December 1989, A8.

2. Geoff Heinricks, "Whose news? Business Circles the *Globe*," *This Magazine* 23, no. 3 (September 1989), 14–21.

3. Edward Herman and Noam Chomsky, *Manufacturing Consent: The Political Economy of the Mass Media*, new rev. ed. (New York: Pantheon, 2002 [1988]), 1–2.

4. Noam Chomsky, *Deterring Democracy* (New York: Farrar, Straus and Giroux, Hill and Wang, 1992), 357–71; Noam Chomsky, *Necessary Illusions: Thought Control in Democratic Societies* (Toronto: CBC Enterprises, 1989), 131–32.

5. See, for example, Alex Carey, *Taking the Risk Out of Democracy: Corporate Propaganda versus Freedom and Liberty*, ed. Andrew Lohrey (Urbana and Chicago: University of Illinois Press, 1997). I wonder if the demand for a language of science to replace ordinary language does not spring from the same sources. Consider the phrases "the confused impressions of the crowd" and "superficial examination" to describe the sources of ordinary language, in the opening passage of Emile Durkheim's sociological classic *Suicide: A Study in Sociology*, trans. John A. Spaulding and George Simpson, ed. George Simpson (New York: Macmillan, Free Press, 1951):

   > Since the word "suicide" recurs constantly in the course of conversation, it might be thought that its sense is universally known and that definition is superfluous. Actually, the words of everyday language, like the concepts they express, are always susceptible of more than one meaning, and the scholar employing them in their accepted use without further definition would risk serious misunderstanding. Not only is their meaning so indefinite as to vary, from case to case, with the needs of argument, but, as the classification from which they derive is not analytic, but merely translates the confused impressions of the crowd, categories of very different sorts of fact are indistinctly combined under the same heading, or similar realities are differently named. So, if we follow the common use, we risk distinguishing what should be combined, or combining what should be distinguished, thus mistaking the real affinities of things, and accordingly misapprehending their nature. Only comparison affords explanation. A scientific investigation can thus be achieved only if it deals with comparable facts, and it is the more likely to succeed the more certainly it has combined all those that can be usefully combined. But these natural affinities of entities cannot be made clear safely by such superficial examination as produces ordinary terminology; and so the scholar cannot take as the subject of his research roughly assembled groups of facts corresponding to words of common usage. He himself must establish the groups he wishes to study in order to give them the homogeneity and the specific meaning necessary for them to be susceptible of scientific treatment. (41)

6. For example, James Winter, *Common Cents: Media Portrayal of the Gulf War and Other Events*, (Montreal: Black Rose Books, 1992).

7. Noam Chomsky, "The Mortal Sin of Self-defence," *Z Magazine*, December 1989, 14; Chomsky, *Deterring Democracy*, 292. In general, on the previous paragraph in the text see Herman and Chomsky, *Manufacturing Consent*, chapter 2. For detailed attention to the case of El Salvador in the U.S. media see *Necessary Illusions*.

8. Canada. External Affairs. Secretary of State (Right Hon. Joe Clark), "Peacekeeping in Central America—Statement by Secretary of State for External Affairs," *Commons Debates*, 2 December 1987, 11409–412.

9. Editorial, "The Dirty Wars," *Globe and Mail*, 28 October 1987.

10. "The Dirty Wars," *Globe*, 1987.

11. Editorial, "The Dirty Nine-year War of El Salvador," *Globe and Mail*, 28 December 1988, A6; "Arena for El Salvador," 22 March 1989, A6; "Fear Stalks El Salvador," 19 June 1989; "The

Pain and Violence of El Salvador," 18 November 1989. The same features of balanced responsibility and benign U.S. motives characterize a subsequent, short editorial, "To Induce Peace in El Salvador," *Globe and Mail*, 17 May 1990, A6.

12. The point was made bluntly by Robert White, former U.S. ambassador to El Salvador, at a Washington memorial service the day after the massacre: "The Salvadoran government would not survive for one month without U.S. support" ("In League With Assassins," *Sojourners*, January 1990, 33). It is also noted by Charles Fernandes in "In Witness of Their Blood," *Grail*, 6, no. 4 (1990), 50.

13. It was the *Globe's* own reporter Linda Hossie who, two weeks after the publication of editorial "D," reported in "El Salvador's Widening Reality Gap" "one Western diplomat" saying what anybody even slightly knowledgeable of the situation in El Salvador, and certainly the *Globe's* editorial board, knew, namely that "the U.S. administration is trying to liken the government of Alfredo Cristiani to the Christian Democrats it replaced as 'a middle force, pressured between the right and the left' when, in fact, the president's 'main source of power—well, not his main source, but his major source—is the U.S. embassy.'" Of course, both this propaganda fantasy and the facts it serves to obscure had been in place since at least 1979. See sub-section 2.3.2, "The Propaganda Line: A Reformist Junta Trying to Contain the Violence of Left and Right," in the section on Archbishop Oscar Romero in Herman and Chomsky, *Manufacturing Consent*, 49-53: "And the Salvadoran government has continued to be 'moderate' and 'centrist' up to today." (51)

14. An unusually unequivocal statement, post hoc to be sure, is to be found in the last paragraph of a Reuter story out of Washington: "An estimated 73,000 people have died in El Salvador's decade-long civil war—most of them civilians killed by U.S.-trained and supplied security forces" ("Bush Acts to Release Shipments of Military Aid to Salvador Regime," *Kitchener-Waterloo Record*, 16 January 1991, B12).

15. For another example, see Charlotte Montgomery, "El Salvador, Guatemala Assailed on Rights," *Globe and Mail*, 14 June 1989, A8: "After detailed study of cases, Amnesty has concluded that the death squads blamed for much of Guatemala's violence 'are in fact regular members of the police and military operating in plain clothes, but under the orders of their superiors.' Amnesty issued a strikingly similar report on death-squad activity in El Salvador less than a year ago." When, in 1992/93, "The UN Truth Commission published its report on atrocities of the 1980s, [it] attribut[ed] 85 percent of the horrendous record to the security forces, trained, armed, and advised by the United States and another 10 percent to the death squads linked to them and to the wealthy business sector that the United States hopes to keep firmly in power" (Noam Chomsky, *World Orders, Old and New* (London: Pluto Press, 1994), 99). With tacit U.S. approval the El Salvador government responded by "issuing an amnesty for the killers and torturers in gross violation of the peace accords that established the Truth Commission, which stated that the guilty must be punished." (Chomsky, *World Orders*, 99)

16. Angus Taylor (Philosophy, University of Victoria) responded to editorial D's claim that the U.S. "has been attempting 'to strengthen democracy there'" by writing "Surely you jest" in his letter "U.S. Motive is Suspect," *Globe and Mail*, 1 December 1989, A6. Among all the *Globe and Mail* editorials I have read on El Salvador, editorial "D" of 18 November 1989 is alone in employing the expression "Christian Marxist" to describe the FMLN. While this is technically closer to a correct description of that coalition's political orientation, its use-in-context produces a curiously chilling effect. The editorial's opening paragraph reads:

> On Tuesday, Salvadorean university rector Ignacio Ellacuria begged the embattled government of his war-torn country to talk peace with its Christian Marxist rebel foes. The reply came with unspeakable brutality before dawn Thursday.

That is, where the expression might have caused readers accustomed to the damning term "Marxist" to have paused and wondered whether there might not after all be something worthy about these rebel bastards ("Christian" being generally a term of moral worthiness), instead there is the sense of connotative contamination in the other direction; the good of "Christian" becomes poisoned with the evil of "Marxist." Was the Jesuit rector one of these

"Christian Marxists?" No wonder they killed him. And we shouldn't grieve too much about it either. We are better off without these "commie Christians," so the reasoning might go. This is more or less the sentiment of Jeremy Forster's letter to the editor in the *Globe and Mail*, 1 December 1989, A6: after blaming civilian casualties on the FLMN he writes, "The people of Central America certainly need our help, as they need our informed understanding. Instead of dabbling in liberation theology and *other assorted leftist sophistries, the Jesuits* might better promote a program of family planning" (emphasis mine). By way of contrast see McMaster University sociologist Peter Archibald's neat dissection of editorial D's "Meagre Evidence of Support" for its confident claim that the FMLN lacks support among Salvadorans, in his letter to the editor in the *Globe and Mail*, 30 December 1989, D7; see also L. Pena's letter, "Something Missing," 21 December, A6, which points out that, despite apparent even-handedness, "the editor was careful not to point a finger at the United States for at least some responsibility in this sorry situation."

17. "Well, who are the Communists? 'Communists' is a term regularly used in American political theology to refer to people who are committed to the belief that 'the government has direct responsibility for the welfare of the people.' I'm quoting the words of a 1949 State Department intelligence report which warned about the spread of this grim and evil doctrine, which does, of course, threaten our 'raw materials' [in other countries] if we can't abort it somehow" (Noam Chomsky, "Intervention in Vietnam and Central America: Parallels and Differences," in *The Chomsky Reader*, ed. James Peck (New York: Pantheon, 1987), 319).

18. The rather impressive evidence for this view, notably in studies by Lars Schoultz and by Edward Herman, is reviewed by Chomsky in "Intervention in Vietnam and Central America," 330-338, the sources being cited in the footnotes to his "Human Rights: The Pragmatic Criterion," in *Year 501: The Conquest Continues* (London: Verso, 1993), 120.

19. See Peter Eglin, "Deaths in the Family: El Salvador," in *Getting a Life: A Story of Studies in Pursuit of Intellectual Responsibility* (forthcoming), for the full story of the reception of the UCA massacre at Wilfrid Laurier University.

20. Herman and Chomsky, *Manufacturing Consent*, 137-139.

21. Charlotte Montgomery, "Canadian Churches May Send Escort with Aid to El Salvador," *Globe and Mail*, 25 November 1989, A5. The rather different orders of consequences for the Salvadoran aid worker and the visiting Canadian aid official, cooperating to deliver Canadian development aid to El Salvador's poor, when their plans run afoul of the military and the U.S. Embassy, are graphically portrayed in the exceptional movie *Diplomatic Immunity*.

22. Hon. Lloyd Axworthy, "[Reply to Joe Clark]," *Commons Debates*, 2 December 1987, 11413.

23. Editorial, "The Pain and Violence in El Salvador," 18 November; Linda Hossie, "OAS Proposal for Peace Offered in El Salvador," *Globe and Mail*, 18 November 1989, front page; Donn Downey, "Jesuits Decry Killings in El Salvador," *Globe and Mail*, 17 November 1989, A5; Linda Hossie, "El Salvador Frees Jailed Canadian Volunteer," *Globe and Mail*, 21 November 1989, front page; [Just What Was Said] "Jesuits' Killers Must Not Escape Justice (From an editorial in the *New York Times*)," *Globe and Mail*, 21 November 1989, A8; Canadian Press, "Aid to El Salvador Flawed, Canadian Missionary Says," *Globe and Mail*, 22 November 1989, A5; Montgomery, "Salvador Aid to Continue," 23 November.

24. Margaret Mironowicz, "Stop Aid to El Salvador, UW Protesters Demand," *Kitchener-Waterloo Record*, 23 November 1989, B1; Barbara Aggerholm, "Reimer, McLean Pressed to Help Families Escape War in El Salvador," *Kitchener-Waterloo Record*, 25 November 1989, B2.

25. But see "Intelligentsia Under Attack," *Globe and Mail*, 8 December 1989, A6. This letter to the editor by Bill Graham, President of the Ontario Confederation of University Faculty Associations, and Jim Head, President of the Ontario Secondary School Teachers Federation, mourns the loss of the Jesuit educators, reviews the recent history of similar killings, bombings, torture and imprisonment of university faculty, administrators and students in El Salvador, locates it in the context of gross inequality in Salvadoran society, condemns U.S. support for the regime and describes as "unacceptable" Canada's "tacit compliance" with U.S. policy. Though

I have not thoroughly researched the matter, I am unaware of any other such public responses by Canadian academia to the UCA massacre.

26. Herman and Chomsky, *Manufacturing Consent*, 23, quoting S. L. Vaughn, *Holding Fast the Inner Lines* (Chapel Hill: University of North Carolina Press, 1980), 194.

27. Douglas Grant Mine, Associated Press with Reuter News Agency (San Salvador), "Cristiani Cuts Ties with Managua for Alleged Weapons Smuggling," *Globe and Mail*, 27 November 1989, A8.

28. Ron Arias, *People Weekly*, 22 January 1990, 64–65. For a more sceptical view see Isabel Vincent, "Internacionalistas: The Che Guevara Wannabies," *Globe and Mail*, 3 February 1996, D3.

29. San Salvador (CP), "War of Words: El Salvador, Nicaragua Squabble After Arms-flight Crash," *Kitchener-Waterloo Record*, 27 November 1989, C10; San Salvador (Reuter), "U.S. Policy in El Salvador Criticized by Rights Group;" Miami (AP), "Massacre Witness in U.S."

30. San Salvador (AP), "Salvador 'Carnage': Jesuits' Killers Looked Like Soldiers, Witness Says," *Kitchener-Waterloo Record*, 28 November 1989, A3; Washington (AP-CP), "Bush Will Protest Soviet Allies' Action in Central America."

31. San Salvador (AP), "Armed Men Kill Seven in El Salvador Slaughter," *Kitchener-Waterloo Record*, 29 November 1989, F12; San Salvador (AP), "Supporter of Land Owners Killed in Car by Gunmen."

32. Reuter (Managua), "Pilot Reported Dead by El Salvador Speaks to Press," *Globe and Mail*, 29 November 1989, A16.

33. New York Times Service (Managua), "Missiles Part of Anti-U.S. Gambit, Officials Say," *Globe and Mail*, 8 December 1989, A3.

34. Charlotte Montgomery, "Nicaraguan Ambassador Rebuts Arms Shipment Story," *Globe and Mail*, 9 December 1989, A11.

35. Glenn Cooper, "Slanted Toward Americans [Letter]," *Globe and Mail*, 23 December 1989, D7. The story continued in the *New York Review of Books*, 1 February and 15 March 1990.

36. For the general U.S. case see Noam Chomsky and Edward Herman, *The Political Economy of Human Rights*, 2 vols. (Montreal: Black Rose Books, 1979); for Honduras and Panama see Noam Chomsky, "The Manufacture of Consent," in *The Chomsky Reader*, 126; for Israel see Chomsky, *World Orders*, 205–206; for Guatemala consider the following: "The policy of neutrality, the professed 'main pillar [of] President Cerezo's foreign policy,' crumbled in November when his government sent Guatemalan soldiers to San Salvador to support the Cristiani government in its war with the . . . (FMLN) . . . According [to] the daily *Prensa Libre*, a U.S. Air Force Hercules 144 transport plane left Guatemala City for El Salvador, apparently carrying arms or soldiers. The French Press Agency (AFP) reported that 126 of Guatemala's elite counterinsurgency force 'Kaibiles' were transferred to El Salvador" (Toronto Guatemala Solidarity Committee, *Guatemala Update*, Spring 1990). I don't know if this story made it to the "liberal" or "conservative" press.

As for Canada, consider the following by John McMurtry in "Why Does Canada Aid the Oppressors?" *Globe and Mail*, 20 February 1990, A7. Professor McMurtry (University of Guelph, Philosophy) is a wonderful exception, along with some others, to what I have asserted here about Canadian intellectuals' general pattern of response to "constructive bloodbaths" (the term of Chomsky and Herman, *Political Economy of Human Rights*).

According to a recent article for the International Journal by T. A. Keenleyside and Nola Serkasevich, 112 governments received Canadian aid between 1984 and 1987, the majority of them having reasonably good human-rights records. However, more than 70 per cent of the total aid budget of the Canadian International Development Agency has gone to governments which, according to Amnesty International documentation, practice large-scale arbitrary arrest and imprisonment of people for non-violent beliefs or activities, and torture and murder their suspected critics or opponents as "a common part of life."

Providing such aid is not the same as exporting arms but it accomplishes similar ends. As for arms themselves see the annual issue of *Press for Conversion* (the magazine of Coalition to Oppose the Arms Trade) devoted to documenting Canadian arms sales, as well as the annual *Armed Conflicts Report* published by Project Ploughshares. The latter's report on 1994 was given a desultory treatment, which nevertheless reveals some of the awful facts, in Editorial, "Avoiding Sales to Miscreant Armies," *Globe and Mail*, 6 October 1995, A16.

37. Charlotte Montgomery, "El Salvador Begins Public-relations Effort," *Globe and Mail*, 13 December 1989, A5.

38. "Salvadoran President Alfredo Cristiani got a ringing endorsement but lost some money when he stopped by the White House yesterday. The U.S. state department announced El Salvador will get $229 million in economic aid, $59 million less this year than originally budgeted. Military aid of $86 million stays about the same." (Washington (Special), "Cristiani Wins Bush's Praise, But Loses Aid," *Toronto Star*, 2 February 1990, A15).

39. Noam Chomsky, "Letter from Lexington," *Lies of Our Times*, January 1991, 14-15.

40. Reuter, "Bush Acts to Release Shipments of Military Aid to Salvador Regime," *Kitchener-Waterloo Record*, 16 January 1991, B12.

41. Chomsky, "Letter from Lexington," citing editorials of 31 October and 7 November 1990 from *Proceso*, the Jesuit journal published by the University of Central America. See also the report on the release of the interim report on the investigation by the New-York-based Lawyers Committee for Human Rights in Jean Kavanaugh, "El Salvador, U.S. Rebuked for Role in Investigations," *Globe and Mail*, 17 November 1990, A13.

42. Details of the course of the investigation can be found in such reports as "Chronology of the Jesuit Investigation, May 16-August 27 [1990]," reproduced by the National Federation of Salvadorean Workers Union (FENASTRAS) and the Committee of Mothers and Relatives of Political Prisoners, Disappeared and Assassinated of El Salvador "Monsenor Oscar Arnulfo Romero" (COMADRES), both in Toronto, Canada; Lawyers Committee for Human Rights (New York), *A Chronicle of Death Foretold: The Jesuit Murders in El Salvador*, 1990, and *The Jesuit Murders: A Report on the Testimony of a Witness*, 1990; Americas Watch, "El Salvador: The Jesuit Trial—An Observer's Report," *News from Americas Watch*, III, no. XIII (13 December 1991); United States Department of State, *Report of the Secretary of State's Panel on El Salvador, July 1993*; and the report of the Lawyers Committee for Human Rights cited in the previous endnote.

43. United Nations (AP), "Salvadoran Abuses Continue," *Kitchener-Waterloo Record*, Tuesday, 13 November 1990, D16.

44. Reuter (Washington), "Armed Forces Implicated in Murders of 6 Jesuits," *Globe and Mail*, 15 January 1990, A9.

45. (AP), "Salvadoran Abuses Continue."

46. Jean Kavanaugh, "Death Squads Threaten Leftists," *Globe and Mail*, 14 January 1991, A10.

47. Mary Jo Leddy (a member of the Sisters of Our Lady of Sion), *Globe and Mail*, 17 February 1990, D3. For more extended consideration, including quotation, of the social analyses of Martin-Baro and Ellacuria—censored in the American press, despite their availability—see Chomsky, *Deterring Democracy*, 386-92.

48. Kavanaugh, "Death Squads." Notice, by the way, that Bush's announcement restoring military aid was made on January 15 (Reuter, "Bush Acts to Release," *Record*, 16 January), the day after the report of the death squad threat. Notice, too, the *Globe*'s curious definition of "leftist," which appears to include priests, intellectuals, student leaders and others. The phrase "El Salvador's Roman Catholic church and its two leftist political coalitions," which appears in the body of the article, wonderfully exploits the indexicality of "its" to compromise the political independence of the church, in keeping with its use of the descriptor "Christian Marxist" noted above.

49. WORLD IN BRIEF, Reuter (San Salvador, El Salvador), "Activist Found Slain," *Globe and Mail*, 9 July 1991, A11.

Chapter Five

Dan Rather And The Problem With Patriotism: Steps Toward The Redemption Of American Journalism And Democracy

Robert Jensen

THOUGH IT WAS UNINTENTIONAL, SINCE September 11, 2001, Dan Rather has single-handedly provided enough evidence to destroy one of American journalists' central claims about their special place in a democratic society while at the same time helping us see why patriotism is morally unacceptable.

Rather's struggles with the conflicts between his role as a journalist and his desire to be patriotic demonstrated why contemporary U.S. journalism falls well short of its claim to be politically neutral. For this service, journalists should be grateful to Rather, for if we can bury that peculiar ideology of contemporary commercial journalism it might be possible to rebuild a media system that better serves a democratic society and its citizens. At the same time, Rather's declarations about citizenship during wartime have demonstrated why the problem with patriotism is not how to define it properly, but how to eliminate it. For this service, citizens should be grateful, for if we can leave behind that morally and intellectually bankrupt ideology it might be possible to dismantle the American empire to make way for a meaningful American democracy.

Why Dan Rather?

Rather, anchor of the CBS Evening News and the dean of American television journalism, spoke more openly after 9/11 than any other mainstream commercial journalist, appearing on numerous talk shows to discuss his reaction to the tragedy and media coverage. The flashpoint was his appearance less than a week after 9/11 on David Letterman's talk show, for which he was both criticized and lauded for his declaration of loyalty to the president. But much more important than that initial reaction have been comments Rather has continued to make since 9/11 as he has tried—and failed—to reconcile the contradictions in his conception of what it means to be a journalist and a U.S. citizen. In that failure—which is not his alone but the whole profession's—we can see how intellectually incoherent and politically debilitating are the current ideologies of journalism and patriotism.

The basic claim journalists make about their role in society is simple: In a democracy predicated on the notion that the people—not leaders—are sovereign, the people need information independent of the centers of power, especially the government. The larger and more complex the society, the more difficult it is for individuals to gather for themselves that information. Enter the journalists, who offer themselves as independent watchdogs on power who don't take sides in partisan struggles. In the contemporary United States, journalists claim to be neutral sources of information.

Since 9/11, it has been painfully clear that the mainstream commercial news media have not been, on the whole, that much-needed critical, independent voice and are far from neutral politically. Just as important, the current posture of journalism shows that such simplistic claims to political neutrality tend to undermine the ability to be critical and independent; nowhere is that more evident than in discussions of patriotism. Dan Rather helps make this plain as day.

Some have written him off as an aging crank who not only can sound goofy on the air (his sometimes strained colloquialisms have been dubbed "Rather Blather") but, more importantly, doesn't represent the views of most journalists. I see it just the opposite; Rather is a fairly typical journalist, just unusually blunt and honest in public. That's precisely why he so often embarrasses the profession; he isn't good at self-censorship.

Using Rather's comments as a starting point, I will lay out a case against the typical journalistic claim to the importance of political neutrality and the typical American claim to the nobility of patriotism, arguing that both are incoherent and destructive to democracy.

Patriotic Journalism

This argument rests on the simple assertion that patriotism is not politically neutral, which is both obvious and steadfastly ignored. In fact, in the United States invocations of patriotism are routinely coupled with declarations of bipartisanship, evidence that one has gotten "beyond politics." Yet patriotism is inherently political, not only in the way it is used by politicians—often cynically—to justify particular policies regarding war but in the fundamental way it defines citizenship in relation to a nation-state. More on that later, after an examination of Rather's post-9/11 performance.

Rather's first foray into the issue came on the Letterman show on Sept. 17, 2001, when he said: "George Bush is the president. He makes the decisions, and, you know, it's just one American, wherever he wants me to line up, just tell me where, and he'll make the call."[1]

Such a direct declaration of subordination to the authority of a political leader made many—especially many journalists—nervous, and though Rather never retracted the remark he tried to refine his ideas in subsequent discussions. As he consistently reasserted his patriotism without apology, he struggled to articulate it in a fashion consistent with a conception of journalists-as-neutral-observers. For example, Rather—the same man who offered to line up wherever the president ordered—would not wear a flag pin on the air, as some other journalists did. In a September 22, 2001, interview on "CNN Tonight" with Howard Kurtz (the *Washington Post*'s media critic who also appears on the cable news channel), Rather explained: "It doesn't feel right to me. I have the flag burned in my heart, and I have ever since infancy. And I just don't feel the need to do it. It just doesn't feel right to me."[2]

Shortly after 9/11, the American flag became a symbol of "American standing tough" which quickly became fused with "America going to war." So, Rather was correct in recognizing that journalistic neutrality, as it is conventionally understood, would be compromised by wearing a flag. But in that same interview, Rather was asked by Kurtz if he thought journalists, out of a fear of a public backlash, might be reluctant to criticize the administration. Rather's answer exhibited his inability to move past a sense of patriotism as subordination to authority:

> I want to fulfill my role as a decent human member of the community and a decent and patriotic American. And therefore, I am willing to give the government, the president and the military the benefit of any doubt here in the beginning. I'm going to fulfill my role as a journalist, and that is ask the questions, when necessary ask the tough questions. But I have no excuse for, particularly when there is a national crisis such as this, as saying—you know, the president says do your job, whatever you are and whomever you are, Mr. and Mrs. America. I'm going to do my job as a journalist, but at the same time I will give them the benefit of the doubt, whenever possible in this kind of crisis, emergency situation. Not

because I am concerned about any backlash. I'm not. But because I want
to be a patriotic American without apology.

Rather's contradictions are striking. He won't wear a flag pin, but he'll claim to be
patriotic without apology. He will ask tough questions, but if those tough questions elicit responses from officials that seem questionable, he will give officials
the benefit of the doubt. Rather's answer to Kurtz came just 11 days after the terrorist attacks, when one could plausibly believe the shock of the event led people
to speak in ways they might otherwise not. But Rather offered the same assessment on June 4, 2002, on the "Larry King Live" show on CNN, when King asked if
there was "a thin line between patriot and reporter." Rather replied:

> No. I don't think it's a thin line at all. I've never had any difficulty with
> that line. What's sometimes a thin line, and where I do have some diffi-
> culty, is what's appropriate and what's the appropriate time? That's
> what I've just tried to outline in the wake of September 11. And then
> when the war first started, early in October, you know, when there's
> doubt to be given, we should give the military those doubts.

On October 9, 2001, Rather managed to contradict himself in the same interview,
with former NBC and CBS reporter Marvin Kalb. After declaring "I don't think you
can be too patriotic; when in doubt, I would much prefer to err on the side of too
much patriotism as opposed to too little," Rather went on to define a patriotic journalist as a "skeptical and independent journalist, not cynical." For Rather, that
means "the measure of a journalist's patriotism is does he have the wisdom, does he
have the savvy and does he or she have the guts to ask the tough questions, even
though it might be deemed to be quote unpatriotic." Later in that interview he
stated, "As a journalist, I never want to place a single American fighting man or
woman's life in danger. And I'm fully prepared to give the government military
spokesman the benefit of every reasonable doubt on that score."[3] Kalb either didn't
see Rather's contradictions or didn't think they warranted comment.

It is not clear on what principle Rather would refuse to interrogate political
leaders early in a crisis or war. On the surface, it would seem just the opposite rule
should apply; in the wake of an attack like 9/11, it's likely politicians would move
quickly to take advantage of public shock and grief, making journalistic intervention and tough questioning all the more important early, when people are most
emotional and most vulnerable to manipulation. Likewise, given the history of
military officials shielding themselves from scrutiny and covering up mistakes
with claims that releasing information would endanger men and women in the

field, Rather would have to explain how one can ask "the tough questions" while giving military officials the benefit of the doubt.

While many journalists were nervous about Rather's pronouncements, the performance of the commercial mainstream news media after 9/11 suggests he was merely articulating what others believed and were doing; journalistic scrutiny of administration claims for months after 9/11 was timid at best, and claims by American officials that were intensely scrutinized in the foreign press and alternative media were accepted at face value in the U.S. commercial mainstream news media.

Curiously, shortly before that appearance on the June 2002 King show, Rather had given an interview to the BBC in which he ruminated on the dangers of excessive patriotism. On "BBC Newsnight" on May 5, 2002, Rather said:

> I worry that patriotism run amok will trample the very values that the country seeks to defend. In a constitutional republic based on the principles of democracy such as ours, you simply cannot sustain warfare without the people at large understanding why we fight, how we fight, and have a sense of accountability to the very top.

This "surge of patriotism," Rather said, leads to a journalist saying, "I know the right questions, but you know what, this is not exactly the right time to ask them." But, he continued, "It's unpatriotic not to stand up, look [officials] in the eye, and ask the questions they don't want to hear."[4] Though Rather had said in the earlier interview with Kurtz that he didn't fear a backlash from a hyperpatriotic public, to the BBC reporter he compared the problems that American journalists faced regarding patriotism with the price the practice of "necklacing":

> It is an obscene comparison. You know I am not sure I like it. But you know there was a time in South Africa that people would put flaming tires around peoples' necks if they dissented. And in some ways the fear is that you will be necklaced here, you will have a flaming tire of lack of patriotism put around your neck. Now it is that fear that keeps journalists from asking the toughest of the tough questions...And again, I am humbled to say, I do not except myself from this criticism.[5]

Rather's flip-flopping—between (1) declarations that he would defer to authority, followed by (2) promises he would ask the tough questions, except (3) when it wasn't the right time to ask tough questions, followed by (4) an acknowledgment that he and his colleagues weren't asking the tough questions even when they should—was not an aberration from, but an honest account of, the position of most American journalists.

Whatever his confusion about the role of journalists, Rather seems clear about the role of citizens in wartime: The majority will either support administration policy or, when war does come, will quickly get in line. On November 2, 2001, on CNN's "Larry King Weekend," Rather said: "[T]he whole country is right in saying, look, whatever arguments one may or may not have had with George Bush the younger before September 11, he is our commander-in-chief, he's the man now. And we need unity, we need steadiness. I'm not preaching about it. We all know this."

Do we all agree with this call for unity? The existence of an antiwar movement that began organizing immediately after 9/11 suggests otherwise. And, why in a democracy we should value such unity? Unity toward what goal? Given that in a democracy people are supposed to determine the goals, and that invariably there will be many differences of opinion about the proper goals, what can unity mean other than the obedience and acceptance of authority? On "Larry King Live" on November 4, 2002, Rather made that explicit:

> And, you know, I'm of the belief that you can have only one commander-in-chief at a time, only one president at a time. President Bush is our president. Whatever he decides vis-a-vis war or peace in Iraq is what we will do as a country. And I for one will swing in behind him as a citizen...and support whatever his decision is.

In that interview, Rather's conception of the role of the news media in governance came into sharper focus. When arguing that the U.S. military can be too restrictive in the information it releases and access it provides journalists, Rather's rationale for greater openness was that in a "constitutional republic based on the principles of democracies such as our own there that there must be—it is imperative there be a higher degree of communicable trust between the leadership and the led."

This is, in a nutshell, Dan Rather's political theory: As a citizen, he will swing in behind a president's decision to go to war; as a journalist, he will provide the information to create trust between politicians and citizens. The obvious problem is that this inverts the relationship of citizen to elected officials in a democracy. Citizens in a democracy are not supposed to be "the led." In a meaningful democratic system, citizens should not be limited to a role only in the selection of leaders (an incredibly thin conception of democracy) or in the selection of policies from a set of limited choices presented to them by leaders (still a very thin conception). In a democratic system with a rich sense of participation, citizens would have an active, meaningful role in the determination of which issues are most important at any moment and in the formation of policy options to address those issues. And journalists would be their ally in that task.

The Problem with Patriotism

Whatever the differences of opinion—about how much journalists should talk in public about patriotism, or whether they should wear flag pins on their lapels, or how aggressive questioning of officials should be—I know of no mainstream commercial journalist in the United States who publicly renounced patriotism after 9/11. Despite the flak he took for various comments, Dan Rather was probably accurate when he told the Texas Daily Newspaper Association in March 2002: "There's a lot of talk today about being patriotic. And we all want to be patriotic."[6] The only potential disagreements have been about what constitutes patriotic behavior for journalists.

Bill Kovach, chairman of the Committee of Concerned Journalists, was one of the strongest spokespersons for a tough, critical journalism after 9/11. He did not trumpet patriotism, but implicitly endorsed the concept in his defense of journalists:

A journalist is never more true to democracy—is never more engaged as a citizen, is never more patriotic—than when aggressively doing the job of independently verifying the news of the day; questioning the actions of those in authority; disclosing information the public needs but others wish secret for self-interested purposes.[7]

An editor at one of the top U.S. journalism reviews also implicitly endorsed patriotism in arguing that journalists serve their country best when asking "tough, even unpopular questions when our government wages war." He distinguished "patriotism, love of one's country" from "nationalism—the exalting of one's nation and its culture and interests above all others. If patriotism is a kind of affection, nationalism is its dark side."[8]

There is only one problem with all these formulations: Patriotism cannot be distinguished from nationalism; patriotism in general is morally indefensible; and patriotism in today's empire, the United States, is particularly dangerous to the continued health of the planet. I argue that everyone—citizens and journalists alike—should abandon patriotism and strive to become more fully developed human beings with allegiances not to a nation but to humanity. At first glance, in a country where patriotism is almost universally taken to be an unquestioned virtue, this may seem outrageous. But there is a simple path to what I consider to be this logical, moral conclusion.

If we use the common definition of patriotism—love of, and loyalty to, one's country—the first question that arises is, What is meant by country? Nation-states, after all, are not naturally occurring objects. In discussions with various community groups and classes since 9/11, I have asked people to explain which aspects of a nation-state—specifically in the context of patriotism in the United States—they believe should spark patriotic feelings. Toward whom or what should one feel love and loyalty? The answers offered include the land itself, the people of a nation, its culture, the leadership, national policies, the nation's institutions, and the democratic ideals of the nation. To varying degrees, all seem like plausible answers, yet all fail to provide an acceptable answer to that basic question.

Land

Many people associate patriotism with a love of the land on which they were born, raised, or currently live. Certainly people's sense of place and connection to a landscape is easy to understand; most of us have felt that. I was born and raised on the prairie, and I feel most comfortable, most at home, on the prairie. But what has that to do with love or loyalty to a nation-state? Does affection for a certain landscape map onto political boundaries? If I love the desert, should I have a greater affection for the desert on the U.S. side of the border, and a lesser affection when I cross into Mexico? Should I love the prairie in my home state of North Dakota, but abandon that affection when I hit the Canadian border? In discussing connections to the land we can sensibly talk about watersheds and local ecosystems, but not national boundaries. And ties to a specific piece of land (i.e., the farm one grew up on) have nothing to do with a nation-state.

People

It's also common to talk about patriotism in terms of love and affection for one's countrymen and women. This can proceed on two levels, either as an assertion of differential value of people's lives or as an expression of affection for people. The former—claiming that the lives of people within one's nation-state are more valuable than lives of people outside it—is immoral by the standards of virtually all major moral philosophies and religions, which typically are based on the belief that all human life is equally valuable. It may be true that especially in times of war, people act as if they value the lives of fellow citizens more, but for most people that cannot be a principle on which patriotism can rest.

Certainly everyone has special affection for specific people in their lives, and it's likely that—by virtue of proximity—for most of us the majority of people for whom we have that affection are citizens of the same nation. But does that mean our sense of connection to them stems from living in the same nation-state? Given the individual variation in humans, why assume that someone living in our nation-state should automatically spark a feeling of connection greater than someone elsewhere? I was born in the United States near the Canadian border, and I have more in common with Canadians from the prairie provinces than I do with, for example, the people of Texas, where I now live. Am I supposed to, by virtue of my U.S. citizenship, naturally feel something stronger for Texans than Manitobans? If so, why?

Culture

The same arguments about land and people applies to cultures. Culture—that complex mix of customs, art, stories, faith, traditions—does not map exactly onto the often artificial boundaries of nation-states. More importantly, if one rejects the dominant culture of the nation-state in which one lives, why should one have affection for it or loyalty to it?

Leaders

In a democracy it is clear that patriotism can't be defined as loyalty to existing political leaders. Such patriotism would be the antithesis of democracy; to be a citizen is to retain the right to make judgments about leader, not simply accept their authority. Even if one accepts the right of leaders to make decisions within a legal structure and agrees to follow the resulting laws, that does not mean one is loyal to that leadership.

Policies

The same argument about leaders applies to specific policies adopted by leaders. In a democracy, one may agree to follow legally binding rules, but that does not mean one supports them. Of course, no one claims that it is unpatriotic to object to existing policy about taxes or transportation planning. War tends to be the only policy over which people make demands that everyone support—or at least mute dissent about—a national policy. But why should war be different? When so much human life is at stake, is it not even more important for all opinions to be fully aired?

Governmental structures

If patriotism is not loyalty to particular leader or policies, many contend, at least it can mean loyalty to our governmental structures. But that is no less an abandonment of democracy, for inherent in a real democracy is the idea that no single set of institutions can be assumed to be, for all times and places, the ultimate expression of democracy. In a nation founded on the principle that the people are sovereign and retain the right to reject institutions that do not serve their interests, patriotism defined as loyalty to the existing structures is hard to defend.

Democratic ideals

When challenged on these other questionable definitions of patriotism, most people eventually land on the seemingly safe assertion that patriotism in the United States is an expression of commitment to a set of basic democratic ideals, which typically include liberty, justice, and equality. But problems arise here as well. First, what makes these values distinctly American? Are not various people around the world committed to these values and working to make them real in a variety of ways? Given that these values were not invented in the United States and are not distinct to the United States today, how can one claim them as the basis for patriotism? If these values predate the formation of the United States and are present around the world, are they not human ideals rather than American?

The next move many make is to claim that while these values are not the sole property of Americans, it is in the United States that they have been realized to their fullest extent. This is merely the hubris of the powerful. On some criteria, such as legal protection for freedom of speech, the United States certainly ranks at or near the top. But the commercial media system, which dominates in the United States, also systematically shuts out radical views and narrows the political spectrum, impoverishing real democratic dialogue. It is folly to think any nation could claim to be the primary repository of any single democratic value, let alone the ideal of democracy.

Claims that the United States is the ultimate fulfillment of the values of justice also must come to terms with history and the American record of brutality, both at home and abroad. One might want to ask indigenous people and black Americans, victims of the America holocausts of genocide and slavery, about the commitment to freedom and justice for all, in the past and today. We also would have some explaining to do to the people of Guatemala and Iran, Nicaragua and South Vietnam, East Timor and Laos, Iraq and Panama. We would have to explain to the victims of U.S. aggression—direct and indirect—why it is that our political culture, the highest expression of the ideals of freedom and democracy, has routinely gone around the world overthrowing democratically elected governments, supporting brutal dictators, funding and training proxy terrorist armies, and unleashing brutal attacks on civilians when we go to war. If we want to make the claim that we are the fulfillment of history and the ultimate expression of the principles of freedom and justice, our first stop might be Hiroshima.

After working through this argument in class, one student, in exasperation, told me I was missing the point by trying to reduce patriotism to an easily articulated idea or ideas. "It's about all these things together," she said. But it's not clear how individual explanations that fall short can collectively make a reasonable argument. If each attempt to articulate patriotism fails on empirical, logical, or moral grounds, how do they add up to a virtue?

Any attempt to articulate an appropriate object of patriotic love and loyalty falls apart quickly. When I make this argument, I am often told that I simply don't understand, that patriotism is as much about feeling as about logic or evidence. Certainly love is a feeling that often defies exact description; when we say we love someone, we aren't expected to produce a treatise on the reasons. My point is not to suggest the emotion of love should be rendered bloodless but to point out that patriotism is incoherent because there is no object for the love that can be defended, morally or politically. We can love people, places, and ideas, but it makes no sense to declare one's love or loyalty to a nation-state that claims to be democratic.

Beyond Patriotism

My claim is that there is no way to rescue patriotism or distinguish it from nationalism, which most everyone rejects as crude and jingoistic. Any use of the concept of patriotism is bound to be chauvinistic at some level. At its worst, patriotism can lead easily to support for barbaric policies, especially in war. At its best, it is self-indulgent and arrogant in its assumptions about the uniqueness of U.S. culture and willfully ignorant about the history and contemporary policy of this country. Emma Goldman was correct, I believe, when she identified the essentials of patriotism as "conceit, arrogance, and egotism" and went on to assert that:

> Patriotism assumes that our globe is divided into little spots, each one surrounded by an iron gate. Those who have had the fortune of being born on some particular spot, consider themselves better, nobler, grander, more

intelligent than the living beings inhabiting any other spot. It is, therefore, the duty of everyone living on that chosen spot to fight, kill, and die in the attempt to impose his superiority upon all the others.[9]

This is not a blanket denunciation of the United States, our political institutions, or our culture. People often tell me, "You start with the assumption that everything about the United States is bad." But I do not assume that; it would be as absurd a position as the assumption that everything about the United States is good. No reasonable person would make either statement. Nor do I "blame America first," as some often assert about radical analysis. Instead, I take seriously the moral obligation to be accountable for one's own behavior and, in a democracy, to be responsible collectively for the behavior of the nation in which I am a citizen.

To do that, we must move beyond patriotism. We can retain all our affections for land, people, culture and a sense of place without labeling it as patriotism and artificially attaching it to national boundaries. We can take into account the human need to feel solidarity and connection with others (what Randolph Bourne described as the ability "to enjoy the companionship of others, to be able to cooperate with them, and to feel a slight malaise at solitude)[10] without attaching those feelings to a nation-state. We can realize that communication and transportation technologies have made possible a new level of mobility around the world, which leaves us with a clear choice: Either the world can continue to be based on domination by powerful nation-states (in complex relationship with multinational corporations) and the elites who dictate policy in them, or we can seek a new interdependence and connection with people around the world through popular movements that cross national boundaries based on shared values and a common humanity. To achieve the latter, people's moral reasoning must be able to constrain the destructive capacity of elite power. As Goldman suggested, patriotism retards our moral development. These are not abstract arguments about rhetoric; the stakes are painfully real and the people in subordinated nation-states have, and will continue, to pay the price of patriotism in the dominant states with their bodies.

As the Bush administration makes good on its post-9/11 promise of an unlimited war against endless enemies, the question of patriotism is particularly important in the United States. The greater the destructive power of a nation, the greater the potential danger of patriotism. Despite many Americans' belief that we are the first benevolent empire, this applies to the United States as clearly as to any country. On this count we would do well to ponder the observations of one of the top Nazis, Hermann Goering. In G.M. Gilbert's book on his experiences as the Nuremberg prison psychologist, he recounts this conversation with Goering:

> "Why of course the people don't want war," Goering shrugged. "Why would some poor slob on a farm want to risk his life in a war when the best that he can get out of it is to come back to his farm in one piece. Naturally, the common people don't want war; neither in Russia nor in England nor in America, nor for that matter in Germany. That is understood. But, after all, it is the leaders of the country who determine the policy and it is always a simple matter to drag the people along, whether it is a democracy or a fascist dictatorship or a Parliament or a Communist dictatorship."
>
> "There is one difference," I pointed out. "In a democracy the people have some say in the matter through their elected representatives, and in the United States only Congress can declare war."
>
> "Oh, that is all well and good, but, voice or no voice, the people can always be brought to the bidding of the leaders. That is easy. All you have to do is tell them that they are being attacked and denounce the pacifists for lack of patriotism and exposing the country to danger. It works the same way in any country."[11]

If Not Patriotism?

If our political lives should not be organized around patriotism and nation-states, then what? The simple answer is both the local and the global; politics must, over time, be devolved down to levels where ordinary people can have a meaningful role in governing their own lives, while at the same time we maintain a sense of connection to the entire human family, and understand that the scope of high-technology and the legacy of imperialism leave us bound to each other across the globe in new ways. This is a call for an internationalism that understands we live mostly at the local level but can do that ethically only when we take into account how local actions affect others outside our view.

My goal here is not a detailed sketch of how such a system would work; any such attempt would be unrealistic. The first step is to envision something beyond what exists, a point from which people could go forward with experiments in new forms of social, political, and economic organization. Successes and failures in those experiments would guide subsequent steps, and any attempt to provide a comprehensive plan at this stage cannot be taken seriously. It is also important to realize that the work of articulating alternative political visions and engaging in political action to advance them has been going on for centuries. There is no reason today to think that national identification is the only force that could hold together societies; for example, political radicals of the 19th and early 20th centuries argued for recognizing other common interests. As Goldman put it:

> Thinking men and women the world over are beginning to realize that patriotism is too narrow and limited a conception to meet the necessities of our time. The centralization of power has brought into being an international feeling of solidarity among the oppressed nations of the world; a solidarity which represents a greater harmony of interests between the workingman of America and his brothers abroad than between the American miner and his exploiting compatriot; a solidarity which fears not foreign invasion, because it is bringing all the workers to the point when they will say to their masters, 'Go and do your own killing. We have done it long enough for you.' This solidarity is awakening the consciousness of even the soldiers, they, too, being flesh of the flesh of the great human family.[12]

We can, of course, go even further back in human history to find articulations of alternatives. As Leo Tolstoy reminded us in his critique of patriotism published in 1900, a rejection of loyalty to governments is part of the animating spirit of Christianity; "some 2,000 years ago...the person of the highest wisdom, began to recognize the higher idea of a brotherhood of man." Tolstoy argued that this "higher idea, the brotherly union of the peoples, which has long since come to life, and from all sides is calling you to itself" could lead people to "understand that they are not the sons of some fatherland or other, nor of Governments, but are sons of God."[13]

In more secular form, this sentiment is summed up often-quoted statement of the great American labor leader and Socialist Eugene Debs, who said in 1915: "I have no country to fight for; my country is the earth, and I am a citizen of the world."[14]

Can Journalists be Neutral, and Does it Matter?

Whatever one's assessment of the intellectual and moral status of patriotism, one thing should be readily evident: A declaration of patriotism is a declaration of a partisan political position. For purposes of this portion of my argument, it matters not how any particular journalist conceptualizes patriotism or what might be the best way for journalists to make good on their patriotism. Just as rejecting patriotism as a framework is political, so is accepting it. How then can journalists both openly proclaim a political position and continue to make the claim they are politically neutral?

Of course individual journalists hold political positions on many subjects; no journalist claims to be politically inert. The conventional argument is not that journalists are devoid of opinions, but that professional practices of fairness, balance, and objectivity help ensure that the news is gathered and presented in a way that is not inordinately influenced by those opinions. As part of that, journalists typically avoid making public pronouncements about their political beliefs and affiliations. This is where patriotism is different; journalists typically agree that patriotism is a good thing and struggle in public with what it means for their work. On this matter, they are openly political yet see no conflict between this and an obviously contradictory claim to neutrality.

The most plausible explanation is that these journalists take patriotism to be the kind of political judgment that is so universally accepted that to publicly accept it is uncontroversial. For example, it's likely true that all American journalists believe slavery is wrong, and if asked in public no journalist would hesitate to state that belief. The statement would be a moral and political judgment about the rights and obligations of people, but no one would see it as compromising an accompanying claim to neutrality because to argue for slavery would place one well outside current social norms. It would be seen as an indication of pathology, personal and political.

But unless the argument against patriotism is evidence of such pathology —making me, Debs, Goldman, Tolstoy, and many others, both today and in the past, pathological—patriotism can't be in that category of a moral or political truism. The only way to pretend that declarations of patriotism are not political and open to critique is to erase the many arguments against patriotism. Indeed, a review of contemporary American mainstream commercial journalism would suggest that is exactly what happens.

Does any of this matter? Does it affect the news that U.S. readers and viewers get, especially on matters of war and peace? Yes, for this patriotism systematically clouds the vision of American reporters, and not just since 9/11. The most thorough account of this is contained in *Manufacturing Consent*, in which Edward S. Herman and Noam Chomsky extensively review the systematic slanting of the news of foreign affairs toward the official viewpoint of the dominant culture's political elites.[15] But, if one doesn't trust such radical sources, let's return to Dan Rather.

In 1996 Rather gave a talk on journalism ethics at the University of Texas, where I teach. More interesting than the lecture was his response to one question. A student asked Rather about the failures of the news media in covering the 1991 Gulf War—boosterish coverage of the military, failure to examine the Bush administration claims (many of which turned out to be lies), a gee-whiz approach to the high-tech weapons. The student laid out a clear and compelling case for journalistic malfeasance, and Rather acknowledged that he couldn't argue with most of what the young man said.

But, Rather shrugged, in time of war, "journalism tends to follow the flag."[16]

Rather was right, and I suppose we can admire him for being honest. But he seemed to miss the point of the question: Yes, journalists *do* tend to follow the flag, but *should* they? Rather's acceptance of the student's analysis indicated he understood how a democratic system suffers when journalists too readily accept the pronouncements of the powerful during a war, how people can't really make intelligent decisions about policy options without independent information. But his reaction also indicated that he believed the "follow the flag" instinct was inevitable, perhaps a law of journalistic nature.

But, of course, there are no laws of nature for journalists. Instead, there are institutional realities, professional routines, and ideologies that shape behavior, as Herman and Chomsky lay out in their propaganda model. The importance of these influences on the news are obscured by the professional ideology of political neutrality, which keeps both journalists and citizens from understanding the relationship between power and the news media. Any claim to such neutrality is illusory; there is no neutral ground on which to stand anywhere in the world. One need not be overtly partisan or propagandistic to be political. The politics of journalists' choices about which stories to cover, from which angle, using which sources, cannot be eliminated by a claim to have established neutral professional practices. The question is not whether one is neutral, but whether one is independent in a meaningful way from powerful forces.

Mainstream commercial journalists are quick to answer, "Yes, of course we are independent." In fact, government officials rarely attempt to impose legal restraints on journalists, and editors and reporters work relatively free of direct governmental control. (Of course journalists are not independent of the corporations that employ them, but the focus here is on independence from government.) All governments routinely attempt to control the information journalists receive from officials, especially during wartime, but the U.S. government does relatively little, in terms of direct repression, to impede journalists from their work. (One exception to that is in the war theater itself, which is a complex issue I won't take up here.)

What do journalists do with that freedom from most legal control? For the most part during war, not much. The slavish dependence on official sources and the ideology of patriotism keeps the vast majority of American journalists trapped in a fantasy world in which U.S. war aims are always just and anything bad that happens is the product of either an honest mistake or the rogue action of a "bad apple" in an otherwise decent system. The result is painful to come to terms with: Times of war—when a democracy most desperately needs a critical, independent journalism working outside the ideological constraints of the culture—are precisely when the U.S. commercial mainstream news media fails most profoundly. A final anecdote to illustrate.

During the question period following a 1999 speech at the National Press Club, Dan Rather discussed the decision of U.S. military planners in the attack on Yugoslavia to target that nation's power grid. Sam Husseini, communications director of the Institute for Public Accuracy,[17] pointed out the apparent contradiction between Rather's use of the pronoun "we" in describing U.S. military action while claiming to be a neutral journalist. Rather acknowledged it was a difficult issue, but he made no bones about where he came down on the question: "I'm an American, and I'm an American reporter. And yes, when there's combat involving Americans—criticize me if you must, damn me if you must, but—I'm always pulling for us to win."[18]

Unstated in Rather's response, of course, is the assumption that Americans in combat fight on the right side. But what if U.S. leaders sent Americans into battle for a cause that was not just? What if leaders pursued a war that was, in fact, decidedly unjust? What if the United States fought a war not for freedom and justice but instead to extend and deepen its own control over crucial strategic regions of the world? Let's say, just for the sake of argument, this war took place in a region of the world that held the majority of the easily accessible oil reserves, in an era in which the world's industrial economy ran on oil, and therefore control over the flow of oil and oil profits meant real power. What if American troops were sent into combat for the objective of such control? What if, because of the way U.S. military planners fight wars, one could be reasonably certain that large numbers of civilians would die? Just for the sake of argument, if that were to happen, would it be acceptable for anyone—journalist or ordinary citizen—to be "pulling for us to win"? Should journalists be open to the possibility that the leadership of their country might be capable of such a war plan? And if journalists were not open to such a possibility, would we call them neutral? Would we trust them to provide us with the information we need to make decisions as citizens in a democracy?

As I have argued throughout this essay, Dan Rather's public comments are important not for the way in which they occasionally are idiosyncratic, but for the way in which they are completely conventional. When Rather talked about "pulling for us to win," the most disheartening moment was not the comment itself, which was hardly surprising given Rather's history and public comments. More troubling was that at the National Press Club—in a room full of some of the most experienced and influential working journalists in the nation's capital—the audience broke out in applause.

NOTES

1. L. Brent Bozell, "Media coverage at its best," *Washington Times*, September 25, 2001, p. A-18.

2. All quotes from television broadcasts are, unless otherwise indicated, taken from transcripts retrieved from the Dow Jones Interactive database.

3. "A conversation with Dan Rather," October 9, 2001, "The Kalb Report: Journalism at the Crossroads," CD-ROM. http://www.gwu.edu/~kalb/.

4. Quotes transcribed from
http://news.bbc.co.uk/hi/english/audiovideo/programmes/newsnight/newsid_1991000/1991885.stm.

5. "Dan Rather says U.S. patriotism leads some journalists to self-censorship," Associated Press report, May 16, 2002.

6. Mike Tolson, "Remain objective despite war, Rather tells Texas journalists," *Houston Chronicle*, March 19, 2002, p. 19.

7. Bill Kovach, "Journalism and patriotism," talk to the annual meeting of the Organization of News Ombudsmen, April 30, 2002. http://www.newsombudsmen.org/kovach.html.

8. Russ Baker, "Want to be a patriot? Do your job," *Columbia Journalism Review*, May 2002, pp. 78-79.

9. Emma Goldman, "Patriotism: A Menace to Liberty," in *Anarchism and Other Essays* (New York: Dover, 1969), pp. 128-129.

10. Randolph Bourne, "War is the Health of the State," 1918. http://struggle.ws/hist_texts/warhealthstate1918.html.

11. G. M. Gilbert, *Nuremberg Diary* (New York: Farrar, Straus and Company, 1947), pp. 278-279.

12. Goldman, "Patriotism," pp. 142-143.

13. Leo Tolstoy, "Patriotism and Government," online at http://dwardmac.pitzer.edu/Anarchist_Archives/bright/tolstoy/patriotismandgovt.html.

14. See: http://bari.iww.org/iu120/local/Scribner12.html.

15. Edward S. Herman and Noam Chomsky, *Manufacturing Consent*, rev. ed (New York: Pantheon, 2002).

16. Dan Rather, "Ethics in Journalism," lecture to College of Communication, University of Texas, November 26, 1996.

17. See: http://www.accuracy.org.

18. Dan Rather, speech to National Press Club, Washington, DC, June 25, 1999. Transcript at http://www.fair.org/activism/husseini-rather.html.

Chapter Six

Corporate Hegemony: A Critical Assessment Of The *Globe and Mail's* News Coverage Of Near-Genocide In Occupied East Timor, 1975–1991[1]

Jeffery Klaehn

MOST CANADIANS ARE UNAWARE OF THE genocide or near-genocide in East Timor. Amnesty International[2] has thoroughly documented the extent of the human rights violations and state-sponsored atrocities perpetrated by Indonesia following its December 7, 1975 invasion of East Timor.[2] In his book, *Indonesia's Forgotten War: The Hidden History of East Timor*, Taylor writes that Indonesia's occupation violated 'almost every human rights provision in the United Nations Charter, the Universal Declaration of Human Rights and the International Bill of Rights.'[3] There is a range of secondary literature documenting the extent to which the United States participated in and contributed toward the near-genocide.[4] In contrast, Canada's role has received only scant attention from Canadian scholars.[5]

This research asks whether the *Globe and Mail's* coverage of the historical events in East Timor was hegemonic or ideologically serviceable to the extent that it provided a political and historical benchmark by which to inform the public (or not) and influence (or not) Canadian government policy on Indonesia and East Timor? The question is a crucial one given that the government of Canada was in a position to wield significant diplomatic influence over the 'Question of East Timor' at the United Nations (UN) during the period of 1975 through until 1991.

> Canada had enormous leverage over the slaughters in East Timor and never used it. The media were never concerned and the intellectual community was never concerned. In this respect, Canada has contributed materially to the slaughters.[6]

This research focuses on the *Globe and Mail* coverage of East Timor throughout the 'invasion period,' that is, from the time of the December 7, 1975 Indonesian invasion through to the end of 1980. This was when news coverage of the historical events in East Timor would have been most crucial in terms of (1) organizing public awareness of the Indonesian invasion of East Timor, the occupation and subsequent atrocities and (2) influencing Canadian government policy toward East Timor and Indonesia.

How did Canada's news agenda-setter and self-declared national newspaper cover the news story of the invasion and occupation of East Timor? Moreover, how did it cover Canada's connections to and participation in the story? Secondary sources contend that the media played a propagandistic role.[7] Implicit in these arguments are accusations of deception, cover-up and political propaganda.

East Timor—The Background

East Timor, a former Portuguese colony, was invaded by Indonesia on December 7, 1975. On December 12, 1975 the UN General Assembly adopted Resolution 3845 (XXX) recognizing that the invasion had breached the principle of self-determination as laid out in articles 1 and 55 of the UN Charter and in UN Resolutions 1514 (XV) and 1541 (XV).[8]

On December 22, 1975 the UN Security Council adopted Resolution 384 which called upon Indonesia to withdraw from East Timor 'without delay' and called upon 'all states to respect the territorial integrity of East Timor as well as the inalienable right of its people to self-determination.'[9] The Security Council reaffirmed East Timor's right to self-determination on April 22, 1976, voting in favour of Resolution 389 which once again denounced integration. By this time approximately 60,000 East Timorese had already been killed. Throughout the late 1970s and early 1980s, the General Assembly adopted eight additional Resolutions reaffirming General Assembly Resolution 3845, rejecting Indonesia's position that East Timor had been lawfully integrated,[10] reaffirming East Timor's right to self-determination and calling for an immediate military withdrawal.[11]

Indonesia's illegal occupation of East Timor was one of the most brutal in post-war history.[12] According to Noam Chomsky, the death toll, relative to the population, is the worst case of mass slaughter since the Holocaust.[13]

Amnesty International tells us that at least 200,000 East Timorese perished as a result of Indonesia's invasion and occupation, between a quarter and a third of the territory's pre-1975 population.[14]

Indonesia's invasion and occupation of East Timor constituted an act of aggression,[15] included war crimes and/or 'crimes against humanity' under international and Canadian criminal law,[16] and 'violated almost every human rights provision in the UN Charter and the Universal Declaration of Human Rights and the International Bill of Rights.'[17] The record of repression, state-sponsored atrocities and human rights violations are well-documented.[18]

Indonesia enacted programs of forced relocation causing induced starvation and disease,[19] initiated programs of forced sterilization and birth-control,[20] and undertook psychological programs within East Timor oriented toward pacification and social engineering.[21]

East Timor in Canadian Foreign Policy[22]

Following Indonesia's invasion of East Timor, Canada could not bring itself to support the ten UN Resolutions that expressed 'grave concern at the loss of life,' called upon 'all States to respect the inalienable right of the people of Portuguese Timor to self-determination, freedom and independence,' rejected 'the claim that East Timor had been integrated into Indonesia,' drew 'the attention of the Security Council to the critical situation in East Timor,' and called upon the Indonesian military to 'withdraw without delay.' Canada was the largest Western investor in Indonesia at the time of the invasion.

In September 1987 Canada's representative to the UN Human Rights Sub-Commission voted against putting East Timor back on the UN Human Rights Commission agenda. Not until 1992, in the wake of the Santa Cruz massacre of November 12, 1991, did Canada's official stance at the UN change as the UN Commission on Human Rights condemned, for the first time, Indonesia's human rights record in East Timor. In 1993 Canada co-sponsored a resolution critical of Indonesia, and supported a similar statement in 1994.[23]

Canada was in a position to wield significant diplomatic influence at the UN during the crucial invasion years. A range of secondary sources suggest that Canada's opportunistic foreign policy was motivated by political and economic self-interest. Sorenson (1990) writes that,

> In short, the case of East Timor serves as a grim lesson in political realities.
> Canada's profitable relations with Indonesia have ensured that violations
> of international law and extensive human rights abuses are ignored.[24]

Given that the government of Canada was implicated in the near-genocide by virtue of its pro-Indonesian voting record on East Timor resolutions at the UN, the story was not quite so remote as Canada's geographic proximity to East Timor would suggest. Foreign policy is one way in which the government of Canada is implicated in the East Timor near-genocide.

Canadian Aid to Indonesia and East Timor

Canadian Overseas Developmental Assistance (CODA) to Indonesia nearly doubled after Indonesia invaded East Timor in 1975—from $19.52M in 1974-1975 to $36.7M in 1975-1976. Canada 'has continually been among the top 10 [donors] since its 1975 invasion of East Timor.'[25] Further, 'the bulk of CODA to Indonesia is bilateral, that is government-to-government aid,' 'designed as welfare to support Canadian business (or business-like institutions like universities) by requiring the "aided" country to buy the donor's goods.'[26] The 'goods' have entailed material and intellectual capital, and academics across the spectrum of disciplines have participated in joint development projects.

Canadian Investment in Indonesia

When considering the importance of Canada's business ties to Indonesia, total foreign trade is less significant than direct Canadian investment in Indonesia. Economic incentives for Canadian-based multinationals have included reparations of profits, exemptions from import duties, generous tax holidays, and availability of cheap, non-unionized domestic labour, mostly women.[27] Canada was the largest Western investor in Indonesia at the time of the 1975 invasion of East Timor. Historically, the largest Canadian-based investor in Indonesia has been PT INCO.

The Case of PT INCO in Indonesia

Since first locating in Indonesia in 1968, INCO has invested more than $1.5B in its nickel-mining operations there. In the initial stages of these operations, the Crown's Economic Development Corporation (EDC) approved two loans totalling $57.25M. Additional funding was provided by credit agencies in the U.S., Japan, Norway, Britain and Australia.[28]

Expansion in the Indonesian market allowed INCO to limit its reliance on a far less cost effective Canadian work force. Downsizing its Canadian operations resulted in a more favorable wage/benefit ratio. Indonesian mining laws allow the state to seize large tracks of land belonging to the local peoples, who were forced to sacrifice their land, lifestyle, and traditional means of subsistence.[29] Like the majority of its foreign aid, taxes paid by corporations such as INCO have traditionally been diverted to Indonesia's military elite, in addition to invisible money involved in private security and bribes.[30]

Canadian Military Exports to Indonesia

Although Indonesia is able to acquire the bulk of its military arsenal from other countries, predominantly the U.S., successive Canadian governments have authorized military export permits that have allowed Canadian arms manufacturers to export duel-purpose (civilian and military) military goods to Indonesia.[31] Not all export licenses result in actual exports. According to the Department of Foreign Affairs and International Trade[32] the ratio 'is often as low as 10%.' Hence, the value of export licenses is normally only a fraction of the value of actual permits issued. However, Canada's willingness to authorize permits stands in direct opposition to Canada's own Import/Export Act, which prohibits the sale of Canadian-made military goods to 'countries engaged in hostilities' and/or to 'countries whose governments have a persistent record of serious violations of human rights.' There is a burden of proof indicating that Indonesia meets both these criterion. Canada has also hosted several military trade fairs and bazaars, promoting Canadian military exports to Indonesia.[33]

A Critical Review of Herman and Chomsky's PM of Media Operations[34]

Herman and Chomsky's 'propaganda model' of media operations (PM) argues that elite media interlock with other institutional sectors in ownership, management, and social circles, effectively circumventing their ability to remain analytically detached from the power structure of society, of which they themselves are presumed to be integral parts.[35] The net result of this, the PM contends, is self-censorship without significant coercion. The PM constitutes an institutional critique of media performance and theorizes media performance as an outcome of market forces. It concedes that the powerful have individual objectives but presumes that dominant elites share common political, economic and social interests.[36] The PM presumes that media behaviour will reflect these interests in such ways that are 'functional' for dominant elites and social institutions.

The PM theorizes that media serve 'political interests,'[37] 'mobilize' (or not) sympathetic emotion for victims and outrage against victimizers, and routinely 'divert' public attention away from some stories and news items while concurrently directing attention toward others.[38] The model postulates that media routinely make selection choices that establish and define 'worthy' and 'unworthy' causes. It predicts there will be qualitative and quantitative differences in the treatment accorded *'unworthy victims'* (victims of oppression and/or state terrorism that is perpetrated by the capitalist democracies), and *'worthy victims'* (victims of oppression and/or state terrorism perpetrated by official enemy states). Disparities in treatment will be observable in sourcing and evaluation, such that 'worthy victims' will be accorded more coverage, more prominent coverage and more humanistic treatment than unworthy victims.[39]

In sum, then, the PM predicts that news discourse will feature (1) the promotion of ideologically serviceable themes and system-supportive disinformation;[40] (2) a low volume of news coverage devoted to reporting on *'unworthy victims'*; (3) dominance of official discourse; and (4) a very tight, controlled range of *'permitted opinion'* and debate on central topics.[41]

The PM emphasizes that media personnel internalize beliefs and attitudes which in turn influences media performance.[42] This is a social psychological argument that is presumed but not directly tested by the PM.[43] It was echoed by one of the journalists I interviewed in my research for this paper:

> A lot of journalists are genuinely clueless about the forces to which they are responding. Some are malleable, others try to act with integrity and are perpetually surprised at the blocks they encounter. Others suss out the system and either get out or act in concert with it. Those are the ones who often move up in the system. I've had journalists and editors tell me about the way things work very straightforwardly. Some combine both. There are a surprising number of higher up editors and producers who know they must accommodate the interests of ownership and other powers (in the case of public broadcasting) but within these constrictions, are still committed to as much muckraising as possible.[44]

There are two central methodological techniques associated with the PM. The first is to study *'paired examples'* of co-occurring historical events. Disparities in treatment can lend insight into interpreting media behavior. The second, favored by Chomsky in his polemical writings, is to explore the 'boundaries of the expressible' or range of 'permitted opinion' on crucial topics.

> One appropriate method is to consider the spectrum of opinion allowed expression. According to the propaganda model, one would expect the spectrum to be bounded by the consensus of powerful elites while encouraging tactical debate within it.[45]

This research utilizes both methodological approaches. The *Globe and Mail* was selected because it is Canada's key 'national medium'[46] and influences the tone and direction of lower-tier media.[47] In this context, the *Globe and Mail* has been described as Canada's news 'agenda-setter.'[48]

If the data conform with the predictions of the PM, the coverage will feature propagandistic elements observable in choices of story selection and in the quantity and quality of the news coverage accorded the near-genocide in East Timor.

Covering the Invasion: The Distribution of the Globe and Mail Coverage of East Timor, 1975-1991

The distribution of the coverage in the year 1975 was as follows: prior to the December 7 invasion, the *Globe and Mail* published 29 articles on East Timor up to and including December 6, 1975. Following Indonesia's invasion, the coverage declined significantly. The distribution of its coverage of the invasion itself, during the month of December 1975, is as follows: one article on the day after the invasion (December 8), one article on each of the following three days (December 8, 9 and 10), and one article on each of December 15, 20, 23, and 30.

During 1976 the *Globe and Mail* published a one-paragraph article on January 5 and a two-paragraph piece on January 16 reporting on the invasion. This was the extent of its coverage of the invasion throughout the entire year of 1976.

Four additional articles on East Timor were published during 1976, three of which reported on its annexation. It published one article on East Timor in 1977, a single paragraph article on March 1, which was headlined 'Australians charge 100,000 killings.' Throughout the next 16 months there was no additional coverage of East Timor published in the *Globe and Mail*.

On October 9, 1978 the newspaper published an investigative piece by Mick Lowe, headlined '60,000 have died in unseen war.'

Throughout 1979 it published three small articles on East Timor.

This was the extent of the *Globe and Mail* news coverage of crucial invasion period. The coverage included no discussion whatsoever of Canada's diplomatic or material contributions to the near-genocide. In fact, the coverage makes no mention of Canada in relation to Indonesia or the unfolding near-genocide in East Timor.

Canada is effectively *omitted* or *'edited out'* of the unfolding news story at this stage. This evident omission can be seen to conform with the hypotheses advanced by the PM.

Table 1 provides a summation of the quantity of the *Globe and Mail's* East Timor coverage from 1975 to March 20, 1991 and provides a summation of the distribution of the coverage.

Table 1: Search of Globe and Mail Articles relating to East Timor, December 7, 1975–December 31, 1991

Year	Total Articles	East Timor Mentioned in Passing	Articles About East Timor	Editorials	Letters to Editor re: East Timor
1975	36				
Feb 75:	1		1		
Aug–Sept:	22	1	21		
Oct–Dec 6:	6	1	55		
Dec 7–31:	7		77		
1976	6		6		
1977	1		1		
1978	1		1		1
1979	3		3		
1980	5	1	3		1
1981	5	3	2		
1982	9	5	3		1
1983	10	5	5		
1984	18	6	2		10
1985	7	3	2		2
1986	4	3	1		
1987	13	3	1	1	8
1988	9	4	2		3
1989	19	2	8		9
1990	12	4	3		5
1991	28	12	12		4

Source: Scharfe (1996: 117)

The quantity and distribution of the *Globe and Mail* East Timor coverage support the hypotheses advanced by the PM. The coverage reduced significantly after Indonesia invaded and dropped to almost nil as the atrocities reached their peak throughout 1978/79. The absolute low volume of news coverage effectively concealed (1) Indonesia's *near-genocidal* aggression and (2) Canada's diplomatic and material contributions from public view.

Analysis of Paired Examples: Comparing and Contrasting the Quantity of News Coverage Accorded East Timor to that Accorded to Cambodia[49]

Following the PM's methodological assumption of seeking paired examples, this section provides a detailed comparison of the quantity of coverage accorded East Timor and Cambodia by both the *Globe and Mail* and the *New York Times*. As Eglin notes, the two cases are well-suited for the purposes of such a comparison given that (1) the 'genocide' in Cambodia was comparable in relative scale to the mass killings or near-genocide in East Timor and (2) given that it coincided with the period (1975-1979) of the worst atrocities, killings and deaths.'[50]

Table 2 provides a summation of the number of major articles accorded East Timor and Cambodia by the *Globe and Mail* during the period of 1977-1991. The sharp contrast and observable disparity in treatment conforms with the PM.

Table 2: Globe and Mail Coverage of East Timor and Cambodia, November 1, 1977–December 31, 1991

Year	Major Articles on East Timor	Major Articles on Cambodia
Nov–Dec, 1977	1	0
1978	1	0
1979	3	6
1980	3	22
1981	2	65
1982	3	34
1983	5	47
1984	2	31
1985	2	74
1986	1	34
1987	1	28
1988	2	68
1989	8	90
1990	3	71
1991	12	53
Total	**49**	**623**

Source: Scharfe (1996: 114)

Ruling Out Possible Explanations for the Low Volume of News Coverage

To argue that the *Globe and Mail* coverage is biased or ideologically inflected because it omits legitimately relevant information raises the question of whether information was available to the media at the time of the coverage. Omissions may only be evident in retrospect. However, there is ample evidence indicating this was not the case here.

> Extremely high casualty figures were already becoming available in 1976. In February 1976, an Indonesian client, Lopez da Cruz, who had been appointed deputy chair of the 'Provisional Government of East Timor' set up by the forces of occupation, asserted that 60,000 Timorese had already died.[51]

There are several possible explanations for the initial poor coverage accorded the unfolding East Timor story. Indonesia imposed tight information controls that prevented journalists from entering the territory after the invasion. Lack of access to the territory is a reasonable explanation for the low volume of coverage. Moreover, the *Globe and Mail* had only three full-time staff foreign correspondents (based in Beijing, London and Washington) at the time of the invasion and relied upon the wire services (principally Reuters and AP), traveling Canadian-based staff correspondents, and freelance writers for its foreign news coverage. Lack of resources is another possible explanation for the low volume of news coverage. Lack of interest among the Canadian public could be offered as a third possible explanation.

Each of these possible alternative explanations are problematic for a variety of different reasons.

While lack of access to the territory is undeniable, Carey observes that despite the restrictions on access and information blackout imposed by the government of Indonesia, East Timor was given fitful attention by the Australian and British media after the invasion.

> A form of collusion existed between Western governments, international corporations and the Indonesian Government to keep East Timor off the agenda given the very lucrative business contracts which existed with Jakarta at this time.[52]

Noam Chomsky argues that the elite American media ignored and suppressed the East Timor story precisely because doing so served broader U.S. (geo) political-economic interests. Chomsky recalls that the *Columbia Journalism Review* asked him to contribute a piece in 1978.[53] Chomsky then suggested an essay discussing the lack of coverage accorded East Timor by the American media. His proposal was rejected on the grounds that the topic of 'East Timor' was 'too remote.' Chomsky remarks, 'the circle is complete,' when 'first, the media suppress a major story, then a journal dedicated to the performance of the media is unwilling to investigate the suppression because it has been so effective.'[54]

Eight months after the invasion Canada's Secretary of State for External Affairs and International Trade Allan J. MacEachen delivered a speech in Jakarta,[55] where he spoke at length about Indonesia's natural resources, large population and strategic importance, all of which, MacEachen stressed at the time, had placed Indonesia 'in a key position to play a role in international affairs.'[56] MacEachen then stressed a 'reorientation of Canada's foreign policy' toward increased economic development, shared objectives and co-operation between Canada and Indonesia, declaring that the government of Canada had been 'impressed by Indonesia's pragmatic leadership...which has resulted in steady economic progress.'[57]

Two years later, in 1978, Canadian ambassador to Indonesia Glen Shortliffe visited illegally occupied East Timor as part of the international delegation of parliamentarians and news correspondents granted supervised access. Although the Canadian news personnel that accompanied Shortliffe were able to view (first-hand) the Biafra-like conditions of the starving, diseased Timorese who were then residing in the Indonesian military-controlled strategic hamlets after having been forcibly relocated by the occupying military forces, there was no media coverage of the diplomatic visit, or of the abject 'victimization' of the East Timorese.[58]

Given that Canadian news journalists undeniably had direct (albeit supervised) access to the territory during this diplomatic visit, there is reason to seriously question the argument that lack of access explains the low volume of coverage accorded the events in East Timor throughout the crucial invasion period and Canada's role in 'aiding and abetting' the near-genocide.

Lastly, that information was available on what was taking place in East Timor throughout the invasion and occupation periods is undeniable. Chomsky and Herman, for instance, devoted an entire section of their book *The Political Economy of Human Rights, Vol. One: The Washington Connection and Third World Fascism*, published in 1979, to the near-genocide in East Timor.[59] Beyond this, however, East Timor was accorded coverage in a range of alternative media throughout the invasion period. At least 22 articles on East Timor were published in alternative media in 1978 alone (at least 16 articles in 1979, and at least 19 articles in 1980). If lack of access is in fact a credible explanation for the low volume of coverage accorded the

East Timor story by Canada's self-declared 'national newspaper' and news agenda-setter, then how does one possibly account for the simple fact that alternative media, with far fewer resources available to them, were able to generate so many stories devoted to reporting on and speaking directly of the events taking place there during this time period? The second possible explanation is also seriously compromised given that, by definition, alternative media are availed to far fewer resources than are the corporate, mainstream media.

The last possible explanation for the absolute low volume of coverage accorded the story of East Timor is lack of interest amongst (1) the *Globe and Mail's* readership and (2) amongst the Canadian public generally. This explanation is problematic for the simple reason that the East Timor story can be seen to have been both sensationalistic and dramatic.[60] As an unfolding news story, its dimensions entailed 'invasion,' years of bombing and thousands of confirmed cases of systematic gross human rights violations. The East Timor story included other dramatic elements: forced relocation, induced starvation and disease, pacification, sterilization, and (Western-backed) near-genocide. And, as highlighted above, there were myriad ways in which Canada was directly connected to the near-genocide. If one takes the suggestion that public interest in the story simply was not there, then it begs the question, why not?

On logical grounds, the quantity and distribution of the coverage of the coverage can be seen to have been ideologically-motivated, virtually ensuring that Canada's pro-business agenda would not be challenged.

Exploring the Range of 'Permitted Opinion' in the Globe and Mail Coverage

The findings indicate that throughout the crucial invasion period of 1975-1980, the *Globe and Mail* diverted public attention away from two important considerations: (1) the international nature of the Indonesian invasion and occupation of East Timor and (2) Canada's own diplomatic and material contributions to the slaughters.

Two levels of omission are evident in the *Globe and Mail's* East Timor coverage during the crucial invasion period. At the referential level, omission is evidenced by the absence of context, criticism and humanization from the whole process of representation. At the significatory level, it is evidenced by the absence of alternative ways of signifying actors, action and events, which are framed in particular ways. The sources cited in the *Globe and Mail's* East Timor news coverage published throughout the invasion period were all official (Indonesian-approved) sources.

Indonesian representations of major events, actors, and substantive issues are presented not as claims but rather as *facts*, even in the face of evidence proving the contrary. Since the 1975 invasion Indonesia has consistently claimed that it did not *invade* East Timor but rather *intervened* in the civil war in East Timor. This representation creates context in which Indonesia's actions in East Timor may be characterized as *'intervention'* as opposed to *'invasion,' 'illegal aggression'* and *'occupation.'* Various scholarly sources indicate that the brief civil war in East Timor had ended by November 1975, and that between 2000 and 3000 Timorese had died in the fighting.[61]

Indonesia commenced cross-border armed incursions from West Timor in November, 1975. On November 28, 1975, the de facto FRETILIN government declared unilateral independence for East Timor in order to defend its territorial integrity at the UN.[62] Indonesia then invaded outright on December 7. The *Globe and Mail's* chronology mirrors the government of Indonesia's both in terms of both what it declares to be fact and what it excludes.

The *Globe and Mail* coverage established context within which Indonesia's 1975 *invasion* of East Timor was not an act of *aggression* but rather *'intervention'* and later *'war'* with Fretilin. Within this contextual framework, ensuing events may be explained away, justified, and *blamed upon* the resistance movement (Fretilin) within East Timor.[63] By promoting this representation, the *Globe and Mail* can be seen to have facilitated Canada's (geo) political-economic interests.[64] Ideologically serviceable context is established. Concurrently, the government of Canada, together with Canada's corporate and intellectual communities, are not cast as an active partners in the near-genocide.

The *Globe and Mail's* endorsement of the official chronology can be traced back to the pre-invasion period. On November 11, 1975 it published a report, headlined 'Civil Wars that bleed the Third World,' stating that the civil war had yet to end. A smaller article, headlined 'East Timor official seeks help,' published on November 26, 1975, reported (again) that the civil war in East Timor was still ongoing at the time. Articles bylined out of Jakarta prior to the invasion reported that the civil war in East Timor was still ongoing in late November and early December 1975. The political disinformation, coupled with the low volume of coverage accorded the events in East Timor, can be seen to strongly support the PM.

Themes of atrocities, vested interests, political and institutional alliances, while not entirely absent from the discourse, are present in only a cursory way in the coverage published throughout the invasion period.

Narrowness of debate is evidenced by the extent to which the news coverage featured no information and/or debate on (1) the illegality of Indonesia's invasion and subsequent occupation of East Timor; (2) Canada's diplomatic courtship of Indonesia; (3) ethical issues relating to Canadian investment in and aid to Indonesia during the same time period when Indonesia was carrying out 'extermination campaigns' and near-genocide in East Timor; (4) Canada's 'hypocritical' foreign policy toward Indonesia; (5) the involvement of virtually every Canadian university (and Canadian academics) in administering numerous 'aid projects' to Indonesia in unison with CIDA throughout the invasion and occupation periods; and (6) the 'complicity' of the major mass media in 'covering' East Timor as an unfolding news story.

Coverage of the East Timor Story in Other Canadian Dailies

Examination of the news coverage accorded the story by other newspapers throughout the crucial invasion period (1975-1980) enabled additional insight into how the story was treated by the Canadian media and also afforded an opportunity to test the assumption that the *Globe and Mail* is the premiere agenda-setting newspaper in Canada with respect to this particular news story. The Canadian News Index (CNI) was consulted in order to delineate how much coverage other Canadian dailies accorded the East Timor story throughout the crucial invasion period (1975-1980). The CNI listed a total of zero (0) news articles published on East Timor throughout the entire invasion period (1975-1980) by any of the Canadian newspapers considered, including *Calgary Herald* (CH), Montreal *Gazette* (MG), and the Winnipeg *Free Press* (WFP). According to the CNI, there was only one (single) news article on East Timor published in the *Toronto Star* (TS) throughout the entire period.[65] The TS article was published one day after the invasion, on December 8, 1975. By-lined out of Jakarta, the (Reuter-UPI) article stresses, in its second full paragraph, Indonesian foreign minister Malik's claim 'that the Indonesian troops [had] stormed the capital of Dili [sic] at the invitation of pro-Indonesian elements' within East Timor. Its one-line fifth paragraph notes that China had called Indonesia's takeover a 'flagrant invasion.' The sixth paragraph cites Malik and recounts the official Indonesian chronology.

> Malik claimed Indonesia, which immediately declared Dili part of its territory, acted to 'prevent bloodshed' in a civil war which had broken out there between pro-Indonesian forces, members of the People's Democratic Association of Timor (Apodeti), and leftist forces belonging to the Front for an Independent East Timor (Fretilin).

According to the CNI, the *TS* did not publish another news article on East Timor for the next fourteen years. The absolute low volume accorded the invasion, occupation and near-genocide in the Canadian print media can be seen to confirm the PM with considerable strong evidence.

The Findings: Re-Assessing the Propaganda Model

The central hypothesis of this research was that if the data conformed to the PM, there would be a tendency for official discourse to feature prominently into the data, if not dominate it. If debate did find expression in the data, it would be limited. The framing of events would demonstrate a pervasive presence of official representations. Victims would not be humanized by the data, which would be closed rather than open and inclusive. Throughout the invasion period, official representations of the major actions, actors, and substantive issues featured prominently into the *Globe and Mail* news coverage. Thematic content, sources, framing, evident disinformation and propaganda proper are evidenced by the data, strongly supporting the substantive hypotheses advanced by the PM.

The *Globe and Mail* East Timor coverage throughout the 1980s was sporadic. Official, dominant representations of major events continued to feature prominently into the news discourse but marginal changes in the thematic content and range of sources represented throughout the 1980s is evidenced by the data. Where a marginal voice of criticism is most evident in the *Globe and Mail* news coverage of East Timor was in its *letters to the editor* section. It afforded a *space* in which official representations of major actions, actors and substantive issues are questioned, scrutinized and challenged. Within this space, parameters of debate are evidenced.[66] The news reporting, which features minimal debate and omission of substantive information, contrasts sharply in this regard, and, by virtue of placement, was accorded greater prominence within the newspaper than were letters to the editor.

Concluding Remarks

In assessing the extent to which the *Globe and Mail's* East Timor news coverage conforms with the hypotheses advanced by the PM, this research suggests that the *Globe and Mail* affirmed rather than challenged Canada's actions and policies during the period in which the coverage appeared. The promotion of ideologically serviceable disinformation is systematic in the *Globe and Mail's* East Timor news coverage, and is observable in terms of both individual story headlines and story content.

The *Globe and Mail* failed in its public responsibility to provide adequate news coverage, first to the major events, actions and actors involved in the East Timor '*story*' and, secondly, to the (myriad) relevant Canadian connections. More extensive coverage can be seen to have been warranted given the horrific and sensational nature of the near-genocide, and given the involvement of the international community, Canada in particular.

The vital role of Canada's key national medium is of particular importance given that its news coverage throughout the late 1970s and 1980s can be seen (1) to have served as a conduit for official, established truths and (2) to have facilitated Canadian's pro-business foreign policy toward Indonesia.

Insofar as the coverage provided a benchmark by which to influence Canadian government policy on Indonesia and East Timor, the *Globe and Mail* can be seen to have performed a significant hegemonic function, one oriented toward legitimization and political accommodation. The significance of political legitimacy is marginal given that assent was achieved simply by keeping the Canadian public relatively ignorant of the near-genocide. However, the data indicates that legitimacy was virtually ensured, via the suppression of dissenting voices and promotion of ideologically serviceable themes, disinformation and political propaganda proper. Eglin provides additional evidence that the *Globe and Mail* acted as a conveyer of state and corporate propaganda. Throughout this time period, the government of Canada's actions and policies toward Indonesia and East Timor can be seen to have been oriented toward the accommodation of Canada's own (geo) political-economic interests. The absolute low volume of news coverage virtually ensured that decision-making would be unchallenged. It can be concluded that the interrelations of state and corporate capitalism and the corporate media effectively circumvented fundamental democratic processes.

Dedicated to the memory of Suzanne Kondratenko
(March 3, 1974–September 11, 2001)

NOTES

1. This chapter was first published in *Gazette: The International Journal of Communication Studies*, 2002, Vol. 64(4): 301-321. Reprinted by permission of Sage Publications Ltd.

2. Amnesty International, *East Timor: Violations of Human Rights, Extra-judicial Executions, 'Disappearances', Torture and Political Imprisonment* (London: Amnesty International, 14 May 1985); Amnesty International, *Indonesia & East Timor—Power and Impunity: Human Rights Under the New Order* (London: Amnesty International, 28 September 1994).

3. John Taylor, *Indonesia's Forgotten War—The Hidden History of East Timor* (London: Zed, 1991), 78.

4. Noam Chomsky and Edward S. Herman, 'East Timor: Genocide on the Sly', in *The Political Economy of Human Rights, Vol. One: The Washington Connection and Third World Fascism* (Montreal: Black Rose, 1979); Noam Chomsky, *The Chomsky Reader*, James Peck (ed.) (New York: Pantheon, 1987); Carmel Budiardjo, 'Indonesia: Mass Extermination and the Consolidation of Authoritarian Power,' Alexander George (ed.) *Western State Terrorism* (New York: Routledge, 1991); Matthew Jardine, 'International Report: APEC, the U.S. and East Timor,' *Z Magazine* (Jan 1995:34-39).

5. On the surface, the lack of scholarship is puzzling given that virtually every Canadian university has participated in Indonesian development projects administered through the Canadian International Development Agency (CIDA).

6. Noam Chomsky, cited in Elaine Briere, 'A Country Now Forgotten,' *This Magazine* 25 (1) (June/July 1991): 22-24.

7. Elaine Briere, 'Tribulations of a tribal nation: Why does Canada condone the subjugation of East Timor?' *Globe and Mail*, 6 December 1988, A7; Elaine Briere, 'Feeding the Cyclops,' *Briarpatch* May 1988, 20-23; Elaine Briere, 'East Timor: Genocide Continues,' *Briarpatch* Oct 1988, 35; Elaine Briere *Bitter Paradise: The Sell-Out of East Timor* [video documentary], (Mission, BC: Snapshot Productions, 1997); D. Maitland, 'Remember them' [Letter to the Editor], *The Kitchener-Waterloo Record*, 6 Nov 1992; Peter Eglin, 'Complicity in Genocide,' *Ontarion*, 21-27 Feb 1995, 12; Peter Eglin, (forthcoming) *Getting A Life: A Story of Studies in Pursuit of Intellectual Responsibility*; Peter Eglin et al., 'Canada, Canadian Corporations, Canadian Universities, Canadian News Media and Complicity in Genocide in East Timor,' Paper presented at the joint session of the Canadian Law and Society Association with the Canadian Sociology & Anthropology Association on *State Terrorism/State Violence in the Good and Peaceable Kingdom'* Learneds, Calgary, 12-14 June 1994; Sharon Scharfe, *Complicity: Human Rights in Canadian Foreign Policy—The Case of East Timor* (Montreal: Black Rose, 1996); Jeffery Klaehn, 'East Timor concealed,' *The Cord*, 15 Oct 1993; Jeffery Klaehn, 'Corporate Hegemony: The Institutional Nature of Indonesian Genocide in East Timor' [unpublished MA thesis] *University of Guelph*, (1995); Jeffery Klaehn, 'For gain...for shame: For 24 years Canada has been too reluctant to criticize Indonesia's brutal treatment of East Timor,' *The Kitchener-Waterloo Record*, 25 September 1999, D3; John McMurtry, 'Why does Canada aid the oppressors,' *Globe and Mail*, 20 Feb 1990, 7; John McMurtry, 'Stop aid to Indonesia' [Letter to the editor] *Globe and Mail*, 15 April 1992.

8. Scharfe, *Complicity*, 82-3.

9. Heike Kreiger, ed., *East Timor and the International Community: Basic Documents* (Cambridge International Series, Vol. 10. Cambridge: Cambridge University Press, 1997), xxiii.

10. Budiardjo, 'Indonesia: Mass Extermination and the Consolidation of Authoritarian Power', 199.

11. Scharfe, *Complicity*, 83.

12. W. Carey, 'East Timor: The Making of an International Issue 1974-99,' *The Brock Review* 7, no. 1/2 (1999), 29.

13. Noam Chomsky, *Deterring Democracy* (New York: Hill and Wang, 1992), 204.

14. Amnesty International, *Indonesia and East Timor—Power and Impunity*.

15. James Dunn, *Timor: A People Betrayed* (Milton, Qld.: Jacaranda Press: 1983); Carmel Budiardjo and Liem Soei Liong, *The War Against East Timor* (London: Zed, 1984); Scharfe, *Complicity*, Chapter 2.

16. McMurtry, 'Why does Canada aid the oppressors'; Peter Eglin, 'Partnership in an Evil Action: Canadian Universities, Indonesia and Genocide in East Timor,' *Brock Review* 7, no. 1/2 (1999), 58-100.

17. Taylor, *Indonesia's Forgotten War*, 178.

18. Amnesty International, *East Timor: Statement of Amnesty International Concerns in East Timor* (London: Amnesty International, 29 April 1980); Amnesty International, 'East Timor: Violations of Human Rights—'; Amnesty International, *Indonesia/East Timor: Summary of Amnesty International Concerns in Indonesia and East Timor* (London: Amnesty International, April 1987); Amnesty International, *Indonesia/East Timor: Summary of Amnesty International Concerns in Indonesia and East Timor* (London: Amnesty International, May 1988); Amnesty International, *Indonesia/East Timor: A Summary of AI's Concerns* (London: Amnesty International, 1990); Amnesty International, *East Timor: The Santa Cruz Massacre* (London: Amnesty International, 1991); Amnesty International, 1994; Asia Watch, *Human Rights in Indonesia and East Timor* (New York: Asia Watch, March 1989); Asia Watch, *East Timor: The November 12 Massacre and its Aftermath* (New York: Asia Watch, December 1991); Asia Watch, *East Timor: Asia Watch Criticizes Commission Report* (New York: Asia Watch, Jan 1992); Asia Watch, *The Limits of Openness: Human Rights in Indonesia and East Timor* (New York: Asia Watch, Sept 1994).

19. Frank Chalk and Kurt Jonassohn, *The History and Sociology of Genocide* (New Haven, Conn: Yale University Press in co-operation with the Montreal Institute for Genocide Studies), 411; John Taylor, *The Indonesian Occupation of East Timor, 1974-1979: A Chronology* (London: Catholic Institute for International Relations, 1990), 17-20; Scharfe, *Complicity*, 55; D. Selby, 'Indonesian expansionism: the case of East Timor,' *Human Rights* (Cambridge: Cambridge University Press, 1987), 43.

20. Scharfe, *Complicity*, 52; Mirand E. Sissons, *From One Day to Another: Violations of Women's Reproductive and Sexual Rights in East Timor* (Fitzroy, Victoria: East Timor Human Rights Centre, 1997), 34.

21. G.C. Gunn, *A Critical View of Western Journalism and Scholarship on East Timor* (Sydney, Australia: Journal of Contemporary Asian Studies, 1994), 232.

22. Selections from this section first appeared in Eglin et al, 'Canada, Canadian Corporations....'

23. Canada has facilitated direct investment in Indonesia and bilateral trade since the invasion (see Scharfe, *Complicity*, 190-192).

24. John Sorenson, 'Canadian Role in Indonesia Opportunistic,' *Winnipeg Free Press*, 12 December 1990.

25. Scharfe, *Complicity*, 157-8.

26. Eglin, 'Partnership...,' 67.

27. Briere, 'Tribulations'; Briere, 'Feeding the cyclops'; Briere, 'Genocide continues'; Briere, *Bitter Paradise*; McMurtry, 'Why does Canada aid the oppressors'; Klaehn, 'Corporate Hegemony...'; Klaehn, 'For gain...'; Scharfe, *Complicity*.

28. Scharfe, *Complicity*, 169, 189; *The Indonesian Kit*, Second edition (Vancouver: East Timor Alert Network, 1993), 37; J. Swift, *The Big Nickel: INCO at Home and Abroad* (Toronto: Between the Lines, 1977), 81.

29. Eglin et al, 'Canada, Canadian corporations....'

30. Chomsky and Herman, 'Genocide on the sly', 212.

31. For details on Canadian trade in military goods, see Scharfe, *Complicity*, 194-206.

32. External Affairs and International Trade Canada, *Program for Export Market Development* (Ottawa: External Affairs and International Trade Canada, 1995).

33. Scharfe provides detailed analysis of Canadian military exports to Indonesia and notes that Foreign Affairs does not trace the end use or user of Canadian military export products; see *Complicity*, 197-204.

34. It bears mentioning that Edward S. Herman was the principle author of the first chapter of *Manufacturing Consent*, in which the filter mechanisms are laid out.

35. This view echoes Miliband, who wrote that 'There is nothing particularly surprising about the character and role of the major mass media in advanced capitalist society. Given the economic and political context in which they function, they cannot fail to be, predominantly, agencies for the dissemination of ideas and values which affirm rather than challenge existing patterns of power and privilege, and thus to be weapons in the arsenal of class domination'; Miliband, cited in Wallace Clement, *Canadian Corporate Elite: Analysis of Economic Power* (Toronto: McClelland & Stewart, 1975), 278.

36. The debate here effectively mirrors the Marxist response to the liberal-bourgeois thesis within Canadian sociology.

37. Noam Chomsky, *Necessary Illusions: Thought Control in Democratic Societies* (Toronto: CBC Enterprises, 1989), 153.

38. As Cohen put it, media 'may not be successful in telling people what to think' but there is much evidence that they are 'stunningly successful in telling people what to think about'; see Bernard C. Cohen, *The Press and Foreign Policy* (New Jersey: Princeton University Press, 1963), 13.

39. Edward S. Herman and Noam Chomsky, *Manufacturing Consent: The Political Economy of the Mass Media* (New York: Pantheon, 1988), 35.

40. Herman and Chomsky, *Manufacturing Consent*, 2.

41. See also Edward S. Herman, 'The Propaganda Model Revisited,' *Monthly Review* [reprinted online at http://musictravel.free.fr/political/political7.html] (July 1996); Edward S. Herman, 'The Propaganda Model: A Retrospective,' *Journalism Studies*, no. 1 (2000); Chomsky, *Necessary Illusions*; James Winter, *Common Cents: Media Portrayal of the Gulf War and Other Events* (Montreal: Black Rose, 1992); James Winter, 'Media Think: The Role of the Media in Supporting the Establishment,' *Canadian Communications: Issues in Contemporary Media and Culture*, Second edition (Toronto: Prentice Hall, 2002); John McMurtry, *Unequal Freedoms: the Global System as an Ethical Market* (Toronto: Garamond Press, 1998); Jeffery Klaehn, 'A Critical Review and Assessment of Herman and Chomsky's Propaganda Model of Media Operations,' *European Journal of Communication* 17 (2) (2002).

42. For additional reading, see H. Gans, *Deciding What's News* (New York: Pantheon, 1979); Richard V. Ericson, Patricia Baranek and Janet Chan, *Negotiating Control: A Study of News Sources* (Toronto: University of Toronto Press, 1989); Gaye Tuchman, *Making News: A Study in the Construction of Reality* (New York: Free Press, 1978).

43. Also see Robert Hackett, *News and Dissent: The Press and the Politics of Peace in Canada* (New Jersey: Ablex, 1991); Lance Bennett, *News: The Politics of Illusion*, Second edition (New York: Longman, 1988).

44. A range of scholarly literature takes up the political-economy of news production. See, for example, Cham Eyal, James Winter and Maxwell McCombs, 'The Agenda-Setting Role in Mass Communication' in Michael Emery and Ted Curtin Smythe' in *Readings in Mass Communication: Concepts and Issues in the Mass Media*, Sixth edition (Wm. C. Brown, 1986), 169-174; Peter Desbarats, *Guide to Canadian News Media* (Toronto: Harcourt Brace Jovanovich, 1990); Norman E. Isaacs, *Unintended Gates: The Mismanaged Press* (New York: Columbia University Press, 1986); Joyce Nelson, *Sultans of Sleeze: Public Relations and the Mass Media* (Toronto: Between the Lines, 1989); Ben Bagdikian, *Media Monopoly* (Boston: Beacon Press, 1987); Robert McChesney, *Corporate Media and the Threat to Democracy* (New York: Open Media Pamphlet Series, Seven Stories Press, 1997); Edward S. Herman, *Triumph of the Image: Essays on Economics, Politics and the Media* (Boston: South End, 1995); Edward S. Herman, *The Myth of the Liberal Media: An Edward Herman Reader* (New York: Peter Lang Publishers, 1999); Norman Solomon and Peter Cohen, *Wizards of Oz: Behind the Curtain of Mainstream News* (Common

Courage Press, 1997); McMurtry, *Unequal Freedoms*; Winter, *Common Cents*; Klaehn, 'A Critical Review and Assessment....'

45. Chomsky, *Necessary Illusions*, 59.

46. Desberats, *Guide to Canadian News Media*, 227; G. Heinricks,'Whose news? Business circles the globe,' *This Magazine* 23, 3 September 1989, 14-21; Hackett, *News and Dissent*, 95.

47. Other Canadian media, such as television and radio, reach a greater proportion of the Canadian population, and can also generate public interest in foreign policy issues.

48. Hackett notes that the *Globe and Mail* is 'disproportionately read by the affluent and powerful' and observes that 'Globe reports often fuel debate in the House of Commons'. The *Globe and Mail* can thus be seen to be both politically and ideologically influential within Canada; see *News and Dissent*, 95.

49. Selections of this section first appeared in Eglin *et al*, 'Canada, Canadian corporations....'

50. Peter Eglin, 'Proposal for four small research projects on the relationship of Canadian Intellectuals to the 'Genocide' in East Timor,' *East Timor Alert Network*, 4 Aug 1992.

51. Budiardjo, 'Mass extermination...,' 199.

52. Carey, 'East Timor: The making of...,' 46.

53. Noam, Chomsky, *Towards a New Cold War: Essays on the Current Crisis and How We Got There* (London: Sinclair Browne, 1982), 337-348.

54. Chomsky, *Towards a New Cold War*, 471, fn. 3.

55. As noted, Canada's close economic ties to and diplomatic courtship of Indonesia are two logical reasons why the unfolding events in East Timor can be seen to have warranted significant news coverage in the Canadian media.

56. Allan MacEachen, 'Canada and Indonesia—The Dialogue Has Begun Well,' Speech *by Allan MacEachen to Jakarta Press Club*, Jakarta, 25 Aug 1976.

57. MacEachen, 'Canada and Indonesia....'

58. As noted, the *Globe and Mail* coverage reduced significantly in 1978 with only one article published throughout the entire year.

59. Herman and Chomsky, 'Genocide on the Sly.'

60. See Jeffery Klaehn, 'Canadian Complicity in the East Timor Near-Genocide: A Case Study in the Sociology of Human Rights.' *Portuguese Studies Review*. 2004, Vol. 11(1): 49-65.

61. Scharfe, *Complicity*, 45; Selby, 'Indonesian expansionism', 42; Jardine maintains that the civil war ended even earlier, on September 24, 1975; see *Genocide in Paradise*, 16.

62. Budiardjo and Soei Liong, *The War Against East Timor*, 1-8.

63. This representation conforms with the '*chronology*' of the major actions, issues and events laid out by the Department of Foreign Affairs of the Republic of Indonesia (July 1992) in their document entitled *East Timor: Building for the Future*. This document was sent to me upon request by the Indonesian embassy.

64. The *Globe and Mail* can also be seen to have accepted, endorsed and legitimized Indonesia's illegal annexation of East Timor vis-a-vis its bylines.

65. 'Indonesia takes over Portuguese Timor,' 8 December 1975.

66. See, for example, McMurtry, 'Why does Canada aid the oppressors'; McMurtry, 'Stop aid to Indonesia'; also see Jeffery Klaehn, (forthcoming) 'Taking Note of Genocide on the Sly: Analysis of Letters to the Editor on East Timor in the *Globe and Mail*.'

REFERENCES

Amnesty International (1980) *East Timor: Statement of Amnesty International Concerns in East Timor*. London: Amnesty International, 29 April 1980.

Amnesty International (1985) *East Timor: Violations of Human Rights, Extra-judicial Executions, 'Disappearances,' Torture and Political Imprisonment*. London: Amnesty International, 14 May 1985.

Amnesty International (1987) *Indonesia/East Timor: Summary of Amnesty International Concerns in Indonesia and East Timor*. London: Amnesty International, April 1987.

Amnesty International (1988) *Indonesia/East Timor: Summary of Amnesty International Concerns in Indonesia and East Timor*. London: Amnesty International, May 1988.

Amnesty International (1990) *Indonesia/East Timor: A Summary of AI's Concerns*. London: Amnesty International, 1990.

Amnesty International (1991) *East Timor: The Santa Cruz Massacre*. London: Amnesty International, 1991.

Amnesty International (1994) *Indonesia & East Timor. Power and Impunity. Human Rights Under the New Order*. London: Amnesty International, 28 Sept 1994.

Anderson, B. (1995) 'East Timor and Indonesia: Some Implications' in Peter Carey and G. Carter Bentley (eds) *East Timor at the Crossroads: The Forging of a Nation*. Honolulu: University of Hawaii Press.

Andrews, P. (1989) 'Looking at what the media don't say: controversial Noam Chomsky sees subtle US thought control.' *Seattle Times*, 29 June, D4.

Asia Watch (1989) *Human Rights in Indonesia and East Timor*. New York: Asia Watch, March 1990.

Asia Watch (1991) *East Timor: The November 12 Massacre and its Aftermath*. New York: Asia Watch, December 1991.

Asia Watch (1992) *East Timor: Asia Watch Criticizes Commission Report*. New York: Asia Watch, Jan 1992.

Asia Watch (1994) *The Limits of Openness. Human Rights in Indonesia and East Timor*. New York: Asia Watch, Sept 1994.

Bagdikian, Ben (1987) *Media Monopoly*. Boston: Beacon Press.

Ballinger, J. (1992) 'The new free trade heel: Nike's profits jump on the backs of Asian workers.' *Harper's*, Aug.

Bennett, Lance (1988) *News: The Politics of Illusion*. Second ed. New York: Longman.

Bottomore, Tom (1993) *Elites and Society*. Second ed. New York: Routledge.

Branegan, J. (1992) 'Empire of the sons—and daughter.' *Time*, Feb 3: 24–27.

Briere, Elaine (1988) 'Tribulations of a tribal nation: Why does Canada condone the subjugation of East Timor?' *Globe and Mail*. 6 Dec, A7.

Briere, Elaine (1988) 'Feeding the cyclops.' *Briarpatch*, (May): 20–23.

Briere, Elaine (1988) 'East Timor: genocide continues.' *Briarpatch*, (Oct): 35.

Briere, Elaine (1991) 'A Country Now Forgotten.' *This Magazine*, 25 (1), June/July: 22–24.

Briere, Elaine (1997) *Bitter Paradise: The Sell Out of East Timor* [video documentary]. Mission, British Columbia: Snapshot Productions.

Briere, Elaine and Dan Devaney (1990) 'East Timor: The Slaughter of a Tribal Nation,' *Canadian Dimension*, 24 (7), Oct: 31–35.

Briere, Elaine and S. Gage (1993) *The Indonesian Kit*. Second ed. Vancouver: East Timor Alert Network.

Brooks, Daniel and Guillermo Verdecchia (1991) *The Noam Chomsky Lectures: A Play*. Toronto: Couch House.

Brownstone, M. and C. Demers (1994) *External Review of the University of Guelph's Involvement in the Sulawesi Regional Development Project*. Guelph, Ontario: University of Guelph.

Budiardjo, Carmel and Liem Soei Liong (1984) *The War Against East Timor*. London: Zed.

CIDA (Canadian International Development Agency) (1975/1976) *Canada and Development Cooperation, Annual Review, 1975-1976*. Ottawa: CIDA.

—. (1976) *Annual Report*. Ottawa: CIDA.

—. (1992) *CIDA Programs in Asia—Indonesia, June*. Ottawa: CIDA.

—. (1993) *CIDA Programs in Asia*. Ottawa: CIDA.

—. (1993) *CIDA in East Timor*. Ottawa: CIDA.

—. (1993) *Indonesia Country Policy Framework, Canada-Indonesia Cooperation Program*. Ottawa: CIDA.

Carter, R. (1958) 'Newspaper Gatekeepers and their Sources of News,' *Public Opinion Quarterly*, 22: 133-144.

Carey, W. (1999) 'East Timor: The Making of an International Issue 1974-99' in *The Brock Review* 7 (1/2) 1998/99.

Chalk, Frank and Kurt Jonassohn (1990) *The History and Sociology of Genocide*. New Haven, Conn: Yale University Press (in co-operation with the Montreal Institute for Genocide Studies).

Chomsky, Noam (1973) *For Reasons of State*. London: Collins.

Chomsky, Noam (1982) *Towards a New Cold War: Essays on the Current Crisis and How We Got There*. London: Sinclair Browne.

Chomsky, Noam (1985) *Turning the Tide: US Intervention in Central America and the Struggle for Peace*. London: Pluto.

Chomsky, Noam (1987) *The Chomsky Reader*, ed. James Peck. New York: Pantheon.

Chomsky, Noam (1988) *Language and Politics*, ed. Carlos Peregin Otero. Montreal: Black Rose.

Chomsky, Noam (1989) *Necessary Illusions: Thought Control in Democratic Societies*. Toronto: CBC Enterprises.

Chomsky, Noam (1991) 'International Terrorism: Image and Reality,' pp. 12-38 in Alexander George (ed) *Western State Terrorism*. New York: Routledge.

Chomsky, Noam (1991) 'The Gulf Crisis' *Z Magazine* (Feb): footnoted version.

Chomsky, Noam (1991) 'Letter from Lexington' *Lies of Our Times* (Aug).

Chomsky, Noam (1991) 'What We Say Goes: The Middle East and the New World Order' *Z Magazine* (May).

Chomsky, Noam (1991) 'Aftermath' *Z Magazine* (October): footnoted version.

Chomsky, Noam (1992) *Deterring Democracy*. New York: Hill and Wang.

Chomsky, Noam (1993) *Letters from Lexington: Reflections on Propaganda*. Toronto: Between the Lines.

Chomsky, Noam (1993) *The Prosperous Few and the Restless Many*, interviews with David Barsamian. Berkeley, CA: Odonian.

Chomsky, Noam (1993) *Year 501: The Conquest Continues*. Boston: South End.

Chomsky, Noam (1997) *Class Warfare*. Vancouver: New Star.

Chomsky, Noam (1997) *Media Control: The Spectacular Achievements of Propaganda*. Open Media Pamphlet Series. New York: Seven Stories Press.

Chomsky, Noam (1998) *The Common Good*. Interviews with David Barsamian. Berkeley, CA: Odonian.

Chomsky, Noam and Edward S. Herman (1979) 'East Timor: Genocide on the Sly' in *The Political Economy of Human Rights, Vol. One: The Washington Connection and Third World Fascism*. Montreal: Black Rose.

Clement, W. (1975) *Canadian Corporate Elite: Analysis of Economic Power*. Toronto: McClelland & Stewart.

Cohen, Bernard C. (1963) *The Press and Foreign Policy*. New Jersey: Princeton University Press.

Desbarats, P. (1990) *Guide to Canadian News Media*. Toronto: Harcourt Brace Jovanovich.

Dobbin, Murray (1998) *The Myth of the Good Corporate Citizen: Democracy Under the Rule of Big Business*. Toronto: Stoddart.

Domhoff, William G. (1979) *The Powers That Be: Processes of Ruling Class Domination in America*. New York: Viking.

Dunn, James (1983) *Timor: A People Betrayed*. Milton, Qld.: Jacaranda Press.

Eglin, Peter (1995) 'Complicity in Genocide.' *Ontarion*, Feb 21-27.

Eglin, Peter (1999) 'Partnership in an Evil Action: Canadian Universities, Indonesia and Genocide in East Timor.' *Brock Review* 7 (1/2) 1998/1999, pp. 58-100.

Eglin, Peter, Jeffery Klaehn, Bill Ripley and Sharon Scharfe (1994) 'Canada, Canadian Corporations, Canadian Universities, Canadian News Media and Complicity in Genocide in East Timor.' Paper presented at the joint session of the Canadian Law and Society Association with the Canadian Sociology & Anthropology Association on 'State Terrorism/State Violence in the Good and Peaceable Kingdom,' Learneds, Calgary, June 12-14.

Ericson, Richard V., Patricia Baranek and Janet Chan (1989) *Negotiating Control: A Study of News Sources*. Toronto: University of Toronto Press.

ETAN (East Timor Alert Network) (1989) 'East Timor and Canadian Investment in Indonesia' and 'The War in East Timor.' Vancouver, ETAN.

ETAN (1991) 'East Timor and the Gulf War.' Vancouver, ETAN.

ETAN (1992a) 'New Study reveals 273 killed in Dili massacre.' Press release issued in Lisbon by Jose Ramos-Horta on September 3, 1992.

ETAN (1992b) 'East Timor newsletter.' September, Toronto, ETAN.

ETAN (1993) 'East Timor newsletter.' July, Toronto, ETAN.

Eyal, Cham, James Winter and Maxwell McCombs (1986) 'The Agenda-Setting Role in Mass Communication,' pp. 169-174 in Michael Emery and Ted Curtin Smythe (eds) *Readings in Mass Communication: Concepts and Issues in the Mass Media*. Sixth Edition. New York: William. C. Brown.

External Affairs and International Trade Canada (1992) *Survey of Bilateral Economic Relations Between Canada and Indonesia*. Ottawa: External Affairs and International Trade Canada.

Finn, Ed (2000) *Who Do We Try To Rescue Today? Canada Under Corporate Rule*. Ottawa, Ontario, Canada: Canadian Centre for Policy Alternatives.

Fishman, Mark (1980) *Manufacturing the News*. Austin, Texas: University of Texas Press.

Foreign Affairs Canada (1999) 'Fact Sheet—Indonesia, April 1999.' Ottawa: Foreign Affairs Canada.

Galtung, Johan and Mari Ruge (1973) 'Structuring and selecting news,' pp. 62-72 in Stanley Cohen and Jack Young (eds) *The Manufacture of News: A Reader*. London: Sage.

Gans, H. (1979) *Deciding What's News*. New York: Pantheon.

Gunn, G.C. (1994) *A Critical View of Western Journalism and Scholarship on East Timor*. Sydney, Australia: Journal of Contemporary Asian Studies.

Hackett, R. (1991) *News and Dissent: The Press and the Politics of Peace in Canada*. New Jersey: Ablex.

Heinricks, G. (1989) 'Whose news? Business circles the globe.' *This Magazine*, (23, 3 Sept):14-21.

Herman, Edward S. (1982) *The Real Terror Network: Terrorism in Fact and Propaganda*. Boston: South End.

Herman, Edward S. (1995) *Triumph of the Image: Essays on Economics, Politics and the Media*. Boston: South End.

Herman, Edward S. (1996) 'The Propaganda Model Revisited' in the *Monthly Review* (July); reprinted online at http://musictravel.free.fr/political/political7.htm

Herman, Edward S. (1999) *The Myth of the Liberal Media: An Edward Herman Reader*. New York: Peter Lang Publishers.

Herman, Edward S. (2000) 'The Propaganda Model: A Retrospective.' *Journalism Studies* 1 (1): 101-112.

Herman, Edward S. and Noam Chomsky (1988) *Manufacturing Consent: The Political Economy of the Mass Media.* New York: Pantheon.

Herman, Edward S. and Gerry O'Sullivan (1991) '"Terrorism" as Ideology and Cultural Industry,' pp. 39-75 in George Alexander (ed) *Western State Terrorism.* New York: Routledge.

Hughes, P. (1993) 'Quiet Complicity.' *Briarpatch* (March): 22.

Isaacs, Norman E. (1986) *Unintended Gates: The Mismanaged Press.* New York: Columbia University Press.

Jacoby, Russell (1987) *The Last Intellectuals: American Culture in the Age of the Academe.* New York: Noonday Press.

Jamieson, Don (Secretary of State, External Affairs Canada) (1976) 'Canada Pledges Continued for the World Organization.' Statement by Secretary of State Don Jamieson, at the 31st Session of the UN General Assembly, New York, 29 Sept 1976.

Jardine, Matthew (1993) 'Weapons for genocide.' *San Francisco Examiner*, May 31, A17.

Jardine, Matthew (1995) 'International Report: APEC, the US and East Timor.' *Z Magazine* (Jan):34-39.

Jardine, Matthew (1996) 'Pacification, Resistance, and Territoriality: Prospects for a Space of Peace in East Timor.' *GeoJournal* 39 (4), pp. 397-404.

Jardine, Matthew (1997) *East Timor: Genocide in Paradise.* Arizona: Odonian.

Jolliffe, Jill (1978) *East Timor: Nationalism and Colonialism.* St. Lucia, Qld.: University of Queensland Press.

Kadine, K. (1990) 'The CIA supplied Suharto with death lists in 1965.' *Inside Indonesia* (June):12-13.

Klaehn, Jeffery (1993) 'East Timor concealed.' *The Cord*, Oct 15.

Klaehn, Jeffery (1994) 'Hypocrisy prevails over international human rights politics.' *The Ontarion*, Feb. 1.

Klaehn, Jeffery (1999) 'For gain…for shame: For 24 years Canada has been too reluctant to criticize Indonesia's brutal treatment of East Timor.' *Kitchener-Waterloo Record*, Sept. 25, D3.

Klaehn, Jeffery (2002) 'A Critical Review and Assessment of Herman and Chomsky's Propaganda Model of Media Operations' in the *European Journal of Communication*, 17 (2): 147-182.

Klaehn, Jeffery (2002) Review of Edward S. Herman and Noam Chomsky, *Manufacturing Consent: The Political Economy of the Mass Media* (revised edition), *Cultural Dynamics* 14 (3): 327-329.

Klaehn, Jeffery (2003) 'Model Construction, Various Other Epistemological Concerns: A Reply to John Corner's Commentary on the Propaganda Model.' *European Journal of Communication* 18 (3): 377-383.

Klaehn, Jeffery (2003) 'Behind the Invisible Curtain of Scholarly Criticism: Revisiting the Propaganda Model.' *Journalism Studies* 4 (3): 359-369.

Klaehn, Jeffery (2004) 'Canadian Complicity in the East Timor Near-Genocide: A Case Study in the Sociology of Human Rights.' *Portuguese Studies Review* 11 (1): 49-65.

Klaehn, Jeffery (2005) 'Understanding Power – An Interview with Noam Chomsky' in *Bound by Power: Intended Consequences.* Montreal: Black Rose Books.

Klaehn, Jeffery (2005) 'On the Disease of Corporatism and Its Outcomes – An Interview with John McMurtry' in *Bound by Power: Intended Consequences.* Montreal: Black Rose Books.

Klaehn, Jeffery *(forthcoming)* 'Taking Note of Genocide on the Sly: Analysis of Letters to the Editor on East Timor in the G&M.'

Kreiger, Heike (ed.) *East Timor and the International Community: Basic Documents.* Cambridge International Series, Vol. 10. Cambridge: Cambridge University Press.

Lee, M. and N. Solomon (1990) *Unreliable Sources: A Guide to Detecting Bias in the News Media.* New York: Carol.

MacEachen, Allan (Secretary of State, External Affairs Canada) (1976) 'Canada and Indonesia – The Dialogue Has Begun Well.' Speech by Allan MacEachen to Jakarta Press Club, Jakarta, 25 Aug 1976.

MacEachen, Allan (Secretary of State, External Affairs Canada) (1976) 'Canada and Australia Expand Their Untroubled Relationship.' Remarks by Allan MacEachen to Australian National Press Club, Canberra, 3 Sept 1976.

Maitland, D. (1992) 'Remember them' [Letter to the Editor] *Kitchener-Waterloo Record*, Nov 6.

Masse, B. (1992) 'Why won't Canada follow its own human rights rules?' *Peace Magazine* (May/June):12-13.

McChesney, Robert (1997) *Corporate Media and the Threat to Democracy*. New York: Open Media Pamphlet Series, Seven Stories Press.

McLeod, B. (1991) 'Cut off arms to Indonesia.' *Toronto Star*, Dec 13.

McMurtry, John (1990) 'Why does Canada aid the oppressors.' *Globe and Mail*, Feb 20, A7.

McMurtry, John (1992) 'Stop aid to Indonesia.' [Letter to the editor] *Globe and Mail*, Apr 15.

McMurtry, John (1994) 'Money is king: Unfortunately, the idea that this is a democratic society is pure hogwash.' *Kitchener-Waterloo Record*, Dec 10.

McMurtry, John (1998) *Unequal Freedoms: the Global Market as an Ethical System*. Toronto: Garamond Press.

Moody, R. (1992) *The Gulliver File, Mines, People and Land: A Global Background*. London: Minewatch.

Nairn, Allan (1992) *Testimony of Allan Nairn before the US Senate Committee on Foreign Relations on Crisis in East Timor and US Policy Towards Indonesia, Feb 17, 1992*.

Nelson, J. (1989) *Sultans of Sleeze: Public Relations and the Mass Media*. Toronto: Between the Lines.

Rai, Milan (1995) *Chomsky's Politics*. New York: Verso.

Regehr, Ernie (1988) 'Military Sales,' pp. 209-220 in Robert O. Matthews and Cranford Pratts (eds) *Human Rights and Canadian Foreign Policy*. Kingston and Montreal: McGill-Queen's Press.

Republic of Indonesia (Foreign Affairs) (1992) *East Timor: Building for the Future*.

Said, Edward (1981) *Covering Islam: How the Media and the Experts Determine How We See the Rest of the World*. New York: Pantheon.

Said, Edward (1994) *The Pen and the Sword, conversations with David Barsamian*. Toronto: Between the Lines.

Saunders, Doug (2002) 'Manufacturing Media Bias' in *Canadian Communications: Issues in Contemporary Media and Culture*. Second Edition. Toronto: Prentice Hall.

Scharfe, Sharon (1994) 'Blood on their hands: Human Rights in Canadian foreign policy' [A Case Study of the Canada-Indonesia Relationship (with specific emphasis on East Timor]. Unpublished MA thesis, Faculty of Law, Carleton University, Ottawa.

Scharfe, Sharon (1996) *Complicity: Human Rights in Canadian Foreign Policy—The Case of East Timor*. Montreal: Black Rose.

Schlesinger, Philip (1992) 'From production to propaganda' in *Media, Culture and Society: A Reader*. London: Sage.

Selby, D. (1987) 'Indonesian expansionism: the case of East Timor.' Chapter Six in *Human Rights*. Cambridge: Cambridge University Press.

Sherwood, S.J., P. Smith, and J.C. Alexander (1993) 'The British Are Coming...Again!' The Hidden Agenda of "Cultural Studies." ' *Contemporary Sociology* 22, 3 (May), pp. 370-375.

Smythe, D. (1978) 'The Political Character of Science (Including Communication Science), Or Science is not Ecumenical,' pp. 171-176 in Armand Mattelart and Seth Siegelaub (eds) *Communication and Class Struggle*. New York: International General.

Sissons, Miranda E. (1997) *From One Day to Another: Violations of Women's Reproductive and Sexual Rights in East Timor*. Fitzroy, Victoria: East Timor Human Rights Centre.

Solomon, Norman and Peter Cohen (1997) *Wizards of Oz: Behind the Curtain of Mainstream News*. Common Courage Press.

Sorenson, John (1990) 'Canadian Role in Indonesia Opportunistic.' *Winnipeg Free Press*. Dec 12.

Stackhouse, John (1996) 'PM Defends Cautious Stand on Indonesian Abuses.' *Globe and Mail*. Jan 18, A16.

Stone, G. (1975) 'A strange war of inside shelling and outside lies.' *Globe and Mail*, 13 Sept.

Swift, J. (1977) *The Big Nickel: INCO at Home and Abroad*. Toronto: Between the Lines.

Taylor, John (1990) *The Indonesian Occupation of East Timor, 1974-1979: A Chronology*. London: Catholic Institute for International Relations.

Taylor, John (1991) *Indonesia's Forgotten War—The Hidden History of East Timor*. London: Zed.

Tuchman, Gaye (1978) *Making News: A Study in the Construction of Reality*. New York: Free Press.

United States Department of State (*c.* 1948) 'Bureau of Foreign Affairs: Military Assistance on Reimbursable Basis: Map Country Indonesia.' Southeast Asia Series, University Publications of America.

Van Dijk, Teun (1983) 'Discourse Analysis: Its Development and Application to the Structure of News.' *Journal of Communication* (2): 11-32.

Van Dijk, Teun (1988) *News Analysis: Case Studies of International News in the Press*. New Jersey: Lawrence Erlbaum.

Van Dijk, Teun (1998) *Ideology: a multi disciplinary approach*. London: Sage.

Webster, David (1992) 'Canada chooses profits over rights,' *Toronto Star*, Nov 12, A25.

Winter, James (1992) *Common Cents: Media Portrayal of the Gulf War and Other Events*. Montreal: Black Rose.

Winter, James (1998) *Democracy's Oxygen: How the Corporations Control the News*. Second edition. Montreal: Black Rose.

Winter, James (2000) 'Media Think: The Role of the Media in Supporting the Establishment' in Bohdan Szuchewycz and Jeannette Sloniowski (eds) *Canadian Communications: Issues in Contemporary Media and Culture*. Toronto: Prentice Hall.

Winter, James (2002) *MediaThink*. Montreal: Black Rose.

Wintonick, Peter and Mark Achbar (1994) *Manufacturing Consent: Noam Chomsky and the Media*. Montreal: Black Rose.

Zachary, A. (1987) 'As the trade winds blow, Canada looks on benignly at Indonesia's genocidal occupation of East Timor.' *This Magazine* (March/Apr): 23-27.

Chapter Seven
The Propaganda Model Under Protest
James Winter and Jeffery Klaehn

THIS RESEARCH WAS INSPIRED BY A CENTRAL debate within sociology and critical theories of media and communication: do the ideological institutions centralize hegemony to effectively endorse, legitimize and facilitate the political and corporate agenda(s) of dominant elites? Instrumentalist theories hypothesize that the major mass media and other ideological institutions in society are predominantly agencies for the dissemination of ideas, values, perspectives and 'necessary illusions' that affirm existing patterns of power and privilege. Herman and Chomsky, leading proponents of the instrumental view of media, hypothesize that media performance is an outcome of market forces. Their 'propaganda model' of media operations (PM) is concerned with assessing ways in which media can be seen to mobilize support for corporate and state monied interests. One central argument of the PM is that media shape public opinion (in part) by controlling how various actions, events, actors and viewpoints are (re)presented within news discourse. The bulk of our data analysis is concerned with exploring how news coverage of the protests in Windsor, Ontario, Canada, at the Organization of American States (OAS) meeting in the summer of 2000 was framed as an unfolding news story.

In exploring the ideological role and policy advocacy function of media, our chapter favors a qualitative methodological approach, one that strives to enable understanding of how meaning(s) are conveyed. The broader social, political and economic context(s), in addition to the exclusion of (dissenting) ideas, themes, viewpoints and 'voices' are highlighted. Favoring micro-level textual analysis, we provide an initial 'map' of the coverage, one that examines how interpretive frameworks are established in and through such practices as news-story selection, treatment and (absence of) adequate context. We recognize both explicit and implicit meanings, and feel this methodology is well suited for identifying how the relevant themes, actors and voices associated with the protest were (re)presented in the news discourse.

Brief Overview of the Broader (Geo)Political-Economic Context

Two world events in the spring of 2002 demonstrated the apparent futility of, first, acquiescing to, and, secondly, resisting, the World Bank and International Monetary Fund (IMF). We refer to the cases of Argentina and Venezuela. Naomi Klein, writing in the *Globe and Mail*, suggests that Argentina was 'the IMF's model student throughout the 1990s,' and that 'massive privatization' included the sell off of services ranging from phones to trains, such that virtually the only assets yet to be privatized 'are the country's ports and customs offices.'[1] Jon Hillson, writing in the *New York Transfer*, comments that 'like other Latin American debt slaves, [Argentina] has already been paid off the principle of its initial loans, but now groans under continental arrears of $750 billion, as interest payments mount. In some national budgets, debt service has reached 40 percent of state expenditures. Buenos Aires has defaulted on, and ceased such payments.'[2] Despite its 'model student' behavior, we would contend that Argentina was in shambles; concurrently, the IMF and neo-liberals can be seen to have demanded further 'structural readjustments' intended to benefit the interests of corporate capital as opposed to the people of Argentina themselves. The value system underlying such action is remarkably consistent with any number of cases that demonstrate the extent to which corporate hegemony endangers fundamental democratic rights and principles.

In the case of Argentina, a financial reporter for the *National Post* reached out to a spokesperson for the conservative Cato Institute for thoughts on possible remedies. Ian Vasquez told the *Post* that 'the Argentine crisis is as much a crisis for the IMF as it is for Argentina. It really has shown the failure of the bailout doctrine.' Few would argue with this assessment, but the reasons and rational offered by the reporter are instructive, particularly if considered through the lens of the PM. For example, consider the following: 'The problem with IMF bailouts, its critics suggest, is that instead of providing financial relief while countries sort out their difficulties, they create a "moral hazard." The countries know they will be bailed out, so they spend recklessly.'[3]

In translation, we would suggest that the term 'reckless spending,' in this context, refers to money spent on the people, rather than being vacuumed up by international investors. Variations on the theme of 'reckless spending' abound within the boundaries of debate established (and policed) by the corporate media, which in turn impacts both political discourse and (ideologized) spectrums of opinion. Consider a Reuters article, carried in the *National Post*, which refers to '[The

IMF], which since December has refused to throw any more money at Argentina in disgust at its inability to rein in runaway public spending...The IMF has called on Argentina's provinces, widely seen as a morass of corruption and excess, to halt decades of runaway spending. It also wants to see a bank rescue plan in place.'[4]

Another article indicated the Canadian government's position in the crisis. Under the headline 'Canada leans of Argentina,' the *National Post* article first states that Finance Minister Paul Martin 'calls for action,' then sets the stage by reporting that 'the Argentine government yesterday resisted demands by the IMF for more provincial budget cuts as a condition for a sorely needed aid package, fearful that new austerity measures would lead to another round of deadly rioting.' Eventually, the article turned to the action that Paul Martin prescribed: 'Mr. Martin met Argentina's Minister of Finance and urged him to look into the treatment of Scotiabank and make sure it is dealt with fairly. He told the *Financial Post* he talked with Jorge Remes Lenicov to press his case that the Canadian bank should not be penalized for the country's economic problems. "We made our point very strongly that you cannot discriminate against foreign banks," Mr. Martin said in an interview after meeting Mr. Lenicov during the spring sessions here of the World Bank and International Monetary Fund.'[5]

An admittedly 'austere' budget from President Eduardo Duhalde in March 2002 which cut spending by about 15 percent was deemed inadequate by the IMF, which indicated that 'substantial measures' were still needed.[6] A column in the *National Post*, published approximately one month later, carried a headline and subhead which we feel nicely sums it all up: 'Reform comes first; an IMF bailout won't resuscitate Argentina's economy. Along with cutting government spending, the debt-strapped country needs to severely curtail the influences of provincial governments and unions.'[7]

William Blum on the CIA-Sponsored Coup in Venezuela in April 2002

As for Venezuela, writing in *Counterpunch*, William Blum summed up the actions of President Hugo Chavez, which led to the CIA-sponsored coup in April, 2002. Blum writes:

Consider Chavez's crimes:

- Branding the U.S. attacks on Afghanistan as 'fighting terrorism,' he demanded an end to 'the slaughter of innocents,' holding up photographs of children killed in the American bombing attacks, he said their deaths had 'no justification, just as the attacks on New York did not, either.' In response, the Bush administration temporarily withdrew its ambassador

- Being friendly with Fidel Castro and selling oil to Cuba at discounted rates

- His defense minister asking the permanent U.S. military mission in Venezuela to vacate its offices in the military headquarters in Caracas, saying its presence was an anachronism for the Cold War

- Not cooperating to Washington's satisfaction with the U.S. war against the Colombian guerrillas

- Denying Venezuelan airspace to U.S. counter-drug flights

- Refusing to provide U.S. intelligence agencies with information on Venezuela's large Arab community

- Questioning the sanctity of globalization

- Promoting a regional free-trade bloc and united Latin American petroleum operations as a way to break from the U.S. economic dominance

- Visiting Saddam Hussein in Iraq and Muhammar Ghaddafy in Libya

Blum concludes, 'The United States has endeavored to topple numerous governments for a whole lot less.'[8]

Argentina, by now an old story, has largely dropped from the corporate media agenda, while the story of the people's uprising against the IMF and World Bank goes virtually ignored, except in the alternative media. We contend that, through its policies, the IMF continues to attempt to punish the people of Argentina in an attempt to compel them to bend to its will. As for Venezuela, a popular uprising thwarted the coup and restored President Hugo Chavez to power, representing a serious setback for the distracted American administration of George W. Bush. Events such as these, involving the IMF and World Bank, we argue, are typically (grossly) distorted by the corporate media, in keeping with the neo–liberal policies of advanced capitalism which they represent and promote. As John McMurty states, the 'freedom of international speculators and investors to dictate to governments everywhere how they are to govern' can be seen to be indicative of globalization of the world economy and extends far beyond any one case study.[9] Increasingly, big business dictates government policy and this has given way to harmful consequences, such that there seems to be no limit to examples of the destructive aspects of the myriad policies which can be seen to have evolved from the profit requirements of capitalist production.[10] As Hale points out, 'Most colonized countries have now gained political independence, but this has not brought about effective economic independence. Their economies are still dominated by forces of the world capitalist economic system over which they have little control.'[11] Mechanisms of control which facilitate corporate rule over domestic social and ecological policies 'include control over capital, control over patterns of investment, domination of market relations, decisive bargaining power in the labor market, and political clout, including the use of force as a last resort.'[12]

The OAS Protest in Windsor in June 2000:
'Protest was a cry for democracy'

The protestors at the Organization of American States (OAS) meeting in Windsor succeeded in drawing public attention to the glaring problems associated with globalization. Is their cynicism warranted?

The real crux of their argument is that the whole notion of free trade is something of a fabrication.

There is an increasing degree of autonomy and freedom granted to capital-holders and transnational corporations by democratic governments to do as they like, how they like, when they like, regardless of the moral or emotional dimensions, cultural or ecological costs.

This was the wake-up call delivered by the protestors in Windsor.

At great public expense, various factions of the state policing apparatus, dressed in storm trooper riot gear, were called upon to meet the mostly young and overwhelmingly peaceful protestors with violent force. Invariably, the scenario played out much the same way as it had at earlier protests in Seattle and Washington. Each instance is an example of opposition to democracy. Resistance to corporate domination was met with physical force and toxic chemical defoliants.

The democratic deficit is glaring and the message from self-declared 'masters of mankind' (Adam Smith's phrase) painfully clear. The public should not have the right to democratically decide under what conditions they wish to live their lives. Moreover, anyone inclined to take up the fight against the agencies of global domination should do so from behind barricades and mesh wire fences that have been erected for the singular purpose of keeping the public out.

What does this say about democracy when democratic society is itself defined as a social order organized through the free, continuous and shared discourse of its members?

'To an alarming extent, we have become convinced that we are collectively powerless in the face of international financial markets. And, with the widespread acceptance of this view, the rich have proceeded to create a world in which the rights of capital have been given precedence over protection against interference from the electorate. In spite of democracy, they have largely succeeded in creating a knave-proof world,' wrote Linda McQuaig in *Cult of Impotence*.

Playing the role of the social critic by refusing to pay homage to the powers that be, the coalition of protestors succeeded in reminding us that current economic and political thinking about globalization offers us an illusion of progress while covering up the fact that profit-driven, neo-liberal economic policies have demonstrated a remarkable propensity to be morally, socially and ecologically irresponsible.

'The known degradation of the planet's air, waters and soil by market processes and products; the usurpation of the world's climates by emissions of its "cost-efficient" production; the destitution of rising numbers of children under its distributive rule; the daily extinction of long-evolved species by its resource extraction methods; the loss of life functions for ever more people by its unregulated laws of supply and demand: these results are each and all undeniable.' This quote, by John McMurtry, a philosophy professor at the University of Guelph, appeared in *Unequal Freedoms: The Global Market as an Ethical System*.

The Windsor protest was important because it was precisely this idea of a common good that the activists wished to see incorporated into public political debate in Canada. If we look beneath the veneer of mainstream economic rationality, it becomes clear many leading politicians have abdicated their responsibility to defend the public interest. Instead of acting in the interests of the common good, democratic governments have demonstrated an allegiance to financial elites by granting wealthy market agents free play to pursue their egoistic interests unimpeded by public interference.

It is governance for the rich, by the rich, the Windsor protestors charged, with decisions taking place at the executive level, within undemocratic organs of corporate capitalism, like the OAS, World Trade Organization and International Monetary Fund.

There is nothing particularly new here. Social classes have grossly unequal power. Democratic governments have repeatedly demonstrated that they are responsive to power.

Increasingly, public servants claim impotence to actively pursue the common good. At the same time, they have repeatedly demonstrated the ability to take quick and decisive action to safe-guard the interests of extremely wealthy market agents.

In short, markets rule. As the Windsor protesters reminded us, one result of this trend is that transnationals have come to have more influence over people's lives than national leaders. In the view of billionaire financier George Soros, global capitalism has replaced communism as the principle threat to democratic societies worldwide.

Look no further than the North American Free Trade Agreement for evidence that neo-liberal free trade arrangements have compromised the ability of democratic governments to regulate domestic affairs.

'The big transnationals want to reduce freedom by undermining the democratic functioning in the states in which they're based, while at the same time ensuring the government will be powerful enough to protect and support them,' wrote Noam Chomsky in *The Common Good*.

Transnationals increasingly wield direct power over the quality of people's lives. They determine what jobs will be available, where these jobs will be located, how much they will pay, who will staff them.

They orchestrate patterns of investment, dominate market economies, influence bargaining power of the labor market and possess significant political clout. Transnationals also determine which dependent economies and ecosystems will be exploited.

Their ultimate goal is embedded in the principle of redistributing wealth and power to those who are already the most wealthy and already the most powerful. Free trade is about providing legal means for transnationals to pursue these ends without limitations or regulatory obstacles. Globalization has entailed a shifting of power, away from the electorate, to financial elites.

However, as Murray Dobbin noted in *The Myth of the Good Corporate Citizen*, 'There are nation-states who have rejected free trade, rejected structural adjustment, rejected corporate rule and the impoverished ideology that drives it. Sweden and Norway, after some backward steps, are still egalitarian states and they put the lie to the propaganda that globalization is inevitable and that resistance is futile. Norwegian and Swedish citizens just said no: they made a democratic choice to maintain civilized lives. Their governments remained loyal to the principles of democracy.'

Isn't it high time Canada did the same?

Occasionally, when the public make their voices heard, as they did in the Windsor protest, 'public servants' feel obliged to listen.

That's democracy. It's a precious concept.

By Jeffery Klaehn
Reprinted from the *Kitchener-Waterloo Record*, June 21, 2000, A13

Biased media coverage of the demonstrations at the 1999 World Trade Organization (WTO) meetings in Seattle, Washington has been the focus of some analysis and research. For example, just after tens of thousands of protestors rallied in Seattle to virtually close down the opening conference of the WTO meeting in November 1999, *New York Time's* correspondent Thomas Friedman wrote that 'knaves like Pat Buchanan' had 'duped' the demonstrators—'a Noah's ark of flat-earth advocates, protectionist trade union yuppies looking for their 1960s fix'—into protesting the WTO.[13] Corporate media coverage of these demonstrations was so ideologically inflected that Seattle organizers set up an Independent Media Centre (see: www.indymedia.org) to get an alternative message out. To illustrate the nature of the coverage in detail, in the Canadian context, we will use a case study of press coverage of the OAS meetings and protests in Windsor, Ontario, Canada, from the summer of 2000. First, however, we will provide some historical context.

The IMF and the World Bank: Background Detail and Relevant Historical Context

The IMF and World Bank were established in 1944 at a conference held in Bretton Woods, a ski resort in New Hampshire. The IMF was to further global trade, stabilize currencies and global financial disruptions. According to Michael Albert, 'The World Bank was intended to facilitate long-term investment in underdeveloped countries, to expand and strengthen economies.'[14] In recent decades, according to

Joseph Stiglitz, the 2001 Nobel economist and former chief economist of the World Bank, it has developed a 'country assistance strategy' for each emerging market nation. This strategy consists of a 'structural adjustment agreement' drafted by the World Bank after analyzing each nation's economy. Then the World Bank hands each country's finance minister the same four step program.[15] Step one is privatization, and entails public enterprises being sold off to the private sector. Step two is capital market liberalization, which allows capital to flee, thus allowing for the possibility of a nation's reserves being drained very quickly. Step three is fiscal austerity and market-based pricing, which amounts to raising prices on food, water and other necessities of basic life. Tax collection is increased, while government spending is dramatically reduced. An example is when the IMF eliminated food and fuel subsidies for the poor in Indonesia in 1998, over the objections of brutal dictator General Suharto. The result was riots. The same sort of predictable 'social unrest' (as the corporate media labeled it) has occurred in Argentina, and, in fact, Stiglitz has termed this 'the IMF riot.' Step four is free trade, which is implemented through arrangements such as NAFTA and the FTAA. These restructuring agreements represent an 'evolution' in the means of control of 'emerging market economies' from the (sometimes messy) coups and imposition of dictatorships via the CIA, detailed by William Blum and others, to the more distant persuasion of economic forces. With Nicaragua, for example, although this took the form of a proxy war, it was followed by an economic blockade and finally the mass infusion of cash to support electoral alternatives (Violetta Chamorro) to the Sandinistas. Economic measures and armaments work hand in hand. At times it has been necessary to resort to outright invasion of countries to turf recalcitrant dictators who will no longer cooperate, such as happened in 1989 with General Manual Noriega of Panama, but usually the despots have retired quietly and without too much fanfare, as did Suharto in Indonesia. In most cases, it is unnecessary to resort to military action, although Kosovo, Afghanistan and Iraq (again) are recent exceptions. This method has human, social and environmental costs which cannot be calculated, but has its own instrumental 'advantages' such as stimulating the U.S. economy, stabilizing U.S. oil prices and ensuring access to oil, buttressing the Pentagon and munitions manufacturers, diverting the attention of the public away from domestic social and economic matters, and softening finance ministers around the globe to the gentler persuasions of 'restructuring.'

Imperialism and military interventions are certainly not new. Indeed, they date back a millennia. But there are several new developments which are note-

worthy, such as restructuring agreements. Another is the WTO which was created in 1995 through the provision of the Uruguay Round of the General
Agreement on Tariffs and Trade (GATT). Prior to this, GATT focussed on promoting world trade by pressuring countries to reduce tariffs. As Michael Albert and
others explain, the corporate-inspired global agenda was significantly increased
by targeting so-called 'non-tariff barriers to trade'—essentially any national pro-
tective legislation which might be construed as impacting trade.[16] '[I]nstead of
only imposing on third world countries low wages and high pollution due to their
weak or bought-off governments, why not weaken all governments and agencies
that might defend workers, customers, or the environment, not only in the third
world, but everywhere?'[17]

We contend that one definitive purpose of globalization is to eliminate the 'interference' of domestic populations from the corporate agenda and, on occasion,
also non-client governments, whose attempts to take matters into their own hands
are typically regarded as a 'crisis of democracy' (Noam Chomsky's phrase). Stiglitz
discusses a number of third world examples, including Indonesia in 1998 under
Suharto. 'The IMF is not particularly interested in hearing the thoughts of its "client
countries" on topics such as development strategy or fiscal austerity. All too often,
the Fund's approach to developing countries has had the feel of a colonial
ruler...[Suharto] was being forced, in effect, to turn over economic sovereignty of
his country to the IMF in return for the aid his country needed. In the end, ironically, much of the money went not to help Indonesia but to bail out the "colonial
power's" private sector creditors.'[18] Consider how such forces play out in Canada;
in order to illuminate, we will provide details which overview one brief example. In
1997 Parliament passed a law restricting the import and interprovincial transport
of MMT, a neuro-toxic gasoline additive, which was harmful to people's health and
the environment. Within days, the U.S. multinational Ethyl Corporation, the sole
supplier of MMT in Canada, invoked the 'expropriation' clause of the investment
chapter of NAFTA to sue the government for $350M for damages and lost income.
With the NAFTA agreement working precisely as it had been designed, the pressure
of significant political public liability mounted on the federal government. On July
20, 1998, they acquiesced, settling out of court before the NAFTA arbitration panel
could rule. According to Kenneth Traynor, a researcher with the Canadian Environmental Law Association, 'In the final cruel irony, the $20 million compensation
payment to Ethyl (one of this country's true environmental villains) for lost profits
and legal costs, exceeds the total 1998 Environmental Canada budget for Enforce-
ment and Compliance programs of $16.9 million.'[19]

In every case brought before the WTO thus far, commercial interests have won, whether it was commercial shrimp fishing versus giant sea turtles, air quality versus oil interests, or U.S. cattle producers versus the European Union's ban on hormone-treated beef. Corporate hegemony endangers fundamental democratic rights and principles, is accommodated by the established order and existing structures of ideological rule, and incurs hidden diseconomies which have entailed and continue to entail enormous costs, impacting a multiplicity of human, social, cultural and environmental concerns. Such hidden diseconomies, for all intents and purposes, are incalculable, and the need for further research in this area is glaring, but an abundance of empirical research already exists. As Tom Bottomore states, 'The world economy is dominated by 500 of the largest multinational corporations, by the nation states in which they have their headquarters, and by those institutions of world capitalism such as the World Bank and the International Monetary Fund which determine and regulate economic development on a global scale. These economic forces, which have concentrated the wealth of the planet to an unprecedented degree, have also impoverished a large part of the Third World of "developing countries" and caused massive damage to the natural environment.'[20]

Corporate Hegemony and the Marginalization of Dissent

From casual observation, little or nothing of the information above may be learned from the country's mainstream media, working in their vested interests and in their role as agents of public indoctrination and corporate legitimation generally. This is evident from even casual perusal of mainstream media content, but it has also been documented systematically by a range of progressive academics, including Herman and Chomsky, Robert McChesney, Norman Solomon, Robert Jensen, Ben Bagdikian, Russell Mokhiber and Robert Weissman, andeconomists such as Brian MacLean, William Krehm, and so forth. On a popular level, economic journalist Linda McQuaig has been writing about these developments for more than a decade, most recently in *All You Can Eat: Greed, Lust, and the New Capitalism*. Of course, in keeping with the predictions of the PM, these 'alternative perspectives' on reality are virtually absent from the mainstream.

According to Murray Dobbin, more than 70 Canadian municipalities have demanded exemption from the General Agreement on Trade in Services (GATS) being negotiated by the WTO. 'The European Commission (which represents the

European Union at the WTO) is asking Canada to completely open all "water collection, purification and distribution services through mains" to foreign competition. European water corporations dominate the global market for water treatment and distribution systems.'[21] Dobbin indicates that restrictions on the foreign ownership of farmland in the four Western provinces are threatened, as are government monopolies such as public auto insurance in British Columbia, Manitoba and Saskatchewan, and public liquor distribution such as it exists in Ontario.[22] Additionally, Canada Post and its subsidiaries such as Purolator, and even public health care and public education may very well be threatened.

At least since APEC in Vancouver in 1997, the WTO in Seattle in 1999, the IMF and the World Bank protests in Washington, D.C. in April 2000, various organizations, labor groups, and individuals have brought the 'social unrest' of the so-called 'emerging markets' into what we thought were the already developed market economies of Canada, Italy, the U.S., Switzerland, and so forth. If these are indeed, as Susan George has written, part of an 'international citizens' movement which has disturbed the gatherings of the masters of the universe,' then it begs the question: how are they reported by the mainstream press?[23]

The 30th General Assembly of the Organization of American States was held in Windsor from June 4-6, 2000. It was the tenth anniversary of former Canadian Prime Minister Brian Mulroney's initiative making Canada a member. It was also the first time the OAS met in Canada, although they met again in Quebec City in 2001, with predictable results. The Windsor convention attracted about 3000 protestors, and about 2200 police, with another 4000 police on the U.S. border side of Detroit. The police arrested 78 people during the OAS Summit, mostly for breach of the peace, though only 15 resulted in charges, and all of these charges were eventually dismissed.

Data Analysis: Assessing the News Coverage

The *Windsor Star* carried a total of about 150 stories and letters about the three-day event. The newspaper's coverage began at the end of May, with accounts of how downtown businesses were preparing for the convention business, while preparing themselves from the expected onslaught of protestors. A study of all the material concerning the OAS in the *Windsor Star* indicated that almost all of the critical, contextual and informative material was contained in the 'letters to the editor' section, restricted to about 100 words or less. News stories, editorials and columns focused almost exclusively on the violence and related topics, with few exceptions.

Topics Covered in the Windsor Star Coverage of the OAS Meeting

- Business preparations, planned closings, boarding of windows
- Neighboring police in nearby Chatham offer backup
- Food preparations for dignitaries, meals to be offered
- Hospitals on alert, 'Code Orange Advisory' at Windsor Regional Hospital
- Emergency plan for city says unruly protestors to be dunked in pools
- One hospital set aside for protestors, another for dignitaries and delegates
- Borders brace for traffic snarl
- Detroit outlaws ammonia, chlorine, slingshots downtown
- Arrested protestors may go to nearby Leamington jail
- CIBC bank boarding up windows
- *Windsor Star* downtown office to close
- Contingency plans for downtown businesses: how to get broken windows fixed
- OAS pavilion showcases children and human rights
- Police undergo teargas training
- Police to use snow plows to remove barricades
- Madeleine Albright to miss Summit, on trip with Bill Clinton
- Barriers to transform Windsor: all protestors fault
- Mayor says barricades necessary for protection
- Number of protestors unknown; estimates range from 3 to 10,000
- Organized labor to bus in people in protest
- Plywood barricades set up downtown
- Shutdown coalition holds teach-in at university
- Several hundred RCMP and OPP officers in student residences
- Mayor urges calm (before storm)
- First protestors arrested in park; tourists ignored

- Radical protestors from Washington plan Detroit protest
- More than 500 police in Windsor and Detroit brace for protests
- Wording on protest signs
- Poverty the enemy, says Canadian Prime Minister Jean Chretien; free trade means prosperity
- Puppeteer protestor arrested
- Film-makers use protest to film backdrop for action scenes
- Bus driver kept delegates on board; feared for safety with protestors
- Warehouse used temporarily for jail
- Business is down, cops all over downtown
- Police say should have required parade permits
- Labor considers formal protest over police use of pepper spray
- OAS brought $10M to city

There were five stories of about 121 in total which mention the word 'capitalism.' Four stories mentioned the World Bank, and two mentioned the IMF. Six stories mentioned the WTO. Two stories mentioned 'privatization.' No stories or letters to the editor mentioned the terms: structural readjustment, market liberalization, hot money, money supply, social unrest, prices, fiscal austerity, MMT, harmonization, 'the race to the bottom,' social programs, economic interests, cultural policies, labor laws, giant sea turtles, or homone-injected beef. Five stories mentioned oil, but two of these were about mineral oil used to treat pepper sprayed protestors, while one story mentioned vegetable oil, one was in reference to 'foil' and the other to 'turmoil.'

The references to 'capitalism' and many of the other key terms were vague, disjointed and de-contextualized. For example, in a report on the diverse objectives of participants at the summit, the *Star* stated that 'First of all, of course, protestors hate even the idea of the OAS meeting unless it is to denounce global capitalism.' No further explanation is provided with regard to motivations or what global capitalism actually entails in this context.[24] The same report contained the following more lengthy explanation and defense of free trade: 'Richard Bernal, delegate, Ambassador and Permanent Representative for Jamaica to the OAS: "One of the issues that has come up here and is of concern to us is the operation of the trade unit. The trade

unit is very important in terms of doing research for policy and in providing technical assistance to countries in the free trade zone of the Americas. We're very interested in free trade because as a small economy, we're a very open economy. We see
the establishment of a hemisphere-wide free-trade area as something we can benefit from.'' Another story simply listed some of the wording of protestors' placards
as follows: 'Hemispheric security? Not with Uncle Death in charge'; 'Oppose U.S.
militarism of the Americas'; 'Human rights now in all the Americas'; 'Asylum for
workers, no discrimination'; 'What world do you protect?'; 'Who's streets? Our
streets'; 'Free trade—free for whom?'; 'WTO and OAS—the lies and the mess'; 'OAS
= terror'; 'Funny, I don't recall voting for a one-world government.' These cryptic
descriptions substituted for serious analysis and background information which
would have lent credence to the protestors and would have worked to create an impression of them as something other than radicals and/or threats to public security
(and/or the common good).

One of the few attempts to understand the protestors and their causes, published ten days after the summit concluded, contained an interview with a young
protestor who said he frequently pulled out his guitar to relax.

> "It's a good way to take the seriousness out of it all," he says. "When
> you're constantly indoctrinating yourself and other people about the
> dark sides of the world and how everything is just kind of going to hell
> for everyone who's not a first world consumer, it can get really depress-
> ing. So it's cool just to play music sometimes."[25]

Quotations such as this reinforced the picture of the protestors as radicals, indoctrinated hippies, depressed and, for that matter, depressing.

Another story began, 'After a long day of protesting against corporate capitalism, the average protestor isn't likely to shell out for a restaurant meal. That's
why Food Not Bombs is on the scene in Windsor.'[26] This is open to a multiplicity
of available readings, but at the same time, the dominant meaning encoded
within the lead implies that the 'average protestor' is impoverished. Concurrently, one could read it as implying that Social Darwinism is very much alive and
well in terms of both in real-world practice (the agencies of global capitalism and
the policies they advance) and the spectrums of thought and opinion advanced by
the ideological network (the characterization of these policies, and of the moral-
ity/intelligence/social class of those who would dissent). We recently had the opportunity to interview one of the protestors who was there (on the scene) in
Windsor, and s/he had this to say with respect to the ways in which such
(slanted) discourse (as delineated above) tends to characterize protestors:

I find it incredibly offensive. I've an MA in Business Administration, am quite gainfully employed in Toronto, and, for that matter, my yearly salary is in excess of the mean annual income within Canada; whatever that's worth. I went to Windsor because I'm concerned…about economics, debt slavery, pollution, working conditions…women's rights…it's wrong to have such dialogue taking place behind closed doors…I personally try to stay as informed as possible…I've problems with these things and felt like joining in to express my views…this makes me what…*deviant?*…that's generalizing, and stereotyping…it's putting things in the simplest possible terms…

Another *Windsor Star* story we assessed illustrates how these 'terms' can be highly critical but de-contextualized. The story quotes one of the protestors:

"Our goal was to expose the OAS as part of the jigsaw puzzle of global corporate capitalism and we did that…stop focussing on the miniscule," said Tim Scott, an American union activist arrested Sunday for breaching the peace. "They focus on miniscule acts of property damage. They're not focusing on the lives being destroyed and the tremendous suffering that's happening because of the IMF, WTO, OAS and FTAA."[27]

The terms are not explained—how many newspaper readers would actually know what the acronyms stand for, we would ask—background details are not provided, and the words of the protestor are simply left hanging there—radical, bald, forsaken, sounding like the slick, pat phrases of the brainwashed. This is especially so when such a quote is combined with photographs and depictions of violent confrontations in which the photo cut-lines indicate that it was 'protestors confronting police' and not the other way around. Another problem, of course, is that there are few official spokespersons for the broad anti-corporate globalization movement, so media tend to pick someone out of the crowd, interviewing individual protesters with varying degrees of comprehension and ability to articulate. Media also used the occasion to limit the scope of the movement and to openly question its potential—purportedly using the protesters' own voices:

The question on the minds of coalition members is how far their campaign will go. They call it a "global movement" and have convinced some politicians and authors to take notice. Naomi Klein, a Toronto author and columnist, has just published a book about the movement. Worldwide, however, the movement peaks and wanes, with the anti-sweatshop faction being the most influential in initiating policy change.[28]

No quotations are provided here for backup justification(s), to indicate just whose mind the journalist is exploring. Meanings are simply (and flatly) imposed, and successful battles against the MAI are conveniently ignored.

In an article two days after the protests, one reporter described how art was used as a protest medium, 'from effigies and wall hangings to street theatre and song.' He said that much of the art was crude, 'slapdash affairs, literally thrown together with duct tape and wall paint,' but that it all had 'the same intention: hammer home a message. Rather one-note perhaps, but this week's message was largely along the lines of "capitalism kills!"' For the journalist, in this case a relatively progressive but exceedingly frustrated former graduate student, this would represent a huge victory: getting these few words of dissent past his editors and into the paper.[29] And he did actually make an attempt to elaborate with an example:

> "The Mexican government formed paramilitary troops to force people off their land after free trade started," says Zapateatro actor Fernando Hernandez, who points out that the uprising in Chiapas started the day after NAFTA began. For indigenous people, there are no other sources of income. They live off the land. Or work in slave labor. The ones who benefit from free trade are the large corporations.[30]

While obviously a very limited picture of what is going on and what the protests are about, this account is nonetheless (obviously) critical, and one that is overwhelmed by the volume of coverage devoted to other events, perspectives and representations: police, violence and pepper spray. The Zapatista uprising also dates back to 1994.

An exception was a story run on June 2, in the lead up to the convention, as part of the "OAS COUNTDOWN" coverage, which was otherwise mostly composed of articles about police and downtown businesses. The story was about a speech given by CAW president Buzz Hargrove who was quoted about a WTO ruling just the day before which removed preferential tariffs for the Big Three auto manufacturers: the backbone of the Windsor economy. The story was written by the newspaper's labor reporter: a position which has since been eliminated.

> Hargrove said he finds it "frustrating as hell" that governments don't object more to decisions made by "faceless bureaucrats" in organizations like the OAS, WTO, World Bank and International Monetary Fund...For more than a decade, governments have instead been capitulating to a corporate-driven agenda for free trade, lower taxes, deregulation and

privatization, Hargrove said. But with incomes of working-class families remaining stagnant or declining at the same time "people are crying out for governments to step in and defend their interests," he said.

Of course, this information is pertinent not just because it is labor's perspective, which is usually ignored, but because the WTO ruling could affect business interests in Windsor.

Any critical references were more than offset by guest columnist material holding such positions and the protesters' views up to ridicule as 'collateral noise' and 'absurd caricatures,' and defending the OAS. 'These caricatures are so far off the mark as to be absurd. Worse, they indicate that the persons involved have not asked basic questions about the OAS and have, therefore, forfeited their credibility,' John W. Graham, board member of the Ottawa-based Canadian Foundation for the Americas wrote in a lengthy guest column.

Three more items in the *Windsor Star* should be singled out as exceptions. The first of these was in a column run once every two weeks, by a local, moderately progressive former bookstore owner and former city counselor, Sheila Wisdom. Her column about the OAS ran nine days after the meetings ended. In it, she began by denouncing the radical and violent protesters, and blaming them for creating the violence that obscured the issues. The implication is that if it hadn't been for the (apparent, impending) violence, the media would have been able to focus on the issues, as though it was a choice between the two. 'The radical element, by declaring a goal of shutdown,' she wrote, 'turned the Windsor meeting of the OAS into an issue of power. They aimed to be more powerful than the civil authorities. They aimed to shut down a major world institution.' Of course, they were merely aiming to shut down a meeting and not an institution. Thanks to the violent protesters, she continued, 'we are still left with questions about what in these relatively obscure international agencies—such as the World Trade Organization, the World Bank and the OAS—inspires such passion in both peaceful protesters and radicals.'

Ms. Wisdom quoted the former Premier of Manitoba and former University of Windsor political science professor, Howard Pawley, who 'says one reason for the passion is a recent change in mood in some of his students. Where students were apathetic and disinterested only a couple of years ago, he is now seeing a level of political concern that hasn't been seen in decades.' We are to take from this that student activism is the result of a kind of spontaneous combustion on the part of these young people. Pawley then identified alienation and a lack of control on the part of youth, and reintroduced the WTO decision regarding the Autopact.

To Pawley, the underlying anxiety for most groups centres on the growing influence of these organizations. He says that the protesters "don't feel they have a voice." Some international organizations are making rulings that will affect people but there is little or no recourse for those who disagree. An example of this is the recent decision of the World Trade Organization to strike down the remaining elements of the Auto Pact. Three powerful bodies in Canada—government, business and labour—had lobbied against this decision, only to lose. This reinforces the idea that power is being shifted from our elected officials to distant bureaucracies. And our old means of democratic influence don't seem to apply.

Here, Pawley and Wisdom have managed to identify a major concern: the shift in the locus of power and the ramifications for democracy, although these are not situated in the international context, and only the one example is given. Also, this is but one column in all of the articles provided concerning the OAS, and would not go a long way towards counteracting all of the other misinformation, or overcoming all of the negative portrayals of violence and anarchism.

The second story was carried on the second day of the OAS meetings, and reported on a rally by the Canadian Labour Congress the day before. The story was written by the then-labor reporter, Gary Rennie, and the focus was on how labor denounced the police, and said the only thing missing was the tanks which are present in Colombia, and other Third World confrontations. The story contained the following brief quotations from labor leaders and the NDP:

"We march for the millions of workers trapped in poverty." —Labour leader from Panama

"Let's get the OAS to start standing up for human rights ahead of profit-seeking corporations." —Alexa McDonough, NDP Leader

"What's happening in the Americas is happening to us too," said Darcy. She said the seven deaths from poisoned drinking water in Walkerton resulted from the policies of privatization and cuts to government programs now being urged for adoption in Latin American countries. —Judy Darcy, president of CUPE.

"Francisco Ramirez, a trade union lawyer in Colombia who spoke in Windsor a month ago, is now hiding from death squads in his own country." —Buzz Hargrove.

The final story actually quotes from Noam Chomsky, which, needless to say, is very unusual for the *Windsor Star*. The story quoted some criticisms of the OAS and some praise, concluding that it is "far from perfect," but still "relevent"(sic). Amid the people quoted we find Chomsky, as follows:

> "The OAS has had a conflicted history…it can't function as a community of equals because the countries are so overwhelmed by the U.S.," says Noam Chomsky, internationally known linguist and philosopher. "Like the UN, it can do only as much as the great powers allow it to do. However, the OAS is an important, if weak barrier against U.S. intervention."

This is the only quotation from Chomsky. It is followed in the story by this protracted opposing view from John Graham, an 'authorized knower' whose lengthy opinion piece was published the same day, along with others.

> The OAS is "far from perfect," agrees John Graham, board member of the Ottawa-based Canadian Foundation for the Americas (FOCAL). But, the Americas would be "much worse off" without it. "The OAS helps iron out the road from dictatorship to democracy and the blessing of the OAS gives legitimacy and credibility to a government when it makes that change," says Graham. Twenty years ago, at least 75 per cent of all Latin American governments were dictatorships or under military rule, he notes. Today, officially, there is only one dictatorship—in Cuba. But the precarious state of many other countries emphasizes the need for a collective watchdog such as the OAS, which helps prevent democracies from backsliding, says Graham. "Ecuador is a mess, Colombia is a total mess, Haiti is a towering shambles and in Venezuela in recent days there's been riots in the streets because the president is not tolerant of opposition," said Graham. "But, in spite of that, the OAS is very significant and needed." For Colombian native Marcella Diaz, the OAS is needed to lead those without power out of a life of oppression. As a university student, Diaz remembers being tear-gassed during protests and fearing being gunned down by drug lords on city streets. "The OAS is a lifeline for us," says Marcella Diaz, who moved to Windsor from Colombia in 1990. "Without the OAS, there would be no watchdog keeping an eye on what governments are doing and helping them maintain their fragile democracies." Graham, who acknowledged that the OAS needs to be improved, condemned any attempts to shut down the OAS. "The work of the OAS is not made easier by characters running around saying 'shut it down' and accusing it of evil stuff

which is not part of its mandate," said Graham. "Many of these people are gulled into thinking it is a nasty association of wicked global imperialists which is nonsense." Nobina Robinson, executive director of FOCAL, is vehement in her distaste for such action. "Rage for rages sake does nothing to help their brethren in the hemisphere, they need to educate themselves, focus on priorities and mobilize resources," said Robinson.

Hence, the brief and rather harmless quote from Chomsky is used as a form of inoculation, a tiny amount of viral matter which is injected into the mainstream corpus, in order to do battle with their vastly superior and healthy antibodies. Predictably, Chomsky's views as a leading dissident are used in *support* of the OAS and *against* the protesters, as his selected words defend the OAS as "an important, if weak barrier against U.S. intervention," and by implication, criticize those who oppose the OAS.

Conclusions

Overall, for the *Windsor Star*, organizations such as the OAS are democratic in nature; they represent solutions rather than problems. In its role as a major means of social control, the *Star*, like other corporate media, and our professor of political science quoted above, all see a 'crisis of democracy' in the violent, misguided and indoctrinated embodiment of the protesters, who must be eradicated, so that normalcy: peace, order and 'good government' may return.

The repetitive patterns in these representations, from coverage of labor day, to strikes and the labor movement generally, to broader social movements such as the Days of Action protesting Harris and Chretien's policies in Ontario from 1997 to 1999, to these anti-corporate globalization protests, and for that matter the coverage of the economic picture and class divisions generally, as well as marginalized groups such as feminists, gays and lesbians, visible minorities, all reflect white corporate, capitalist, patriarchal interests: Michael Moore's *Stupid White Men*.

Herman and Chomsky note, 'modes of handling favored and inconvenient materials (placement, tone, context, fullness of treatment) [will] differ in ways that serve political ends.'[31] The PM predicts that in certain cases media will exemplify tendencies toward ideological closure and will be aligned with elite interests. As highlighted elsewhere in this volume, however, it *also* predicts a range of debate within media discourse, which in fact facilitates the effectiveness of social control vis-à-vis the illusion of a genuinely level playing field. The quantity and quality of the news coverage assessed here conform with the predictions of the PM.

An intensive analysis of all *Windsor Star* coverage of the OAS meetings demonstrated a lack of important contextual information: for example, about the bodies such as the IMF, World Bank, and OAS, which the protests concern. In the absence of this information, the protesters appeared to be irrational, and radical, and their causes could be summarily dismissed by reporters, readers, and right-thinking individuals. What coverage existed was predominantly sensationalized, focusing on impending violence, which never occurred. This served to further radicalize the protests, and to justify the neo-liberal agenda surrounding free trade agreements, the WTO, etc. As Herman notes, in responding to critics of the PM,

> There is now an almost religious faith in the market, at least among the elite, so that regardless of evidence, markets are assumed benevolent and non-market mechanisms are suspect…the transnational media corporations have a distinct self-interest in global trade agreements, as they are among their foremost beneficiaries.[32]

The almost exclusive use of right-wing authorized knowers as sources provided the bias of official discourse, and is of course in keeping with the third filter of the PM. Where protesters were quoted, it was a means of discrediting them. Finally, even Noam Chomsky was used as a means of discrediting the protesters and their causes.

NOTES

1. Naomi Klein, 'IMF: Go to hell,' *Globe and Mail*, March 19, 2002.
2. Jon Hillson, 'Reporter's notebook from Argentina,' New York Transfer, April 24, 2002. Available online at Argentina Watch (www.zmag.com).
3. Jacqueline Thorpe, 'Financial crisis called a watershed for IMF policy: massive bailouts may end,' *Financial Post*, April 29, 2002. The idea of 'moral hazard' is defined as: 'The risk that a party to a transaction has not entered into a contract in good faith, has provided misleading information about its assets, liabilities, or credit capacity, or has an incentive to take unusual risks in a desperate attempt to earn a profit before the contract settles.' The Risk Institute, http://newrisk.ifci.ch/
4. Brian Winter, 'Argentina mulls re-pegging peso: may risk IMF wrath to stave off banking collapse, more riots,' *National Post*, (Reuters), April 25, 2002.
5. Peter Morton, Canada leans on Argentina: Martin calls for action; officials tell Dodge Scotiabank unit could reopen this week,' *Financial Post*, from news services, April 22, 2002.
6. Gilbert Le Gras, 'IMF scrubs quick fix for Argentina: macroeconomic measures still deemed insufficient,' *National Post*, (Reuters), March 14, 2002.
7. George Bragues, 'Reform comes first; an IMF bailout won't resuscitate Argentina's economy. Along with cutting government spending, the debt-strapped country needs to severely curtail the influences of provincial governments and labor unions.' *National Post*, April 18, 2002.
8. William Blum, 'The CIA and the Venezuela coup: Hugo Chavez: a servant not knowing his place,' Counterpunch, Latin America Watch, April 14, 2002.
9. John McMurtry, 'A day in the life of the new world order' [letter to the editor] in the *Globe and Mail*, April 1, 1995, p. D1. Also see any number of books by Noam Chomsky, including *The*

Noam Chomsky Reader (New York: Pantheon, 1987); *Language and Politics* (Montreal: Black Rose, 1988); *Necessary Illusions: Thought Control in Democratic Socities* (Toronto: CBC Enterprises); *Deterring Democracy* (New York: Hill and Wang, 1992); *Letters from Lexington: Reflections on Propaganda* (Toronto: Between the Lines, 1993); *The Prosperous Few and the Restless Many* (Berkeley, CA: Odonian, 1993); highly recommended as well is Noam Chomsky and Edward S. Herman, *The Political Economy of Human Rights: Volume One: The Washington Connection and Third World Fascism* (Montreal: Black Rose, 1979).

10. With respect to industrial pollution, Sylvia Hale notes that 'In practice, environmental costs, like social welfare costs, are generally left out of business equations. They form hidden diseconomies or real costs that, if actually paid by the companies responsible for the pollution, would greatly reduce their profits, and might well turn these apparent profits into deficits. But such costs are not counted by corporations because normally it is not the corporations that pay them. The people and other creatures whose lives are damaged or destroyed by the pollution pay the price.' Sylvia Hale, *Controversies in Sociology*, Second Edition (Copp Clark Limited: Toronto, 1995), pp. 272-273.

11. *Ibid.*, p. 250.

12. *Ibid.*, p. 251.

13. Seth Ackerman, 'Prattle in Seattle: the media and the WTO,' EXTRA! (13:1), Jan/Feb 2000, p. 14.

14. Michael Albert, 'What are we for?,' www.zmag.org

15. The four step program and the interview with Stiglitz are taken from Gregory Palast, 'IMF's four steps to domination,' www.zmag.org. See also, Joseph Stiglitz, *Globalization and Its Discontents* (Norton: New York, 2002).

16. Michael Albert, 'A Q&A on the WTO, IMF, World Bank and Activism' from Z Magazine's WTO Primer, www.znet.org. See also Stiglitz, *Ibid.*

17. *Ibid.*, p. 3.

18. Stiglitz, *Ibid.*, pp. 40-41.

19. Ken Traynor, 'MMT fuel additve scandal?' Briarpatch, Sept 1998.

20. Tom Bottomore, *Elites and Society*, Second edition (New York: Routledge, 1993).

21. Murray Dobbin, 'The view from the West: Europe has its eye on Canadian water—and more.' *Winnipeg Free Press* online, May 2, 2002.

22. *Ibid.*

23. Susan George, 'Democracy at the barricades,' Le Monde Diplomatique, August 2001, www.zmag.org. (As translated by Barbara Wilson.)

24. Craig Pearson, 'OAS General Assembly: Day 2, participants' summit objectives diverse,' The *Windsor Star*, June 6, 2001.

25. Quoted in Pearson, *Ibid.*, emphasis added.

26. John Goranson, 'OAS General Assembly: Day 2, guerrilla caterers' get food to masses, food was donated,' *Windsor Star*, June 6, 2000. That Food Not Bombs was labeled 'guerrilla caterers' is also instructive in terms of the predications of the PM.

27. *Ibid.*

28. Goranson, *Ibid.*

29. For a description of the role of journalists in the social construction of news, see James Winter, *Democracy's Oxygen: How Corporations Control the News* (Black Rose, Montreal, 1996).

30. Craig Pearson, 'OAS perfect medium for artistic ingenuity,' *Windsor Star*, June 8, 2000.

31. Edward Herman and Noam Chomsky, *Manufacturing Consent: The Political Economy of the Mass Media* (New York: Pantheon, 1988). Herman and Chomsky charge that news coverage devoted to government (state) policy in general (foreign and domestic) is typically 'framed' in order to effectively legitimize and facilitate the (geo)political-economic interests of dominant elites.

32. Edward S. Herman, "The Propaganda Model Revisited," *Monthly Review*, July, 1996.

Chapter Eight
Newspaper Discourses On Environment[1]
Robert Babe

> Media bias on behalf of productive interests has resulted in inadequate
> [environmental] coverage or presentation of issues and fewer resources
> allocated to coverage. —Hessing and Howlett, Canadian Natural Re-
> source and Environmental Policy

ACCORDING TO THE EMINENT CANADIAN economic historian and media theorist, Harold Innis, news " dwells in a one-day world,"[2] making it well suited to the
interests of advertisers and the fashion industry. Those controlling the press system, Innis maintained, have little interest in continuity; their major goal is to promote hedonism and consumption. Innis contended more generally, as have Noam
Chomsky and Edward S. Herman, that the élites in any society, by definition, control the dominant means of communication, and normally exercise their "monopoly of knowledge" in ways that enhance their perceived self-interest. In this
chapter we put the Propaganda Model to the test by analyzing environmental
news coverage by leading Canadian newspapers.

As noted by the Brundtland Commission (the United Nations World Commission on Environment and Development), among many others, economy and
ecology in our day are on a crash course. However, following Innis, Chomsky and
Herman, one would expect that the daily press, financed by advertisers and usually owned by multimedia organizations if not indeed conglomerate interests,
will downplay the conflict between our economic system and the environment.

This is not to say that there will not appear in the press, on occasion, envi-
ronmentally-sensitive articles. But the Innisian claim would be that these are the
exceptions that prove the rule, that despite such smatterings of ecologically-
sound reporting and opinion, by far the major thrust of the press is to promote
hedonism and consumption.

Media discourses on economy and environment are, of course, highly influential. They help set the tone and subject matter of the public's discourses—in the

words of communication theorist Maxwell McCombs, media help "set the agenda"[3] for the public.

Before proceeding, a few words of qualification. The following data and analyses do not deal with radio or television broadcasting; in the case of CBC, at least, this is likely an important omission. Internet sources (apart from on-line versions of the newspaper titles referenced below) are not analysed, even though the internet can be an important source of environmental information for some. Nor are all Canadian daily newspapers studied here; rather, the chapter focuses primarily on the *Globe and Mail*, arguably the premier Canadian print journal, with some comparisons of its environmental coverage to that of the *Toronto Star* and the *National Post*. Although two of these three dailies purport to be "national newspapers," there is definitely an Ontario—even Toronto—focus. These qualifications need to be kept in mind when interpreting the analysis that follows.

World Scientists' Warning, and Models of the Press

On November 18, 1992, fifteen hundred scientists released a document entitled "World Scientists' Warning to Humanity." Among the signatories were 92 Nobel laureates (over fifty percent of all living Nobel recipients). They declared:

> Human beings and the natural world are on a collision course. Human activities inflict harsh and often irreversible damage on the environment and on critical resources. If not checked, many of our current practices put at serious risk the future that we wish for human society and the plant and animal kingdoms, and may so alter the living world that it will be unable to sustain life in the manner that we know.[4]

The World Scientists further claimed that virtually all aspects of our natural habitat—the atmosphere, water, soil, forests, biodiversity—are experiencing "critical stress." They warned,

> A great change in our stewardship of the earth and the life on it, is required, if vast human misery is to be avoided and our global home on this planet is not to be irretrievably mutilated.

The World Scientists noted that rich and poor nations alike bear responsibility for rapid deterioration in environmental conditions: the rich on account of "overconsumption," and the poor because of excessive population growth. Regarding the rich, the World Scientists asserted: "The developed nations are the largest polluters in the world today; they must greatly reduce their overconsumption, if we are to reduce pressures on resources and the global environment." They therefore called for "a new ethic—a new attitude towards discharging our responsibility for caring for ourselves and for the earth."

For anyone regarding the press as an "objective" gatherer and disseminator of news, or as a platform for the unconstrained expression and exchange of ideas and opinions, or as the public's watch dog checking abuses of power by exposing malfeasance (the doctrine of the "fourth estate"), the paucity of coverage of the World Scientists' Warning must be perplexing: as noted by David Suzuki,[5] however, the "Warning " was not reported by the *New York Times*, by the *Washington Post*, or by the *Globe and Mail*; nor was their statement covered by the major U.S. television networks; likewise, the CBC was silent.[6] (On the other hand, as Suzuki notes ironically, "the O. J. Simpson trial and President Clinton's alleged sexual behaviour [were] inordinately reportable".)[7]

It is well known that some 80 percent of newspaper revenues derive from advertising, as opposed to 20 percent from subscriptions or single copy sales. From a business perspective, as Dallas Smythe observed, the editorial content of a newspaper (sometimes referred to as the "news hole") is the cost publishers incur to assemble readers for advertisers; newspaper owners sell readership to advertisers, and "content" is their cost of producing this "audience commodity."[8] Moreover, from a business perspective, this "content" should not detract from, and indeed ideally should contribute to, the effectiveness of the surrounding ads.[9] In brief, editorial content, from this perspective, should not be inconsistent with the consumption ethic in general, or with printed inducements to procure advertised goods and services in particular. The World Scientists Warning to Humanity obviously failed to satisfy this criterion. After all, the World Scientists stated pointedly: "The developed nations are the largest polluters in the world today; they must greatly reduce their overconsumption, if we are to reduce pressures on resources and the global environment."

Overall Content of the Press

To attain a better idea of the content comprising the daily press, I performed a content analysis on 12 issues each of the *Toronto Star*, the *National Post*, and the *Globe and Mail* for the period of June 3–June 8, 2002 and May 3–May 9, 2003. Tables 1 and 2 are based on the first of these periods; these tables summarize the general orientation of these three large Canadian daily newspapers, generally thought to cover a spectrum of right/neo-conservative to centrist/liberal.

Table 1: Content of Three Toronto Papers, % Area per Category, June 3–8, 2002*

	National Post	Globe and Mail	Toronto Star	Average
Category	(%)	(%)	(%)	(%)
News/Commentary	119.8	21.2	17.7	19.6
Advertising	31.5	49.3	52.7	44.5
Sports	7.4	7.9	10.8	8.7
Consumption/Lifestyle	41.3	21.6	18.8	27.2
Total	**100**	**100**	**100**	**100**

*Excludes special supplements such as Pull-Out Book Reviews Section, Colour Comics, Business Magazines, advertising inserts, etc.

Table 2: Content of Three Toronto Newspapers, Number of Articles by Category (Excludes Advertising), June 3–8, 2002*

	National Post	Globe and Mail	Toronto Star	3 Paper Average
Category	Articles / %	Articles / %	Articles / %	Articles / %
News/Commentary	310 / 25.8	373 / 38.4	380 / 38.0	354 / 34.1
Sports**	154 / 12.8	146 / 15.1	219 / 21.9	173 / 16.2
Consumption/Lifestyle	738 / 61.5	449 / 46.4	401 / 40.1	539 / 50.6
Total	**1202 / 100**	**986 / 100**	**1000 / 100**	**1066 / 100**

* Excludes special supplements such as Book Reviews Section, Weekend Colour Comics, Business Magazines, advertising inserts, etc.

** Sports statistics and standings counted by headings; financial tables counted by headings

In Table 1, the content of the three presses is divided into four categories:

- *News & Commentary* consists of "news" excluding human interest, sports, and life-style. It comprises coverage of local, regional, national and world events, backgrounders to such events, and commentaries. The subject matters run the gamut from economy, business and politics to accidents, crime, and the weather.
- *Advertising* includes both display ads and classified advertisements.

- *Sports* concern the activities and performance of athletic teams and athletes, and normally appear in the sports section (although coverage of "big" games may be positioned on the front page).

- *Consumption/Lifestyle* includes special supplements (food, automotive, travel, real estate) designed to stimulate consumption, with the editorial content supporting targeted advertising. As well this category includes personality profiles/interviews, movie reviews, and other content on the entertainment industries (apart from that contained in the business section); and also the daily comics, cross words, horoscopes and so forth. This category excludes separate (detachable) supplements and weekend colour comics.

To compile Table 1, the area occupied by items of these categories was measured and aggregated. For Table 2, a "frequency of occurrence" mode of measurement was used; that is, every item in each category received equal weight regardless of size. For Table 2, the category "advertising" was dropped, primarily because hundreds of two and three line classified ads in small print could, if included, render the table misleading.

From the tables above, the relatively low priority accorded news and commentary, and the relatively high priority accorded consumption/lifestyles is evident. For the three presses, advertising plus consumption/lifestyles took up over 70% of the space, whereas news and commentary comprised less than 20% of the printed space. In terms of number of entries, only about one-third of the non-advertising items constitute "news and commentary;" two-thirds pertain to "entertainment/lifestyles/sports." It is apparent from these data that whatever else the daily press may be, predominantly it is an agency promoting consumption/lifestyles/leisure/entertainment.

Environmental Press Coverage

Let's turn now to the nature of the environmental coverage. Table 3 highlights environmental coverage during the week in June 2002, and Table 4 for the week in May 2003; this latter week was significantly different from the one in 2002 due to the onset of SARS in Toronto and escalating concerns regarding West Nile Virus.

In these tables, items are considered "environmental" if they call attention to the dependence of life on nature/environment. Several of the items are anything but "environmental," however, in the sense of advocating care for the planet.

Table 3: "Environmental" Stories: Globe and Mail, Toronto Star, National Post, June 3–8, 2002, by Topic

Topic	Globe and Mail	Toronto Star	National Post	Total
	# / %	# / %	# / %	# / %
Infectious diseases (SARS, West Nile, cholera)	1 / 11	1 / 8	0 / 0	2 / 6
Ocean fisheries	0 /0	1 / 8	1 / 10	2 / 6
Extinctions/endangered species	1 / 11	0 / 0	1 / 10	2 / 6
Toxins/pesticides/ pollution	2 / 22	7 / 54	3 / 30	12 / 37
Forestation/ deforestation	1 / 11	0 / 0	0 / 0	1 / 6
Biotechnology	0 / 0	0 / 0	0 / 0	0 / 0
Nuclear	0 / 0	0 / 0	0 / 0	0 / 0
Natural disasters	0 / 0	0 / 0	0 / 0	0 / 0
Global Warming/Kyoto	3 / 33	3 / 23	5 / 50	11 / 34
Other	1* / 11	1** / 8	0 / 0	2 / 6
Total	**9 / 100**	**13 / 100**	**10 / 100**	**32 / 100**

*Animal Rights

**"Earthweek": 8 short items as a "diary of the planet"

During the week of June 3–8, 2002, for example, the *National Post* ran five items on global warming/Kyoto. Undoubtedly a report issued that week by the U.S. Environmental Protection Agency (EPA), acknowledging the existence of global warming and attributing it to human activity, caught the paper's eye and ire. One of these articles, positioned on the front page, announced that the Earth Summit, to take place in Johannesburg, South Africa at the end of the summer, would cause more greenhouse gas emissions through delegates travelling to the conference than would "half a million ordinary Africans in a year."[10] A second, bearing the headline "More Bad Science," was authored by university economist Ross McKitrick, an outspoken critic of the scientific consensus on global warming;[11] McKitrick attacked not just the EPA study, but the competency of the EPA generally, and Environment Canada too. A third *National Post* article covered President Bush's dismissal of the EPA report; Bush said it was written by "bureaucrats."[12] A fourth acknowledged that humans probably do cause global warming, but maintained that rather than trying to reduce greenhouse emissions the proper strategy would be to view global warming as inevitable and enact measures to help humans adapt to it.[13] The fifth article, accompanied by a large picture of President Bush holding a young child in his arms, summarized the White House position that "tackling global warming on a massive scale is not cost-effective."[14] In all, there were but 32 "environmental" articles (about 3 percent of all articles) in the three papers during the week in June 2002—a modest number to be sure. And many of these, as we have seen, in fact dismissed environmentalists' concerns.

Table 4: "Environmental" Stories: Globe and Mail, Toronto Star, National Post, May 3–9, 2003, by Topic

Topic	Globe and Mail	Toronto Star	National Post	Total
	# / %	# / %	# / %	# / %
Infectious diseases (SARS, West Nile, cholera)	27 / 50	37 / 58	23 / 68	84 / 59.2
Ocean fisheries	12 / 27	6 / 9	6 / 18	24 / 16.9
Extinctions/endangered species	0 / 0	1 / 2	0 / 0	1 / 0.7
Toxins/pesticides/pollution	4 / 9	13 / 20	0 / 0	17 / 12.0
Forestation/deforestation	1 / 2	1 / 2	0 / 0	2 / 1.4
Biotechnology	1 / 2	0 / 0	0 / 0	1 / 0.7
Nuclear	1 / 2	1 / 2	1 / 3	3 / 2.1
Natural disasters	1 / 2	4 / 6	4 / 12	9 / 6.3
Global Warming/Kyoto	0 / 0	1 / 2	0 / 0	1 / 0.7
Other	0 / 0	0 / 0	0 / 0	0 / 0
Total	**44 / 100**	**64 / 100**	**34 / 100**	**142 / 100**

Comparatively, environmental coverage for the period in 2003 covered by Table 4 was intense; this is because of the attention afforded infectious diseases. A second major environmental topic, highly charged politically, was the federal government's ban on cod fishing and its reduction and redistribution of snow crab limits, setting off bitter exchanges between federal and provincial politicians and even leading to the burning of ships in New Brunswick. Those two topics—infectious diseases and Atlantic fisheries—accounted for three quarters of the "environmental" coverage by the three newspapers. Apart from those two topics, there were 34 other "environmental" items published by the three papers between May 3-9, 2003 (excluding the Sunday editions)—a total very close to the number appearing in the selected week of 2002.

Another way of summarizing the environmental coverage of these periods is presented in Table 5, which concerns the view of nature/environment propagated by the "environmental" items. One view of nature is that nature is wild, dangerous, capricious; human activity, in this view, must therefore try to "tame" nature to make it more predictable, controllable and safe. A second view is that nature is our home and that it sustains life; often this view is accompanied by the position that nature is now endangered through human activities, and that we should, therefore, either care for it (stewardship) or endeavour to tread lightly on it so as to interfere as little as possible with its balance. To complete the picture, a third category is presented in Table 5 consisting of items in which neither view is either expressed or implied.

Virtually all stories on SARS and West Nile Virus, as well as natural disaster stories, foster the view that nature is dangerous and that humans must try to dominate it. On the other hand, items pertaining to fishing quotas indicate that human activity can disrupt nature's life-sustaining cycles; stories on pollution and deforestation also may imply a conservationist stance. Kyoto/global warming stories, on the other hand, could fit into any one of the three categories depending on the tack taken: if global warming is said to be part of an inevitable process of natural climate change, the story qualifies as nature being depicted as dangerous (even though, it is generally said in such articles, humans should adapt to change rather than try to prevent it); if global warming is attributed to human activity, then it would fit into the category of humans interfering with nature's balance (even though, here too, the recommendation often is that we should learn to live with climate change, rather than slow it down); if the article simply recounts disagreements on the issue, it would be categorized as not taking a position.

As is evident from Table 5, SARS/West Nile certainly caused the view of nature to become much more menacing than was presented in the week studied in

2002. In the first period, nature was deemed dangerous in 7 of 32 articles (22%), whereas humans were acknowledged to be threatening nature in 15 of the 32 articles (47 %); in May 2003, however, nature was deemed dangerous in 67 % of the articles, and humans seen as threatening nature in only 27 percent of the items. Nature viewed as dangerous is, of course, much more consistent with a consumption ethic than is the view that humans are damaging nature.

Table 5: Views of Nature in Environmental Coverage, Three Toronto Papers, June 3–8, 2002, and May 3–9, 2003

Topic	Globe and Mail	Toronto Star	National Post	Total
	June 2/May 3	June 2/May 3	June 2/May 3	June 2/May 3
Nature is dangerous	2 / 25	1 / 43	4 / 27	7 / 95
Nature is threatened	5 / 15	7 / 20	3 / 4	15 / 39
No position	2 / 4	5 / 1	3 / 3	10 / 8
Total	**9 / 44**	**13 / 64**	**10 / 34**	**32 / 142**

From this overview of the content of the daily press and review of the amount and nature of environmental coverage, we turn now to a detailed analysis of a particular environmental issue: Kyoto/global warming.

Case Study: Coverage of Global Warming/Kyoto Protocol

Background on Kyoto and Global Warming

The world is getting warmer.[15] The 1990s are judged to have been the warmest decade of the millennium, and the twentieth as the warmest century.[16] Although some still claim that this warming is "natural" and unrelated to human activity, the majority of scientific opinion maintains that global warming is largely "anthropogenic," that is human-induced.

In the 1980s, studies began linking global warming to the combustion of fossil fuels.[17] Currently, human activity releases over 22 billion tonnes18[18] of carbon dioxide into the atmosphere each year.[19] Carbon dioxide levels today are thought to be 30 percent greater than pre-industrial levels. The concern is that "greenhouse gases," such as carbon dioxide, block solar heat from radiating from Earth into space. According to some projections, average global temperatures could rise by 5.9°C (10.6°F) by the end of this century if greenhouse gas emissions are not reduced.[20]

The first scientific conference on the issue, the World Conference on the Atmosphere, was held at Toronto in 1988, with delegates from 46 countries attending.[21] In their closing statement, the scientists declared: "Humanity is conducting an unintended, uncontrolled, globally pervasive experiment whose ultimate consequences could be second only to a global nuclear war." Hence they urged a 20-per-cent reduction in CO_2 emissions, based on 1988 levels.[22]

In 1990, in its first report, the Intergovernmental Panel on Climate Change (established by The World Meteorological Organization and the United Nations Environment Program), concluded that the world would need to reduce greenhouse gases by 60 percent merely to stabilize carbon dioxide levels in the atmosphere. Global warming was also an explicit concern of The World Scientists in 1992. Also in 1992, the UN Framework Convention on Climate Change was signed, which aimed to stabilize, by the year 2000, world emissions of greenhouse gases at 1990 levels. Unfortunately, the voluntary reductions countenanced by that treaty were not effective and hence, in 1997, representatives of 160 countries gathered at Kyoto, Japan, and signed "the Kyoto Protocol," described by the Canadian government as " the first global agreement that establishes binding targets for cutting greenhouse gas emissions."[23] Canada's target was set at a 6% reduction from 1990 levels by the year 2012.

The Kyoto Protocol was to become legally binding, however, only when ratified by at least 55 countries collectively accounting for at least 55 percent of the world's emissions.[24] These dual criteria were established because emissions from developing countries, including China and India, are much lower per capita than those of industrialized countries; moreover, the negotiators believed those countries would be less able to absorb the initial costs of reducing emissions. (Third World countries currently emit about 35 percent of world greenhouse gases and account for 80 percent of the world's population). It was anticipated, however, that Third World nations would be brought into a revised agreement upon the expiry of the Kyoto Agreement in 2012. In May 2002 The European Union ratified the treaty, followed in June by Japan. As of early December 2002, over 80 countries had ratified the Protocol, but collectively they still fell short of the 55% emissions requirement.[25]

A major reason for this shortfall was the fact that in March 2001, American President G. W. Bush announced that the U.S., which had been a major force in drawing up the Kyoto treaty in 1997, would not ratify it; Bush called the treaty "economically irresponsible." He claimed that ratification would cost the U.S. economy $400 billion and 4.9 million jobs.[26] Later, Bush unveiled his "Clean

Skies" plan, which linked reductions in greenhouse emissions to growth in GNP.[27] Since the U.S. accounts for about 25 percent of the world's human-made carbon-dioxide emissions, U.S. rejection meant that virtually all other industrialized countries needed to ratify the Protocol for it to become binding.

Canada, of course, came under immense business pressure to "harmonize" with the U.S., and until early September 2002 it was generally assumed that Canada too would not ratify Kyoto. It was a surprise for many, therefore, when on September 2, 2002 Prime Minister Chrétien announced at the United Nations Earth Summit at Johannesburg, South Africa, that he would ask Parliament to approve ratification of the agreement before the end of the year.[28] Although Canada accounts for only about 2% of world CO_2 emissions, Canada's signature, plus that of Russia (17 percent of emissions), was needed for the Protocol to take effect. (The latter country promised to finalize ratification in 2003, but as of November 2003 had yet to do so).

In response to Mr. Chrétien's announcement, thirty-five business groups, including the Canadian Chamber of Commerce, the Canadian Association of Petroleum Producers, the Canadian Manufacturers and Exporters Association, and the Canadian Council of Chief Executives, formed The Canadian Coalition for Responsible Environmental Solutions. At the peak of its campaign this coalition, assisted by National Public Relations, was spending a quarter of a million dollars a week on television ads advocating a "made-in-Canada solution" instead of Kyoto.[29]

Imperial Oil, Canada's largest integrated petroleum company, was likewise opposed, and it launched its own campaign. According to Imperial Oil:

> Meeting Canada's Kyoto target by domestic action only would require the energy-use-reduction equivalent of shutting down all industrial activity in Ontario and Quebec combined, of taking every second vehicle in Canada off the road...No other country in North or South America will be subject to Kyoto limits.[30]

Imperial championed a "made-in-Canada approach," which, in its words "reflects the realities of increasing North American economic integration and is compatible with the approaches being taken by our economic partners."[31] This "approach," according to Imperial Oil, would consist of (1) ongoing scientific research to better understand global warming (Imperial has yet to affirm the existence of global warming); (2) continuing to take "economic steps" to improve energy efficiency; and (3) continued research on innovative technologies. During the height of its campaign Imperial sponsored a "scientific conference" featuring anti-Kyoto speakers. It also published opinion pieces in the daily press. In a *National Post* article entitled, "Canada's Missing Governance on Kyoto," for example, Imperial's chairman and CEO, Tim Hearn, declared flatly: "Canada will…be the only nation in the Western Hemisphere…to be constrained by Kyoto."[32] (Hearn's monumental error in geography—he forgot entirely about Western Europe—was soon parroted by the *Globe and Mail*'s editorial writers, as we'll note more fully below).

Imperial found a ready and vocal ally in Alberta Premier Ralph Klein, even though rival integrated oil companies, like Suncor Energy[33] and Shell Canada,[34] were quite reserved in their criticisms. Klein crossed the country, denigrating both Kyoto and the Prime Minister, and this was all of course dutifully reported by the daily press.

Another strident opponent was the Canadian Manufacturers & Exporters Association. In its booklet, *Pain Without Gain: Canada and the Kyoto Protocol*, it projected gloomily that "production closures across Canadian industry could result in the permanent loss of 450,000 jobs in manufacturing alone by 2010." The Association also projected dire consequences for individual Canadians. According to the Association, we would all have to:

- Drive less often, drive smaller cars, or take public transit that would, in turn, require massive infrastructure spending on the part of governments;

- Re-insulate our homes, change our furnaces, windows and appliances;

- Pay up to 100% more for electricity, 60% more for natural gas, and 80% more for gasoline; and

- Pay more taxes, in part to finance Canada's purchase of emission credits.[35]

There was a modicum of academic hostility. Two outspoken critics—Christopher Essex, a mathematician at the University of Western Ontario, and Ross McKitrick, an economist at the University of Guelph—published *Taken By Storm: The Troubled Science, Policy and Politics of Global Warming* just in time to enter the fray.[36] Their position was enthusiastically endorsed by *Globe and Mail* columnist, Margaret Wente (more on this below). Other "climate scientists" too contended in the *Globe* that climate change was not human-induced (more on this below as well).

Indeed, much of the battle over Kyoto took place in the pages of the *Globe and Mail*, giving rise (in one sense) to perhaps the most intensive period to that point of environmental coverage in the paper's history. It is to that coverage that we now turn.

Globe and Mail Coverage

This section provides an in-depth review and analysis of the *Globe and Mail's* coverage of Kyoto for the period September 3, 2002, the day after Prime Minister Chrétien announced that Canada would ratify the Protocol, to December 11, 2002, the day after the House of Commons endorsed ratification. The *Globe and Mail* is, arguably, Canada's most influential newspaper.

The *Globe's* coverage of Kyoto, as we will see, was not primarily "environmental." Rather, Kyoto was treated above all as a story of political conflict: the provinces vs. federal government; Alberta Premier Ralph Klein vs. Jean Chrétien; Prime Minister-in-waiting, Paul Martin vs. Jean Chrétien; the energy and manufacturing sectors vs. the federal government. It was a story too of Chrétien "clinging to power," of the change of focus in his governance after he had announced his retirement, and of whether he would be able to control his MPs in the eventual vote in the House of Commons. And it was a story of political uncertainty—who or what would Ontario Premier Ernie Eves support?

In the *Globe*, Kyoto was also often treated as an economic/business/financial story—what ratifying the treaty would do to or for employment, profits, investment, balance of trade, innovation, and other economic/financial indicators. What it was *not*, primarily, at least in the pages of the *Globe and Mail*, was a story of the impact of global warming on the capacity of the planet to sustain life, or the impact of the Kyoto Protocol on global warming.

In fact, to an inordinately large extent, the *Globe's* Kyoto coverage was derived from disaffected interests who, by means of public relations strategies, attained free media exposure to publicize their views in efforts to turn public opinion against the accord. There were, consequently, multitudinous *pseudoevents*[37]—special studies, conferences, speeches, polls, interviews, announcements, name callings, threats, news leaks, sound bites, as well as press releases and letters—much of which was duly and "objectively" reported as "news."

In this section, we first provide an overview of the *Globe's* coverage for the period, then look at several continuing themes in the coverage in greater detail.

Overview

On April 16, 2003 we accessed from the *Globe's* web site all stories listed under the headings: "Kyoto," "Greenhouse," "Climate Change," Global Warming" "Martin Mittelstaedt," and "Alanna Mitchell." We also visited Yahoo News Canada for *Globe* stories on Kyoto, and consulted our extensive collection of clippings. Excluded in the quantitative analysis below, however, are letters to the editor.

For the period September 3–December 11, 2002, we identified 137 items (excluding letters to the editor) in the *Globe* dealing with Kyoto and/or climate change/global warming. As our initial exercise, we classified the articles by main focus: environment, legal/political, or business/financial/economic. Of course, all of the 137 articles in a sense are "environmental," as without a concern for climate change there would be no Kyoto Protocol. Nonetheless, for the great majority of items in the *Globe*, environmental consequences of greenhouse gas emissions and/or the efficacy of the Protocol in reducing these emissions were mere background, often implicit, to the political or economic/financial thrust of the stories and commentaries. We identified only 18 items of the 137 (13%) as having an environmental focus; those articles are listed in Table 7 below.

As well, there was often overlap between a legal/political and economic/business/financial focus due to the simple fact that Kyoto was of political controversy due to its apprehended economic/financial impact; nonetheless, in practice, most articles gave predominant emphasis either to political struggles or to dollar impacts, thereby making distinctions quite easy. Examples of "Legal/Political" articles are: "PM Makes Bid for Green Legacy";[38] "Klein Prepares Battle Over Kyoto";[39] and "Albertans Turn Against Kyoto in Poll."[40] Examples of "Business/Economic/Financial" articles are: "Ottawa Pegs Kyoto Job Risk at 200,000";[41] "Stop Whining: Kyoto Equals Jobs";[42] and "Another Oil Sands Firm Cuts Back, Blaming Kyoto."[43] The results of this initial classification and tabulation are presented in Table 6.

Table 6: Focus of Kyoto/Global Warming Coverage, Globe and Mail, September 3–December 11, 2002*

Major Focus	*Number of Items*	*% of Total*
Environment	18	13.1
Legal/Political	65	47.4
Business/Econmics/Finanacial	54	39.4
Total	**137**	**100**

*Excludes letters to the Editor

We now take a closer look at those few articles actually dealing with climate change/global warming. Of the 18 articles focusing on the environment, 10 were explicitly or implicitly favourable to Kyoto and/or other immediate action to curb greenhouse gas emissions, 1 was neutral, and 7 were hostile. It is also worth noting that of the ten pieces favouring Kyoto and/or other immediate action against greenhouse gas emissions, 4 were written as commentaries by non-*Globe and*

Mail authors, and 4 were written by the *Globe*'s Environment or its Earth Sciences reporters (more on this below). Only two were written by non-environmental staff at the *Globe*. Following are short summaries.

Kyoto/Global Warming Items with "Environmental" Focus, Globe and Mail, September 3–December 11, 2002

Items Explicitly or Implicitly Favourable to Kyoto:

David McGuinty, "Overdraft at the Nature Bank."[44] McGuinty, president and chief executive officer of the National Round Table on the Environment and the Economy, assails economics and accounting practices for not taking into account non-market costs and benefits. We are rapidly depleting "natural capital...whose services make life possible on a biological level; these services include air and water purification, productive soils, wildlife, climate regulation, flood control, and pollination of crops." Since Kyoto will lead to monetization and trading of carbon-reduction credits, it is to be welcomed.

Alanna Mitchell, "Your Own Private Kyoto."[45] The *Globe*'s Earth Sciences Reporter lists various, rather painless ways individuals can reduce emissions of greenhouse gases, thereby contributing to Kyoto targets.

Martin Mittelstaedt, "Firms Breaking Promises on Emissions, Study Says."[46] The *Globe*'s Environment Reporter writes: "Most of Canada's largest corporate greenhouse-gas emitters have failed to honour voluntary pledges to limit pollution responsible for global warming, says a new study by the Pembina Institute and the David Suzuki Foundation..."

Alanna Mitchell, "Greenhouse Pollution Rate Increasing, Data Reveal."[47] The Earth Sciences Reporter cites data showing "that rather than slowing this pollution, Canadians are accelerating it."

Alanna Mitchell, "Arctic Ice Melting Much Faster Than Thought."[48] The story recounts, among other things, that "polar bears are likely to die off when the Arctic ice vanishes."

David Barber, "Chill Prediction."[49] The article concerns dwindling Arctic ice. The author writes: "Humankind is still evolving from a mentality of 'doing battle' with nature for survival; but those days are gone and now we must think of ourselves as nature's stewards, because our habitat, like that of the polar bear, is threatened."

Thomas Homer-Dixon, Karl Braganza, James Risbey, and David Karoly, "Kyoto Skeptics Miss the Point."[50] The article, by climate scientists, is a rejoinder to a skeptical global warming piece by other climate scientists.

Maurice Strong, "Don't Blow It, Canada."[51] The former head of Petro-Canada and former Secretary to the Bruntland Commission states we must act on the best evidence available (as do oil companies when deciding where to dig for oil), and the great majority of scientists believe greenhouse gases like CO_2 are responsible for global warming.

Gloria Galloway, "The Icing Call of the Arctic One of Lament."[52] Winters are getting shorter in the Arctic, thereby shortening the outdoor hockey season.

Alanna Mitchell, "Doubts Cast on Warming's 'Green' Lining."[53] The *Globe's* "Earth Sciences Reporter" cites a new study projecting that build-up of carbon-dioxide in the atmosphere will stunt plant growth rather than increase it as some had projected.

Item Neutral to Kyoto:

Chris Morris, "Climate Change Affecting Flora."[54] The author of this Canadian Press item writes there are good as well as bad consequences associated with global warming. For example, growing seasons will be longer. Kyoto is not mentioned.

Items Negative to Kyoto:

William Thorsell, "Accept It: Kyoto Won't Stop Global Warming."[55] The *Globe's* former editor argues that since global warming will continue apace with or without human help, better to prepare for global warming than vainly try to stop or slow it down.

Rex Murphy, "Selling Something, Dr. Suzuki?"[56] The *Globe* columnist, in a highly sarcastic tone, disputes David Suzuki's claim, made at a press conference sponsored by some doctors, that 16,000 people die each year in Canada from causes related to global warming. Murphy cites an estimate of 200,000 lost jobs if Kyoto is implemented. The *Globe* subsequently published Suzuki's rejoinder as a letter to the editor.

Michael Den Tandt, "Anti-Kyoto Science Must Have its Day."[57] The *Globe* reporter reviews the position of several "anti-Kyoto" scientists who contend one or more of the following: climate change is constant, inevitable, the past 40 years; the Earth is cooling, not warming; there is nothing to worry about. The author suggests the government hold a referendum on Kyoto so that the issue can be debated fully.

Sallie Baliunas, Tim Patterson and *Allan MacRae*, "Climate Change Is Natural."[58] The authors, representing themselves as "objective" climate scientists (more on this below) conclude, "When it comes to climate change, humans aren't the culprits." They reason that "greenhouse gases, clouds and aerosols in the atmosphere do trap some of the solar radiation reflected from the Earth's surface, causing a natural greenhouse effect that warms the Earth and makes it habitable; those gases comprise less than 0.1 per cent of the air...Water vapour, comprising 99 per cent of greenhouse gases in the atmosphere, provides most of the greenhouse effect, followed by water in all its phases in clouds."

Deborah Yedlin, "CAPP Chose Wrong Tactic on Kyoto."[59] This piece reviews that skeptical position regarding greenhouse gases and global warming put forth by Talisman CEO, Jim Buckee—for example, water vapour accounts for 98% of greenhouse gases; some evidence points to temperatures having dropped between 1940 and 1970 despite an exponential increase in carbon dioxide in the atmosphere.

Margaret Wente, "The Kyoto-Speak Brainwashers."[60] The *Globe* columnist suggests that concern over greenhouses gases is a scam put forward by the majority of climate scientists in efforts to get government grants. Wente states: "The climate is indeed changing. Always has, always will."

Anne McIlroy, "Green Options Fall Short, Study Says."[61] The article explores various ways greenhouse gas emissions could be cut, and concludes that a "Herculean effort may be needed to take the measures that will actually stabilize the climate."

We also classified the 137 entries by headline: positive to Kyoto and/or federal government; negative to Kyoto and/or federal government; and neutral. Examples of favourable headlines are: "Alberta Can't Beat Ottawa in Battle of Kyoto";[62] "Kyoto Investment Can Pay Off";[63] "EnCana CEO's Urge to Kill Kyoto is Misguided";[64] "Good Grief! Kyoto Might Actually Be Good";[65] and "Despite the Hazy Debate, Kyoto May Be Just What Canada Needs."[66] Note how lukewarm or equivocal some of the "positive" headlines are, and how several arise from negative concerns.

Examples of negative headlines are: "Ottawa, Conservationists Disagree on Earth Summit Results;"[67] "Kyoto: The Wrong Note to Go Out On,"[68] and "EnCana Chief to PM: Kill Kyoto."[69] Examples of neutral headlines are: "PM Makes Bid for Green Legacy,"[70] "Canada Confronts Kyoto Challenge,"[71] and "Alberta Planning National Tech Site on Emissions."[72] See table below for the results of this classification and tabulation.

Table 7: Headlines in Globe and Mail: Positive, Negative and Neutral to Kyoto and/or Other Immediate Action on Greenhouse Gas Emissions, September 3–December 12, 2002

	Number	% of Total
Positive	34	24.8
Negative	61	44.5
Neutral	42	30.7

Here we see that one quarter of the Kyoto/global warming/climate change headlines were positive or supportive to Kyoto and/or other immediate action, while 45 percent were negative or unfavourable. (Headlines favouring a "made-in-Canada" solution are deemed negative, as no "made-in-Canada" plan existed).

Of course, a headline does not necessarily reflect the tone of the accompanying article. In Table 8 we classify all 137 articles as to whether the overall thrust was to favour, oppose, or be neutral/balanced toward Kyoto and/or the government's handling of the treaty. In the table we also distinguish between news reports and commentaries/editorials.

Table 8: Number and Percent of Articles Favourable, Unfavourable and Neutral/ Balanced Toward Kyoto, Globe and Mail September 2–December 12 2002

	Favourable	Unfavorable	Neutral/Balanced	Total
Commentary/Editorial	20	31	11	62
News	7	28	40	75
Total	27	59	51	137
% of all items	20	43	37	100

Negative news items/commentaries outnumber positive or favourable items by about 2:1. Only 20 percent of Globe articles favoured Kyoto/immediate action. (And, as we saw previously, even of the environment-focused items, only slightly more than 50% favoured Kyoto/immediate action). Table 8 is quite consistent with Table 7; in general, the thrust of the headline matches the tone of the story.

The most commonly cited reasons for not favouring Kyoto were: it is divisive and unfair to energy-rich regions; it is too costly; it will cause dis-investment and unemployment; it is not proven that global warming is caused by humans; there is too much uncertainty and no plan for implementation; Canada is disadvantaged vis a vis USA; Kyoto will be ineffective; it ignores population growth; Canada will have to buy carbon emission rights abroad (from Russia).

The most frequently cited arguments in favour of Kyoto were: Canada assumes an international leadership role on global warming; the treaty will reduce global warming; Canadians are in favour of Kyoto; the majority of scientists agree that greenhouse gases cause global warming; new technologies and new opportunities will be spawned; there is negligible costs to implementing Kyoto; Kyoto will stimulate employment; Kyoto incorporates pollution in the price mechanism; ratification is needed before a plan will be developed; costs of global warming are seldom considered by economists and businesses; it is proven that reductions in emissions can take place; it is better to proceed internationally than nationally on a global issue.

Yet a further indicator of the over-all thrust of *Globe and Mail* coverage can be gleaned by tabulating who were cited as authorities and/or quoted. Table 9 clearly supports a previous finding that, for the *Globe*, Kyoto was primarily a story of political conflict and of economic/financial consequences, not an environmental story.

Table 9: News Source and Authorities, by Occupation, Globe and Mail Coverage of Kyoto/Global Warming, September 2–December 11, 2002

Business executive	54
Federal Liberal politician	53
Provincial politician	53
Un-elected official	22
Federal Opposition politician	21
Scientist	20
Environmentalist	17
Social Scientist (think tank; pollster)	16
Citizen	7
Celebrity	1

Coverage of Specific Issues

1. Is Human-Induced Global Warming Real?

In several pieces, writers in the *Globe and Mail* queried whether global warming is real, and if real whether humans are responsible. *Globe* columnist Margaret Wente, for example, devoted a 3/4 page spread to the topic, complete with a 1/4-page illustration of sheep gathered before a TV screen on which appears a close-up of yet another sheep. Evidently she had just read Taken By Storm by Drs. Essex and McKitrick, and was completely won over. Fortified by the facts and analysis of that book, Wente pronounced global warming to be a monumental scam. She charged that "science has been corrupted by the official doctrine; governments, including Canada's, hand out millions to people to conduct research into climate change—but only if the research confirms the central thesis." She stated: "Serious scientists have given up trying to explain to the public just why the entire edifice of global warming is an intellectual house of cards;" in the very next sentence, however, she quotes Dr. Essex, whom she termed a "serious player in the world of climate science"—despite his strident attempts to explain to the public that the edifice of global warming is an intellectual house of cards. According to Essex, "Over the past 10 years, the voice of scientists has disappeared from the discussion; we're like spectators with our noses pressed up against the glass." Completely reversing what many consider to be the real power/control aspects of media, Wente wrote:

> But the real eye opener is their [Essex and McKintrick's] account of how the politics of global warming has produced certainty in public discourse. It starts with pressure from environmentalists and the public, who convince policymakers that something should be done, who appoint sympathetic experts to head up massive studies, who hire like-minded people to carry them out, which are then synthesized by bureaucrats into executive summaries from which all doubt and uncertainty have been stripped away. These summaries are said to be the "consensus view," and are used as the ultimate authority invoked by politicians to justify their calls for urgent action...This certainty is then amplified by the media which search out stories that appear to further prove the doctrine.[73]

Note that in the Wente/Essex/McKitrick account, alarm over global warming and the greenhouse effect originated not from scientists who finally converged at a conference in Toronto in 1988 to discuss their concerns, nor with the 1500 scientists who signed the petition "warning humanity," but with "environmentalists and the public" who, she writes, were fatigued by an unusually hot summer in 1988. Note also that, according to Wente, "media" selectively and consistently search out people expressing concerns over global warming to lend credibility to the cause, a contention, incidentally, quite at odds with contributions to the *Globe* for the period considered here.

Then, on November 19, the *Globe* published a piece entitled, "Climate Change is Natural: Believe the Science, not the Rhetoric, We Aren't Causing Global Warming, Say Scientists."[74] The *Globe* described the accreditation of the authors of the article as follows: "Dr. Sallie Baliunas is deputy director at Mount Wilson Observatory and an astrophysicist at the Harvard-Smithsonian Center for Astrophysics; Dr. Tim Patterson is a professor of geology (paleoclimatology) in the Department of Earth Sciences at Carleton University in Ottawa; Allan M. R. MacRae is a professional engineer, investment banker and environmentalist."[75] Three days later, however, to its credit, the *Globe* published a letter to the editor from Andrew Baines of the Department of Laboratory Medicine and Pathology, University of Toronto, giving remarkably different credentials for these authors. According to Professor Baines: "Allan MacRae, an 'environmentalist,' is president and CEO of Odyssey Petroleum; Tim Patterson, a geology professor, has been a geologist and biostratigrapher for the oil industry; Sallie Baliunas is a senior scientist at the Washington-based George C. Marshall Institute (supported by the Exxon Education Foundation) that studies how the Kyoto Protocol impacts on national security." Baines then charged that the authors had "misrepresented the contents of the IPCC [Intergovernmental Panel on Climate Change] report—for example, the accuracy of climate models, tropospheric temperature and the importance of water in CO_2 greenhouse effects."[76]

Let us turn, however, to the original article itself. Here is an excerpt:

> The Kyoto Protocol assumes humankind causes global warming, but climate has always changed. For two million years, the Earth has been in an ice age marked by more than 30 glaciations, during which ice sheets covered most of North America to a depth of several kilometres. In the past 800,000 years, the pattern has been 100,000 years of extensive glaciation, interspersed with brief, warmer interglacials of 15,000 years. The next glaciation is less than 5,000 years ahead.

While the authors agree that the greenhouse effect is real, ("Greenhouse gases, clouds and aerosols in the atmosphere do trap some of the solar radiation reflected from the Earth's surface"), and also that carbon–dioxide, a greenhouse gas, has been increasing in atmospheric concentration ("during the past 300 years, atmospheric carbon dioxide concentrations have risen from 275 parts per million to around 360 parts per million, a 30-per-cent increase; most of the increase has been recent, caused by fossil fuel burning and deforestation"), nonetheless they deny that the causation is from carbon concentrations to global warming; rather, they propose cause in the opposite direction: "Climate change drives major changes in CO_2, not the reverse; carbon dioxide is only a minor contributor in the many factors that influence global climate." They conclude: "There is strong evidence that variation in the sun's energy output is a much more significant driver of surface temperature than human-made greenhouse gases. When it comes to climate change, humans aren't the culprits."

Also to its credit, about a week later, the *Globe* printed a rebuttal by other climate scientists[77] who accused the aforementioned deniers of employing "such a selective reading of scientific theory and evidence that their picture bears little resemblance to the reality understood by the vast majority of climate scientists around the world." Reviewing arguments and evidence presented in the previous article, these authors concluded:

> [Their] opinion is at odds with the latest conclusions of the International Panel on Climate Change—which state that "most of the observed warming over the last 50 years is likely to have been due to the increase in greenhouse gas concentrations"—and with the opinions of the majority of climate scientists. Although the weight of numbers does not guarantee truth, the skeptics are increasingly clutching at straws.

In the absence of a larger context, it would be difficult for a layperson to know just how to interpret the *Globe*'s presenting of this exchange of opinion in its pages. Was the exchange the equivalent of granting space to representatives of the flat earth society in the name of "public debate"? Or was it truly a case of the National Newspaper becoming a forum for experts on an unsettled scientific issue of public concern?

2. Commissioning and Reporting Polls

The first poll during the period of intensive debate was taken by Ipsos-Reid for the *Globe and Mail*, and was reported on page A1 of the October 8, 2002 issue, under the headline, "Albertans Turn Against Kyoto in Poll."[78] The main thrust of the story, as given in the opening paragraphs, was that support for Kyoto by Albertans had declined (from 72 percent to 27 percent since an earlier poll in the spring), putting that province "out of step" with the rest of the country, since a majority of Canadians, according to the report, still supported Kyoto. The article maintained, however, that national support for the treaty, too, had "softened," even though

> …a sizable majority still supports implementing the accord. Across the country, backing for the agreement to fight climate change has fallen 12 percentage points, to 74 per cent from 86 per cent in an Ipsos-Reid poll conducted May 22 to June 2. Twenty-one per cent oppose implementing the deal, up from 10 per cent.

The article then reported, "support for Kyoto has also fallen in the Atlantic provinces, by approximately 19 percentage points, in British Columbia by roughly 15 percentage points, and in Saskatchewan-Manitoba by about 13 percentage points." The article did allow, however, that "the percentage of residents backing the accord in these three polling regions is still in the high 60s and low 70s," and moreover that "more than 80 per cent of Quebeckers and Ontario residents also support Kyoto." Only on p. A4, however, were the actual results of the national poll presented, and those data are sufficiently contradictory to put into doubt the validity of the entire survey. Here are the results, as reported:

Views on the Kyoto Accord: Suggestions for Implementing the Kyoto Accord

1. The government of Canada needs to spend more time in investigating the cost and impact of the Kyoto accord before implementing it.
   Agree: 78%   Disagree: 20%

2. I don't think I have enough information about the Kyoto accord to say whether I support or oppose it.
   Agree: 59%   Disagree: 40%

3. Even if there are some problems with the Kyoto accord, I think it should be implemented because it is a good first step.
   Agree: 74%   Disagree: 22%

4. It is possible for Canada to develop an alternative to the Kyoto accord that is just as effective but would cost the Canadian economy a lot less.
   Agree: 71%   Disagree: 22%

5. The government of Canada should ratify the Kyoto accord and implement it, even if it means significant costs to the economy and changes to the lifestyles of Canadians.
   Agree: 57%   Disagree: 39%

Source: Ipsos-Reid, as reported in the *Globe and Mail* Oct. 8, 2002, p. A4.

For Question 2, 59% of respondents agreed they had insufficient information to make any pronouncement on Kyoto, but in Question 3, 74% confidently opined that Kyoto should be implemented. Likewise, responses to Question 1 indicated widespread opposition to Kyoto, and responses to Question 4 pointed also to strong opposition, but the responses to Question 3 indicated overwhelming support, while the responses to Question 5 identified modest support even if Kyoto entailed "significant costs to the economy and changes to the lifestyles of Canadians." Rather than really measuring public attitudes toward Kyoto, then, the poll probably indicated that respondents are more inclined to "agree" than to "disagree" to questions.

The real significance of the October poll, however, came only with publication of another poll the next month. It too was undertaken by Ipsos-Reid, but this poll was commissioned by the Alberta government. This time respondents were asked to choose one of the following: Withdraw from the Kyoto Protocol and develop a made-in-Canada plan for reducing greenhouse-gas emissions (45 % agreed), ratify the Kyoto Protocol (44 % responded yes), or do nothing. The headline on the front page of the *Globe and Mail* screamed that support for the protocol had "plunged"—from 75% to 45%![79] According to reporter Patrick Brethour,

> Support for the Kyoto Protocol has plummeted, with the country split between ratifying the accord or forging a made-in-Canada approach to tackling global warming, a poll suggests.

He continued,

> The survey by Ipsos-Reid suggests that 45 per cent of respondents preferred the federal government withdraw from the Kyoto Protocol and develop a made-in-Canada plan for reducing greenhouse-gas emissions, while 44 per cent wanted Ottawa to ratify the accord...The lukewarm backing for the Kyoto Protocol countrywide was a marked turnaround from early October, when an Ipsos-Reid poll suggested that 74 per cent of Canadians supported implementing the accord, with 21 per cent opposed.

To its credit, four days later, the *Globe* printed a letter to the editor from Frank L. Graves, president of Ekos Research Associates, a rival polling firm which undertook polling on Kyoto for the federal government. Graves noted that the first poll asked respondents if they favoured Kyoto, whereas the second asked them to choose among Kyoto, a "made-in-Canada solution," and doing nothing. "Unsurprisingly," commented Graves, "when provided with three rather than two choices, the incidence of support for ratification drops."

Indeed, on the basis of the results published by the *Globe*, the proper conclusion would be that support for action against greenhouse gas emissions had increased substantially. In the October poll, almost thirty percent of Canadians felt no action was required, whereas in the November (Alberta government) poll, only about 10 percent either recommended no action or expressed no opinion.

It is interesting that in his original article, Brethour also noted results of an Ekos poll undertaken, as he put it, "for the Liberal Party," a few days earlier, which suggested that " there was massive support for the Kyoto Protocol, with 79 per cent approving ratification; only Albertans opposed ratification." Regarding that poll, Brethour chided, however, that " the poll's methodology was not released publicly."

The story on polling, however, did not end there. On November 5, 2002, the *Toronto Star* quoted Environment Minister David Anderson as claiming that in releasing the results Alberta had "cooked the books" to show that support for Kyoto had fallen. Anderson termed the poll "fraudulent."[80] The *Star*'s article then proceeded to quote Ipsos-Reid Senior Vice-President John Wright as follows:

> We were unaware they [the Alberta government]were going to do this...We were very disturbed at how this was playing out. The way in which this was spun in the media was overenthusiastic...We have not seen from our numbers a plummeting of the Kyoto accord. There is not a significant drop in support. Right now they're being asked to differentiate between an accord they know nothing about and a made in Canada solution they know nothing about.

The *Star* article went on to note that, "because of the uproar, the firm is redoing the poll."

On November 6, the *Globe* turned to a press conference held the day before, attended by "a handful of people" launching a pro-Kyoto campaign by the Sierra Club of Canada.[81] The campaign was supported by several "prominent Canadians" who had become distraught by the spin put on the Ipsos-Reid/Alberta Government poll. The *Globe* reporter listed "broadcaster" David Suzuki, NDP leadership candidate Jack Layton, members of the bands Tragically Hip and Barenaked Ladies, authors Pierre Berton, Michael Ondaatje and Farley Mowat, comedians Cathy Jones and Greg Malone, cyclist Clara Hughes, and actor Gordon Pinsent as supporters of the campaign. Also present was Bob Hunter, Greenpeace co-founder and currently an environmental reporter for CITY-TV, a Toronto television station. According to reporter Gloria Galloway, at the news conference Mr. Hunter called Premiers Klein and Eves "ecological criminals," and he contended that the question in the Ipsos-Reid/Alberta Government poll had been worded to obtain the results desired by Mr. Klein and the oil industry. She then quoted Mr. Hunter as saying:

> Another poll came out today which points out that support for the Kyoto Protocol all across Canada is solid at about 80 per cent, that there has been no slippage and the previous poll...was, in fact, fraudulent...It's not that Canadians have lost interest in the whole thing. It's just that the Alberta government and its buddies are paying a lot of money to hire pollsters to ask stupid questions.

As reported by the *Globe* the next day[82] (Nov. 7), Ipsos-Reid quickly jumped on Mr. Hunter (but not on Environment Minister Anderson!), demanding through their lawyers that Hunter make an immediate apology. From the Ipsos-Reid web site we learn that the apology was both immediate and profuse.[83] In the same article, the *G & M* quoted an Ipsos-Reid official: "The poll does not suggest that Canadians support for the climate-change accord had plunged but indicates that Canadians are open to a "made-in-Canada solution." Also on November 7 the *Globe* published a piece by Darrell Bricker, president of Public Affairs of Ipso-Reid, who wrote:

> At no place in the analysis [of the poll] did we indicate that support for the Kyoto accord had plummeted (Support For Kyoto Plunges: Nov. 2). In fact, the numbers from the poll released on Nov. 1 are not comparable with previously released polls because different questions were asked and answered.[84]

The controversy was visited again on November 8 by columnist Hugh Windsor and yet again by reporter Steven Chase on November 9.[85] Jeffrey Simpson indirectly entered the fray on December 11, trashing polls generally, albeit barely mentioning the Kyoto polls. It is nonetheless useful to extract a portion of Simpson's column since it leads so nicely into the next topic, "trashing the public."

> A big chunk of Canadians are ignorant or barely informed about anything in the public domain. They get most of their information from television, but what they take in doesn't inform them very much. Television, in general, entertains but does not inform. A corollary point: A chunk of the electorate is completely tuned out of everything beyond its immediate world. It doesn't matter what the media, interest groups, governments or political parties do. They can't reach the unreachable ...With so much ignorance about public policy, polls really don't reveal

very much, despite their use by just about everyone. No wonder interest groups dominate debate, because they display passionate intensity about issues. No wonder, too, that they commission polls that in almost every case reveal answers they like—answers that depend on the questions asked.[86]

3. Trashing the Public

Ian Brown wrote a lengthy weekend Focus piece in the Saturday *Globe and Mail* of October 26, 2002 (pp. F1, F8, F9). It was entitled "The Kyoto Stampede," and came complete with a large colour photo of the Alberta bar scene, as well as photos of anti- Kyoto crusaders Peter Lougheed (former Premier of Alberta), and Nexen Inc. CEO, Charlie Fischer. The first part of the article, was really about Calgary night-life. Here is an excerpt:

> Another young woman, Natalie, whose lips are so glossed over they look like two shimmering eels, is pouring upside-down margaritas. This is how it works: With Natalie standing behind him on a chair, Doug Donald, the manager, ("Biscuit" to his friends), tips his head backward between her breasts. She pours tequila and mix into his open mouth from two bottles she wears in a holster. Then pushing her upper arms around her breasts, and her breasts around Biscuit's head, she whacks his noggin back and forth to 'mix' the drink. And what are the first words out of Biscuit's mouth when she's finished? "Kyoto," he says. "It's the uncertainty, right? I don't like anything that upsets the oil patch."

"Kyoto Stampede"

This initial portion of the article, then, not only trivializes the global warming issue, it also denigrates the public. The real meaning of this part of the story is: *Let the experts decide.*

Hence, Brown shifts immediately to the 45th floor office of Peter Lougheed, who was then chairing Premier Klein's External Advisory Committee on Kyoto. Later in the article, he reports also on a series of interviews with Calgary oil-industry representatives, all opposed to Kyoto. Toward the end of his piece, however, Brown returns to the general public, this time quoting a Toronto bus driver. Here is an excerpt:

> A bus driver named Warren Brubaker said he was for Kyoto because "I know how corrupt the oil industry is."
>
> "How do you know?" someone said.
>
> "I just know."
>
> "But why should we ratify Kyoto?"
>
> "Because the Europeans have all ratified it."
>
> "Are you aware there's a made-in-Canada alternative?"
>
> "No, I don't care that I know nothing about Kyoto. Because I read the experts. And they haven't let me down."[87]

Also in the *Globe and Mail* for October 26 was Jeffrey Simpson's column, entitled "The Great Canadian Effort to Save the Planet" (p. A21). There Simpson trivialized not just Kyoto, and of course Jean Chrétien's advocacy of it, but the whole philosophy of trying to care for the Earth for the benefit of future generations. He accomplished this by concocting a mock telephone conversation between himself and "Uncle Fred." Note in the excerpt that follows how Simpson rhetorically uses the language of safe sex to depict global warming:

> "Mildred and I are desperately worried about you, " said Uncle Fred from Gabriola Island. "Are you taking the necessary precautions to save your life?"
>
> "I appreciate the call, Fred," I replied, "but what are you talking about?"
>
> "Didn't you hear what Jean Chrétien said this week? Here, I'll read it to you. He said, 'Some people will be dying in 30 years in Canada because we have not been responsible today.' "
>
> "Chrétien says a lot of incomprehensible things, Fred. What was he talking about this time?"

Simpson then remarked that each summer two or three people are killed by bears, but that doesn't mean all bears should be killed. Likewise for global warming. Fred and Mildred, he suggested, have about the same chance of being killed by global warming as by a bear attack. But let us pick up the conversation a bit later:

> "But David Suzuki says climate change is the end of civilization as we know it. He's very popular with my Gabriola neighbours. We've got to do something to save this planet."
>
> "Okay, did you know that you and Mildred emit 10 tonnes of greenhouse gases between you?"
>
> "I know I sometimes have indigestion that can be embarrassing in public places, but we don't flatuate that much."
>
> "No, no Fred. Not methane. Carbons. They're the baddies., and the average Canadian emits five tonnes of them a year..."

Note how Simpson pits his expertise against the concerned but ill-informed general "public" represented by well-meaning but dim-witted Fred and Mildred. Soon, however, and with little or no resistance, he turns them against Kyoto by emphasizing that *they* will have to use public transit or buy a fuel-efficient car, and retrofit their house, to cut emissions—the self-interested consumer of capitalism in Simpson's story quickly gets the better of their innate publicly-spirited intentions. Note also how responsibility for global warming now seems to rest almost entirely with the Freds and Mildreds of this world, as opposed to the oil companies, the auto manufacturers, and other industrial users of energy. It is also apparent that Simpson borrowed his litany of personal inconveniences from *Pain Without Gain* by the Canadian Manufacturers & Exporters.

4. Accepting Industry Statements as Fact
The *Globe and Mail* editorial of December 9, 2002 was entitled, "The Terms of Canada's Participation in Kyoto." There the *Globe* charged that Chrétien's plan to pass the Protocol before Christmas was "precipitate" and "irresponsible." The editorial ended: "Canada, if it ratifies the accord, will be the only nation in the Western Hemisphere to take on the international obligation to reduce greenhouse gases." This false statement, it would appear, was lifted directly from the pages of the *National Post* and the opinion piece appearing there by Imperial Oil's CEO.

What Was Not Covered
The Propaganda Model laid out by Edward S. Herman and Noam Chomsky proposes that bias in the media is evidenced not only in relation to what is covered and

how it is covered, but also in terms of what is omitted. Here we look briefly at some material, or possible material, that did not make the pages of the *Globe and Mail*.

- *Timothy Gardner*, Reuters, "Suncor CEO Says Prepared for Kyoto: Unhappy About It," September 5, 2003.[88] "Suncor Energy Inc. will push ahead with its marquee Canadian oil sands projects regardless of whether or not Ottawa ratifies the Kyoto Protocol on greenhouse gas reduction, its chief executive said on Thursday..."

- Articles by *Alanna Mitchell*, "Earth Sciences Reporter." Alanna Mitchell was named the best environmental reporter in the world in 2000 by the World Conservation Union and the Reuters Foundation. And in both 2000 and 2001 that organization appraised Mitchell's work as being the best environmental reporting in North America and Oceania. In a speech given at the University of Regina on January 30, 2003, she was outspoken in her insistence that "the earth's climate could be in peril if we don't change our 'dirty' habits."[89] During the period between September 3, 2002 and December 11, 2002, however, this award-winning journalist was barely evident in the pages of the *Globe and Mail* with regard to Kyoto/global warming. According to the *Globe and Mail*'s web site, Alanna Mitchell published 27 articles during this time period, of which only 10 were related to Kyoto/global warming. Of those ten, five appeared within one week of the prime minister's announcement in early September; the remaining five were spread over the ensuing 13 weeks. A number of her stories during this time period had no environmental thrust at all: "Man Killed, Two Injured in 3 Latest Shootings,"[90] "Universities Grapple With Rising Enrolment,"[91] and "CFL Players Catch Woman Leaping to Escape Fire."[92] Why did the *Globe and Mail* all but silence their high-profile Earth Sciences Reporter after the first week following the Prime Minister's announcement?

- Articles by *Martin Mittelstaedt*. Mittelstaedt is the *Globe*'s "Environment Reporter." For the period, we identified only one article in the *Globe* by Mittelstaedt dealing with Kyoto/global warming.[93] (A second article, concerning the re-death of Lake Erie, contains a one sentence reference to global warming).[94]

By contrast, business reporter Patrick Brethour (he of the ill-fated coverage of Kyoto polling) had his byline on 18 articles dealing with Kyoto, while political reporter Steven Chase authored, or helped author, 42 articles on Kyoto (7 being co-authored with Brethour). After Canada ratified the Protocol, however, Mittelstaedt was back again publishing pieces in the *Globe* related to global warming, such as:

- "Putting Out The Fires." The sub headline here states: "Canada's coal-fired power plants are in the pollution big-leagues, writes Martin Mittelstaedt, spewing out a witches' brew of contaminants that clog the air and cause acid rain..."[95]

- "World Faces Water Crisis" Here Mittelstaedt notes: "The world is facing a water crisis due to pollution, climate change and surging population growth..."[96]

- "Arctic Lakes Deemed Warmest in History"[97]

- "Global Warming May Shrink Great Lakes, Report Says"[98]

Why was Mittelstaedt all but unheard during the period of the Kyoto debate? He responded to our question as follows:

> Most of the Kyoto coverage was handled out of Ottawa and Alberta because it was seen as more of a political story. Although I've written a number of the political stories related to Kyoto over the past few years, I've written more extensively on the science of global warming, which is seen as more of an environmental story.[99]

Conclusions

1. The great bulk of the *Globe's* coverage was negative toward Kyoto. There was no "made in Canada" plan in place, so both by implication and directly the *Globe's* favourable coverage of this "alternative" was tantamount to recommending that no organized action be taken against global warming at this time.

2. Most of the *Globe's* coverage did not deal with the accord itself, nor with global warming and the environment, but focused rather on political conflicts and with economic/financial repercussions of meeting Kyoto's targets.

3. Much of the coverage centred on personality.

4. There was no attempt to quantify the benefits of Kyoto, only the costs.

5. None of the coverage explained the range of harms ("costs") from global warming. While there were a few stories describing select negative effects (melting polar ice caps, extinction of polar bears, shortening of the outdoor hockey season), no

article or articles attempted to describe the full range of environmental consequences foreseen to accompany global warming: these range from the submerging of sea coasts, to mass extinctions, to severe weather patterns including droughts, floods and storms.

6. The *Globe*'s Environment Reporter published only one piece relating (indirectly) to Kyoto/global warming during the period of policy debate. The *Globe*'s Earth Sciences Reporter fared somewhat better, but only marginally; one half of her ten pieces appeared in the week following the Prime Minister's initial announcement, just as the forces of opposition were beginning to mobilize.

7. Only one article was critical of the U.S. for withdrawing from Kyoto; it reported on the hostile reception paid to U.S. Secretary of State, Colin Powell, at the UN Earth Summit,.

8. NGO and environmental groups had very little coverage.

9. Non-believers in human-induced climate change were given inordinate space and accorded much greater credibility than was the large majority of scientists who accept global warming.

10. There is a definite pattern of denigrating concerned citizens, both with respect to their knowledge level, and their sincerity in backing an issue that may cost them personally; there is, concomitantly, a deference to business leaders.

11. Even business leaders were selectively interviewed and quoted. Scanty attention was paid to Suncor and Shell, which announced that their plans for oil exploration and investment would remain undiminished, but ample attention was given to energy executives from Imperial Oil, Talisman and EnCana, who were militantly opposed to Kyoto.

12. The thrust of the coverage was to cite opposition to Kyoto, and then, perhaps, to quote a federal defender of the Protocol.

13. When polls could be interpreted as indicating a decline in public support for Kyoto, they were accorded prominent coverage; poll results that could indicate increased support for Kyoto were scarcely reported at all.

In conclusion, there was a definite and pronounced tilt in the *Globe*'s coverage toward the position of certain business leaders, particularly of hostile executives in the energy sector. As noted, one looks in vain during this period for interviews even with executives from Suncor or Shell, whose companies were much less opposed to Kyoto than were the executives from Talisman and Imperial Oil, who received prominent attention in the pages of the *Globe*. Moreover, the paper accorded but modest attention to environmental concerns and appears even to have de-commissioned its environment reporter from writing on the issue. The "modest attention," however, while important, is easy to explain. Kyoto was a case of the Canadian government and significant portions of the business community being in opposition to one another; Kyoto became a story *because* government suddenly announced its intention to ratify the Protocol. In other words, power was divided, and the range of coverage in the *Globe* reflects divisiveness within circles of power.

Having said that, the analysis and evidence of this chapter point firmly to the *Globe's* lack of balance. We might say that while "lip-service" was paid to environmental concerns, those issues were never addressed in their full range and seriousness; the lip-service, we might speculate, served to divert attention from the overall thrust of the reporting, which was one-sided and hardly environmental.

Only seldom does an issue like Kyoto enter the public domain. Most often government and business are in much greater harmony. Where government-business consensus exists, one can anticipate even less diversity in coverage. Coverage of Kyoto is consistent with the Propaganda Model and is in accord with the media thesis set out by Harold Innis.

NOTES

1. Written with the assistance of Mary N. Babe.
2. Harold Innis, "A Plea for Time," *The Bias of Communication*, p. 79.
3. Maxwell McCombs.
4. Document available at: http://www.hgrm.com/warning.htm
5. David Suzuki, *Earth Time: Essays*. Toronto: Stoddart, 1998, p. 36.
6. David Suzuki and Holly Dressel, *From Naked Ape to Superspecies: A Personal Perspective on Humanity and the Global Eco-Crisis*, Toronto: Stoddart, 1999, p. 68.
7. David Suzuki, *Earth Time: Essays*. Toronto: Stoddart, 1998, p. 36.
8. Dallas W. Smythe, "Communications: Blindspot of Western Marxism," in *Counterclockwise: Perspectives on Communication*, edited by Thomas Guback, Boulder: Westview Press, 1994, pp. 266–291; first published in 1977.
9. CanWest Global Communications Corp., owner of the Southam chain, for example, strategically couples news items with targeted advertising. On March 29, 2003, CanWest's *National Post* ran an eight page "Body and Health" section that focused on asthma and allergies; the section was supported entirely by advertisements for Reactine, an over-the-counter asthma and allergy remedy. During the last two weeks of March 2003, CanWest's *Ottawa Citizen*, *Montreal Gazette* and other dailies ran articles on asthma and allergies above ads for Reactine.
10. Charles Clover, "Earth Summit to Study and Augment Greenhouse Gases, *National Post*, June 4, 2002, p. A1.
11. Ross McKitrick, "More Bad Science: Washington's EPA Joins Environment Canada to Produce the Same Old Story," *National Post*, June 5, 2002, p. FP 19.
12. Tom Doggett, "Bush Rejects EPA Report Blaming Humans for Global Warming," *National Post*, June 5, 2002, p. A11.

13. Jonathan Kay, "Kyoto: Both Sides Have Got It Wrong," *National Post*. June 5, 2002, p. A14.

14. Steven Edwards, "U.S. Report Acknowledges Global Warming: Washington Still Believes Tackling Global Warming on a Massive Scale Is Not Cost Effective," *National Post*, June 4, 2002, p. A2.

15. Dinyar Godrej, *The No-Nonsense Guide to Climate Change*, Toronto: New Internationalist Publications, 2001, p. 15.

16. Dinyar Godrej, *The No-Nonsense Guide to Climate Change*, Toronto: New Internationalist Publications, 2001, p. 13.

17. Actually, a "greenhouse effect" had been proposed as early as1824 by Jean-Baptiste-Joseph Fourier, but the warming induced by the Earth's atmosphere was thought to be totally benevolent for over a century. See Gale E. Christianson, *Greenhouse: The 200-Year Story of Global Warming*, Vancouver: GreyStone Books, 1999, p 12.

18. One tonne equals 1,000 kg. or 2,240 lbs.

19. Government of Canada, "Removing Carbon Dioxide: Credit for Enhancing Sinks," http://www.climatechange.gc.ca/english/whats_new/removing_e.html, July 2001.

20. Dinyar Godrej, *The No-Nonsense Guide to Climate Change*, Toronto: New Internationalist Publications, 2001, p. 20.

21. David Suzuki Foundation, "What Is The Kyoto Protocol?", 2002.
http://www.davidsuzuki.org/Climate_Change/kyoto/Kyoto_Protocol.asp

22. Alexa McDonough, "*Globe and Mail*, September 4, 2002, p. A13.

23. Canada, Department of Foreign Affairs and International Trade, "Taking Action on Climate Change," 7 Feb., 2003; http://www.dfait-maeci.gc.ca/department/focus/kyotoporotocol-en.asp

24. Government of Canada, "Canada and the Kyoto Protocol: Overview: Climate Change Affects Us All," http://www.climatechange.gc.ca/english/whats_new/overview_e.html, July 2001.

25. Tom Cohen, Associated Press, "Canada Plans Kyoto Ratification Vote As Soon As Monday, December 4, 2002, Environment News Network http://www.enn.com/news/wire-stories/2002/12/12042002/ap–49101.asp

26. Tom Cohen, Associated Press, "Canada Ratifies Kyoto Protocol Following Months of Debate," December 17, 2002, Environmental News Network
http://www.enn.com/news/wire-stories/2002/12/12172002/ap–49191.asp

27. CBC News, "Backgrounder: The Kyoto Protocol, Canada and Kyoto," September 23, 2002, http://www.cbc.ca/news/features/kyoto_canada.html

28. CBC News, "Backgrounder: The Kyoto Protocol, Canada and Kyoto," September 23, 2002, http://www.cbc.ca/news/features/kyoto_canada.html

29. Steven Chase, "Business Groups Opposed to Kyoto," *Globe and Mail*, 27 September, 2002, p. B3.; Hugh Windsor, "Oil Patch Candour Needed on Ad Campaign," *Globe and Mail*, 13 November, 2002, p. A4.

30. Imperial Oil, "Climate Change and the Kyoto Protocol," 2002, http://www.imperialoil.ca/Canada-English/News/Issues/N_I_Climate.asp

31. Imperial Oil, "Climate Change and the Kyoto Protocol," 2002, http://www.imperialoil.ca/Canada-English/News/Issues/N_I_Climate.asp

32. Tim J. Hearn, "Canada's Missing Governance on Kyoto," *National Post*, 28 November, 2002; http://www.imperialoil.ca/Canada-English/News/Issues/N–I–KyotoTJH.asp

33. Timothy Gardner, Reuters, "Suncor CEO Says Prepared for Kyoto, Unhappy About It," September 5, 2002, (Yahoo! Headlines); http://www.google.ca/search?q=cache: 3JyG8gji–yoC: ca.news.yahoo.com/020905/5/ore8. Also, Patrick Brethour and Steven Chase, "Kyoto Impact Minimal, Suncor Says," *Globe and Mail*, 10 January, 2003, p. A1.

34. Patrick Brethour, "Shell Canada to Spend Billions on Oil Sands: Says Kyoto Concerns Won't Stop Project," *Globe and Mail*, November 29, 2002, p. B3.

35. Canadian Manufacturers & Exporters, *Pain Without Gain: Canada and the Kyoto Protocol*, http://www.cme-mec.ca/kyoto/.

36. Christopher Essex and Ross McKitrick, *Taken By Storm: The Troubled Science, Policy and Politics of Global Warming*, Toronto: Key Porter Books, 2002.

37. Defined by Daniel J. Boorstin as events that take place for the purpose of being reported.

38. Steven Chase, "PM Makes Bid for Green Legacy," *Globe and Mail*, 3 September, 2002, p. A1.

39. Alanna Mitchell, "Klein Prepares Battle Over Kyoto," *Globe and Mail*, 4 September, 2002, p. A4.

40. Steven Chase and Jill Mahoney, "Albertans Turn Against Kyoto in Poll," *Globe and Mail*, 8 October, 2002, p. A1.

41. Steven Chase and Jill Mahoney, "Ottawa Pegs Kyoto Job Risk at 200,000," Globe and Mail, 25 September, 2002, p. A1.

42. Dale Marshall, "Stop Whining: Kyoto Equals Jobs," *Globe and Mail*, 10 September, 2002, p. A17.

43. Patrick Brethour, "Another Oil Sands Firm Cuts Back, Blaming Kyoto," *Globe and Mail*, 7 November, 2002, p. B1.

44. September 4, 2002.

45. October 5, 2002, p. F7.

46. October 18, 2002, p. A4.

47. November 7, 2002, p. A9.

48. November 28, 2002, p. A11.

49. November 18, 2002, p. A17.

50. November 28, 2002, p. A21.

51. December 6, 2002, p. A25.

52. December 7, 2002, p. A31.

53. December. 7, 2002, p. A18

54. September 20, 2002, p. A7.

55. September 9, 2002, p. A13.

56. September 28, 2002, p. A25.

57. November 18, 2002, p. B2

58. November 19, 2002, p. A21.

59. November 29, 2002, p. B2.

60. December 2, 2002, p. A23.

61. 1 November, 2002, p. A9.

62. John Ibbitson, "Alberta Can't Beat Ottawa in Battle of Kyoto," *Globe and Mail*, 3 September, 2002, p. A1.

63. Alanna Mitchell, "Kyoto Investment Can Pay Off," *Globe and Mail*, 7 September, 22002, p. A8.

64. Eric Reguly, "EnCana CEO's Urge to Kill Kyoto Is Misguided," *Globe and Mail*, 14 September, 2002, p. B6.

65. John Ibbitson, "Good Grief! Kyoto Might Actually Be Good," *Globe and Mail*, October 10, 2002, p. A23.

66. Barrie McKenna, "Despite the Hazy Debate, Kyoto May Be Just What Canada Needs," *Globe and Mail*, 20 September 2002, p. B10.

67. Alanna Mitchell, "Ottawa, Conservationists Disagree on Earth Summit Results," *Globe and Mail*, 4 September, 2002, p. A4.

68. Roger Phillips, "Kyoto: The Wrong Note to Go Out On," *Globe and Mail*, 5 September, 2002, p. A19.

69. Steven Chase, "EnCana Chief to PM: Kill Kyoto," *Globe and Mail*, 12 September, 2002, p. B1.

70. Steven Chase, "PM Makes Bid for Green Legacy," *Globe and Mail*, 3 September, 2002, p. A1;

71. *Globe and Mail*, "Canada Confronts Kyoto Challenge, editorial, 5 September, 2002, p. A20.

72. Patrick Brethour, "Alberta Planning National Tech Site on Emissions," *Globe and Mail*, 27 September, 2002, p. B3.

73. Margaret Wente, "The Kyoto-Speak Brainwashers," *Globe and Mail*, December 7, 2002, p. A23.

74. Sallie Baliunas, Tim Patterson, and Allan M. R. MacRae, "Climate Change is Natural: Believe the Science, Not the Rhetoric, We Aren't Causing Global Warming, Say Scientists," *Globe and Mail*, November 19, 2002, p. A21.

75. Sallie Baliunas, Tim Patterson, and Allan M. R. MacRae, "Climate change is Natural: Believe the Science, Not the Rhetoric, We Aren't Causing Global Warming, Say Scientists," *Globe and Mail*, November 19, 2002, p. A21.

76. Andrew Baines, 'Hot air on Kyoto,' letter to editor, *Globe and Mail*, 28 November, 2002, p. A22.

77. Thomas Homer-Dixon, Karl Braganza, James Risbey, and David Karoly, "Kyoto Skeptics Miss the Point," *Globe and Mail*, November 28, 2002, p. A21.

78. Steven Chase and Jill Mahoney, "Albertans Turn Against Kyoto in Poll," *Globe and Mail*, October 8, 2002, p. A1.

79. Patrick Brethour, "Support for Kyoto Plunges," *Globe and Mail*, November 2, 2002

80. Andrew Chung, "Alberta's Kyoto Poll 'Fraudulent': Anderson," *Toronto Star*, November 5, 2002, p. A7.

81. Gloria Galloway, "Kyoto Backer Lambastes Klein, Eves," *Globe and Mail*, 6 November, 2002, p. A5.

82. Jill Mahoney, "Ipsos-Reid Lashes Out At Critics of Kyoto Poll" *Globe and Mail*, November 7, 2002, p. A9.

83. Ipsos-Reid, Press Release, "Activist and CITY TV Commentator, Bob Hunter, Issues Full Retraction and Apology to Ipsos-Reid for Remarks Made on Kyoto Poll," November 8, 2002.

84. Darrell Bricker, "The Kyoto Numbers," *Globe and Mail*, 7 November, 2002, p. A24.

85. Hugh Windsor, "Questions Lurk Beneath Surface of ads on Kyoto," *Globe and Mail*, 8 November, 2002, p. A4; Steven Chase, "Information About Kyoto Insufficient," *Globe and Mail*, 9 November, 2002, p. A12.

86. Jeffrey Simpson, "When They Poll the No-Nothings," *Globe and Mail*, December 11, 2002, p. A21.

87. Ian Brown, "The Kyoto Stampede," *Globe and Mail*, 26 October, 2002, p. F1.

88. Yahoo News Canada, http://www.google.ca/search?q=cache:3JyG8gji_yoC:ca.news.yahoo.com/02905/5/ore8

89. Karla Paragg, "Globe and Mail Journalist Offers the Goods on Kyoto," *The Manitoban*, 12 February 2003.

90. November 11, 2002.

91. November 11, 2002.

92. September 23, 2002.

93. Martin Mittelstaedt, "Firms Breaking Promises on Emissions, Study Says," *Globe and Mail*, 18 October, 2002, p. A4.

94. Martin Mittelstaedt, "Dead in the Water," *Globe and Mail*, 5 October, 2002, p. F1.

95. *Globe and Mail*, March 15, 2003.

96. *Globe and Mail*, March 5, 2003;

97. *Globe and Mail*, April 8, 2003, p. A121.

98. *Globe and Mail*, April 9, 2003, p. A17.

99. E-mail to Robert Babe from Martin Mittelstaedt, dated May 13, 2003.

Chapter Nine

Behind The Invisible Curtain Of Scholarly Criticism: Revisiting The Propaganda Model[1]

Jeffery Klaehn

SOME COMMENTATORS HAVE CRITICIZED the propaganda model for advancing a [perceived] conspiratorial view of media. As Rai correctly points out, the conspiracy theory criticism is 'very common.'[2] That having been said, it is also very problematic, for myriad reasons. The term—conspiracy—implies secret controls that are divorced from normal institutional channels. This is precisely the opposite of that which the propaganda model actually argues. As Herman and Chomsky stress quite clearly at the outset of *Manufacturing Consent*, the propaganda model constitutes a 'free market analysis' of media, 'with the results largely the outcome of the working of market forces.'[3] The conspiracy theory critique conveniently ignores the fact that the propaganda model is a structural model, one that explains patterns of media behavior in terms of normal institutional imperatives.[4] To those who are academically and/or politically opposed to such an analysis, which highlights the ways in which power pervades and structures various social processes, the conspiracy theory label is a convenient means by which to dismiss the propaganda model and its explanatory logic out of hand.

Some critique constitutes a hybrid of criticism and personal attack. One commentator, for instance, asserts that '*manufacturing* consent and certainly *propaganda* imply not just objective irresponsibility on the part of the media [sic], but intent to ignore alternative points of view and manipulate the public. Furthermore...Chomsky and Herman's functionalist imagery is fraught with implications about intent. The implication is clear: the propaganda model is often framed in conspiratorial terms. That Herman and Chomsky deny it is surprising, given that Chomsky is a linguist. It just goes to show that self-interest can warp even brilliant minds!'[5]

Herman and Chomsky cede that deliberate intent is sometimes an intervening factor that can have intended and unintended outcomes, depending upon the
specific case, but their model does not assume conspiracy. Rather, it highlights the
relationship between patterns of media behavior and institutional imperatives.
Clearly the preferred theoretic explanations associated with the model do not assume and/or rely upon conspiracy. Chomsky comments that 'With equal logic,
one could argue that an analyst of General Motors who concludes that its managers try to maximize profits (instead of selflessly laboring to satisfy the needs of the
public) is adopting a conspiracy theory.'[6] The propaganda model, then, assumes
'self-censorship' without coercion and contends that media discourse ought to be
explained in structural terms. If there is conspiracy, it is only conspiracy in the
sense that dominant social institutions routinely make decisions designed to facilitate their own interests.

> The term 'conspiracy theory' is particularly revealing. I've always ex-
> plicitly and forcefully opposed 'conspiracy theories,' and even am well
> known for that...My work (and Ed Herman's, and others') is about as
> much a conspiracy theory as a study of GM that suggests that its man-
> agement seeks to maximize profit and market share. But to the intellec-
> tual classes, to suggest that institutional factors enter into policy is like
> waving a red flag in front of a bull—for very good reasons.[7]

Herman comments that the propaganda model ought to be 'subjected to a test of
evidence,' stresses that 'intent is an unmeasureable red herring' and acknowledges
that critics of the propaganda model included 'liberal and academic media analysts
of the left' following the initial 1988 publication of *Manufacturing Consent*.[8]

To contend that the propaganda model implies conspiracy is to take economies with the truth at the expense of intellectual honesty. The conspiracy theory
label, is precisely that, a label, employed by political and theoretical opponents of
the model as a mechanism utilized to call into question the very legitimacy of the
model. The conspiracy theory criticism is thus completely without merit.

Emphasizing Structural Elements of Social Organization

Critics of the propaganda model have also commented upon a [perceived] tendency
to impose meanings upon newsroom workers and editors from without, while
presuming micro-processes that the model does not directly test. Similar criticism
has been leveled against virtually every macro sociological theoretical perspective
where the focus is on various structural elements of social organization. That is,

because the propaganda model is a structural model, it is not concerned to analyze the practical, mundane or organizational aspects of newsroom work.

Within mainstream sociology, structural models such as structural-functionalism and conflict theory have been tagged with similar criticism simply because these perspectives tend to focus overwhelmingly upon structural elements as opposed to the various micro processes which in turn are the principle concern for other schools of thought within the discipline. Conflict theory is not concerned per se with the sense-making practices of actors (ethnomethodology) whereas structural-functionalism is not concerned to explicate ways in which actors recreate the social world in and through their everyday interactions (social construction). There are numerous additional examples available. Such 'shortcomings,' while surely mentionable, derive from the overall theoretical framework adopted by the various models or perspectives in question, and do not lessen the utility of these models; they simply highlight that various schools of thought have divergent levels of analytical emphasis and focus.

Within the social sciences, macro structural models exist alongside models with a micro-emphasis, resulting in a non-dogmatic multi-perspective discipline with a multiplicity of focus. As noted below, however, critics of the propaganda model, such as Canadian sociologist Peter Archibald, have nonetheless saw fit to assail the propaganda model for not studying micro-processes. Implicit in such critique is, of course, the expectation that the propaganda model should account for more than its formulators actually designed it to do and accomplish.

Underlying such critique is the unreasonable expectation that the propaganda model ought to explain everything, in every context. If this 'standard' were applied universally, to every theoretic model within the social sciences, we would presumably have reason to dismiss every theoretic perspective in one felt swoop, regardless of their utility in fostering an understanding of various recurring patterns which are empirically specifiable. Often, criticisms of the propaganda model are telling devoid of any discussion of available evidence, which tends overwhelmingly to lend significant legitimacy to the model's preferred theoretic explanation(s) for patterns of media behavior.

Critics who allege that the propaganda model is not valid because it does not study micro-processes typically note that the model's explanatory logic is predicated upon a preconceived notion of how power and structural elements pervade subjectivity and consciousness.[9] How can the model and its proponents make any inferences whatsoever pertaining to perceived patterns of media behavior without directly studying micro-processes, the critic might ask. Such critiques are either applying standards selectively or betraying a complete failure to understand how models actually *work* within the social sciences.

Like other theoretic models, the propaganda model begins with a set of assumptions from which various hypotheses are derived, which in turn can be tested empirically. To my mind, this is a strength of the model. It offers an analytical, conceptual framework, one that is concerned to theorize the operation of power in relation to dominant structural elements. The model predicts a correlation between patterns of media behavior and broader institutional and market imperatives, and is oriented toward empirical research. It affords its own methodological techniques which may be utilized in 'testing' its various substantive predictions/hypotheses vis-à-vis consideration of 'boundaries of the expressible' and 'paired examples' in media discourse.

Analogous to the Gatekeeper Model?

Some critics have likened the propaganda model to the 'gatekeeper model' of media. The analogy is flawed. The propaganda model does not assume that media personnel routinely make conscious decisions to align themselves with the interests of elites. It is a structural model and subsequently does not theorize social psychological processes. The propaganda model's overarching concern with power and social class firmly distinguish it from the gatekeeper model.

Despite the gatekeeper model's theoretic inadequacies, Hackett states that it is an appropriate description of the work that newspaper editors actually do 'with regard to news about national and international affairs: They select and disseminate, rather than generate, such news.'[10]

The propaganda model, however, does not predict that news personnel are necessarily 'plotting' how to cover some stories as opposed to others, and so forth, but that meanings are filtered by constraints that are essentially built into the system, such that conscious decisions are typically understood as commonsense.[11]

At the outset of *Manufacturing Consent*, Herman and Chomsky comment that:

> The elite domination of the media and marginalization of dissidents that results from the operation of these filters occurs so naturally that media news people, frequently operating with complete integrity and goodwill, are able to convince themselves that they choose and interpret news "objectively" and on the basis of professional news values.[12]

There is a range of literature devoted to the sociology of news and social construction of reality which addresses and attempts to provide explanations for the various 'intervening processes' which the propaganda model does not theorize.[13] Similarly, there are a range of studies which examine professionalism as ideology and others which devote themselves to intervening processes in general, exploring ways in which ownership, advertising values and corporate influence impact news production.[14] There is also a range of literature which challenges traditional elite theories of media.[15] Although Herman and Chomsky have at various times both written about intervening processes, as noted, the propaganda model proper is firmly a structural model, and as such is concerned with the question of how structural elements influence output, and not concerned, *per se*, with micro-scale processes.

Failure to Theorize Audience Effects?

The propaganda model does not theorize audience effects. It does, however, analyze the extent to which discourse is framed so as to produce or not preferred or 'privileged' interpretations which in turn can be seen to be ideologically serviceable. In doing so, the model does not deny that audiences read media texts in complex ways, nor does it imply that audiences construct meanings in ways that are passive, and not negotiated. What it does do is highlight the fact that perception, awareness and understanding are informed and constrained by the structure of the discourse in question. Some commentators would suggest otherwise. Canadian sociologist Graham Knight, for instance, argues that: 'All interpretations are unavoidably selective and they are informed only to a degree by the structure of the discourse that is being interpreted.'[16] In my view, such theorizing can be seen to be both politically and ideologically inflected. Other scholars contend that media are highly influential in this context.[17] One commentator, for instance, notes that:

> While it is certainly the case that people are not passive receivers of media information (that they may "decode" things in different ways), media texts are nonetheless encoded in very specific ways—they valorize certain voices over others, certain sources over others, as Herman and Chomsky suggest in one of their filters.[18]

In addition, it bears noting that the propaganda model itself does not set out to study audience effects, nor have its formulators ever claimed that media discourse ensures certain 'effects' or outcomes. In fact, as will be noted presently, quite the opposite is actually the case.

To criticize the model for failing to scrutinize that which it was not designed to explore, investigate or assess is perhaps analogous to condemning a book for failing to failing to provide surround sound. The propaganda model does not set out to study effects, nor do its formulators make any claims indicating that the propaganda model unilaterally presumes certain effects. This does not make the model *incomplete,* nor does it imply that the model presumes deliberate intent.

While the words *'propaganda'* and *'manufacture'* may be seen to imply a degree of conscious, deliberate intent, any serious scholar who has actually given careful consideration to the writings of Herman and Chomsky should cede that the model does not presume or theorize effects *or* imply conspiracy.

The propaganda model focuses upon how structural factors influence media discourse and as a result of its macro, structural focus, it (quite consciously and deliberately) is unconcerned with various micro-processes (such as the question of effects). This having been said, the periodic intentionality evident in the language Chomsky sometimes uses—evident in the use of words such as 'manufacture' and/or 'control' and in phrases such as 'brainwashing [under freedom]' —affords grounds for criticism on style if not substance. Concurrently, such language implies a degree of *taken-for-grantedness* with regard to consequent effects, which again avails the model to criticism on style. As will be noted below, however, the propaganda model does not presuppose effects, nor does it predict that audiences do not engage various forms of media in complex, non-negotiated ways. The model is concerned with the question of how the interrelations of state, corporate capitalism and the corporate media can be seen to influence media content. It is toward this end that the methodological techniques associated with the model are specifically oriented.

Any model within the social sciences can be said to have 'blind spots.' The question is, to what degree do these seriously lessen the utility of the model in question? Insofar at the propaganda model is concerned, the answer is not at all. The utility of the model stands. The matter of audience effects is not one that is within its own overall purview. As noted, however, there are a range of studies which do assess effects.

That media *do* have various effects is fairly uncontroversial. A range of scholars stress that media are both culturally and politically influential.[19] James Winter writes that, 'Instead of offering diverse perspectives on events and issues, the corporate media portray an increasingly myopic and orthodox picture of the world around us. The consistency with which they do this has its consequent, intended effect on public opinion and policy formation.'[20]

Taking Ruling-Class Interests and Media Audiences for Granted?

Another criticism of the propaganda model that has been seized upon by its critics pertains to the model's theoretic assumptions regarding the existence of a unified ruling class. Knight argues that the propaganda model 'tends to take notions like ruling-class interests for granted as given and non-problematic. The only important ideological cleavage is the one between the ruling class and the people.'[21] Knight comments further, stating that 'This not only implies that the people are relatively easily manipulated, it also assumes that their interests are relatively homogeneous and non-problematic too.'[22] This view can be seen to derive from a misreading of the model.

First, as will be noted below, Herman and Chomsky's model does not assume or imply that the public is 'easily manipulated,' as Knight derisively suggests, nor does the model predict that the myriad (geo)political-economic interests of dominant elites are 'relatively homogeneous' to the extent that these are marked by total unification. Herman writes that 'the propaganda model does start from the premise that a critical political-economy will put front and center the analysis of the locus of media control and the mechanisms by which the powerful are able to dominate the flow of messages and limit the space of contesting parties. The limits on their power are certainly important, but why should they get first place, except as a means of minimizing the power of the dominant interests, inflating the elements of contestation, and pretending that the marginalized have more strength than they really possess?'[23]

It is true that the propaganda model does not highlight instances when non-elites have influenced mainstream media,[24] but this does not undermine the model being advanced by Herman and Chomsky.

Moreover,

> The market consist of numerous corporations that organize and plan to achieve their narrow goals, and which have been steadily growing in size, global reach and power. At home, they and their political allies are well funded and active; externally, institutions like the IMF, World Bank, the GATT-based World Trade Organization, and the world's governments, work on their behalf. Individual powerlessness grows in the face of the globalizing market; meanwhile, labor unions and other support organizations of ordinary citizens have been under siege and have weakened...In this context, could anything be more perverse politically and intellectually than a retreat to micro-analysis, the celebration of minor

individual triumphs, and reliance on solutions based on individual actions alone?[25]

The propaganda model cedes that the powerful have individual objectives and stresses that these are typically manifest in disagreements over tactics. However, the model assumes that elite institutional sectors have myriad common political, economic and ideological interests. Its conception of the ideological process has much in common with the 'class-based' model of power outlined by Domhoff in *The Powers That Be: Processes of Ruling Class Domination in America.*[26]

The propaganda model's conception of social organization is entirely consistent with analyses demonstrating that corporate concentration and monopoly ownership are undeniable realities.[27] One can infer on fairly logical grounds that contradictions and divergent interests that exist within and between elite sectors are eclipsed by common interests and overlapping institutional interests.[28] In translation, this view of social organization is germane to classical Marxian theory.

As noted, the propaganda model highlights evident correlations between patterns of media behavior and broader institutional and market imperatives. Herman provides a succinct overview of the central 'filter' elements and notes that the close inter-relationships between media and corporations and in turn polity give way to 'a certain degree of solidarity':

> The crucial structural factors derive from the fact that the dominant media are firmly embedded in the market system. They are profit-seeking businesses, owned by very wealthy people (or other companies); they are funded largely by advertisers who are also profit-seeking entities, and who want their ads to appear in a supportive selling environment. The media are also dependent on government and other major business firms as information sources, and both efficiency and political considerations, and frequently overlapping interests, cause a certain degree of solidarity to prevail among the government, major media, and other corporate businesses.[29]

As noted, the assumptions which give rise to the propaganda model's theoretic underpinnings can be seen to be firmly in agreement with the conception of social organization advanced by conflict or political-economic theory within mainstream sociology. The propaganda model assumes that elites are over-represented in government and big business sectors and are the major initiators of action in society. It presumes elites dominate economic and governmental decision-making processes, and assumes that elite sectors share common interests that are largely integrated. For the record, however, Herman and Chomsky do not simply take ruling class interests for granted, as Knight implies. At the outset of *Manufacturing Consent* the authors clearly stated that 'Where the powerful are in disagreement, there will be a certain diversity in tactical judgements on how to attain shared aims, reflected in media debate. But views that challenge fundamental premises or suggest that the observed modes of exercise of state power are based on systematic factors will be excluded from the mass media even when elite controversy over tactics rages fiercely.'[30] Herman and Chomsky suggest that a careful and thorough reading of the major mass media will bear this out and hold that the illusion of genuine debate serves to strengthen the overall 'propaganda system.'[31]

Regarding Knight's claim that the propaganda model implies that the public are akin to 'cultural dopes' and are rather easily manipulated, nothing could be further from the truth.[32] The propaganda model does not imply that media are monolithic, nor does it ignore dissent. Herman and Chomsky had stressed this point in the final pages of *Manufacturing Consent*, writing that 'Government and elite domination of the media have not succeeded in overcoming Vietnam syndrome and public hostility to direct U.S. involvement in the destabilization and overthrow of other foreign governments.'[33] Elsewhere, in the pages of *Necessarily Illusions*, the ability of media audiences to resist and 'defend' against manipulation is taken up yet again, when Chomsky discusses 'intellectual self-defense.'[34]

Chomsky describes the propaganda system as inherently unstable and writes specifically about dissent culture in *Media Control: The Spectacular Achievements of Propaganda*.[35] Herman has often made the point that the propaganda model describes the propaganda system in action, and makes no claim to how effective it may or may not be.[36]

Clearly, then, the assertion that the propaganda model takes media audiences 'for granted' is problematic and, as a critique, highly dubious and less than intellectually honest.

As a means of dismissing the propaganda model from scholarly debates on media performance, however, it continues to be utilized.

The PM—Highly Deterministic?

Another criticism which has been leveled against the propaganda model is that the model is highly deterministic.[37] As noted, the model argues that elite media interlock with other institutional sectors in ownership, management and social circles. These various interlocks, it is concluded, impact the ability of media to remain analytically detached from other dominant institutional sectors. The propaganda model argues that this results in self-censorship without any significant coercion.

Critics alleging determinism presumably fail to subscribe to the reality of social scientific research in that virtually every model involves elements that to various degrees one could baldly refer to as *deterministic*. Certainly the propaganda model is not deterministic in the sense that it presupposes that media are monolithic or entirely closed to debate or period displays of critical dissent. Herman replies specifically to critics who allege determinism and contends that 'critics wisely stick to generalities and offer no critical detail or alternative model; when they do, the results are not impressive.'[38]

Other scholars contend that media are far more pluralistic and far less determined. I will provide one specific example to illustrate. In their essay, 'Framing the Forests: Corporations, the British Columbia Forestry Alliance, and the Media,' which appears in *Organizing Dissent*, Doyle, Elliot and Tindall state that 'media are more open, pluralistic and diverse than the more pessimistic dominant ideology thesis suggests.'[39] The authors go on to suggest that instrumentalist analyses of patterns of media behavior are 'conspiratorial' and (by virtue of default?) somehow less 'sophisticated' than are more pluralistic accounts.[40] These claim statements appear at the outset of their article. What struck me as interesting is that there was no attempt to conceal the ideologized nature of the claims. A theoretic agenda is simply advanced. An alternative model is derisively mischaracterized. The matter, apparently closed with that, is accorded no further comment. Evidence advanced by a range of scholars which reveals the extent to which media content *is* in fact severely constrained by market forces and structures of ownership is conveniently ignored.[41]

This criticism is echoed in *News and Dissent* by Robert Hackett who writes that 'Media are not mere instruments in the hands of particular elites.'[42] I reply to this implicit criticism of the propaganda model by providing a quote from Conrad Black's chief executive officer in which the CEO speaks to the matter of ensuring that the editorial content of Conrad Black's six hundred newspapers will concur with the owner's ideological views: 'If editors disagree with us, they should disagree with us when they're no longer in our employ. The buck stops with ownership. I am responsible for meeting payroll. Therefore, I will determine what the papers say, and how they're going to be run.'[43] Add to this Conrad Black's own telling remark: 'If the small guy's guardian is the media, the small guy is in bigger trouble than I thought.'[44] Now, consider Doyle, Elliot and Tindall's conclusions regarding media constraints: 'Despite the political economy of news media, they [media] are far from being simply an ideological apparatus for capital, as some prominent accounts suggest...'[45] Clearly, there is an observable dichotomy between *reality* and its *representations* as advanced by pluralistic accounts. To my mind, such accounts invariably serve an ideological function, by obfuscating reality rather than revealing.

Interestingly, Hackett states that his own research revealed that openings and opportunities for critical discourse are created by 'contradictions and leaks' within the system.[46] Hackett concludes by noting that oppositional discourse and dissent are more likely to find expression in media when certain 'conditions' are met:

> When it speaks from within the "we" group that the news addresses, when it accepts rather than challenges fundamental ideological and cultural assumptions about the values of liberalism and Western civilization, when it criticizes individual state policies or responds to previous news events rather than offers wholesale alternatives, when it speaks the language of legitimized expertise, and when it can mobilize discourses recognized as authoritative within the framework of a broadly liberal and modernist culture.[47]

These conditions favor the explanatory logic advanced by the propaganda model, thus giving the game away in favor of the propaganda model. And I will dare to go further: each of these 'premises' essentially restate the propaganda model's own general assumptions.

Revisiting the Propaganda Model: A Brief Overview

The propaganda model highlights the multiplicity of ways in which money and power can be seen to influence overall media performance. Its formulators charge that media interests and choices routinely 'amount to propaganda campaigns' and the model they put forth can be seen to highlight the fact that dominant media share close interlocks and common interests with other institutional sectors.

Herman and Chomsky offer clear methodological techniques with which to test the substantive hypotheses advanced by the propaganda model.[48] The method most favored by Chomsky in his lucid and voluminous writings on U.S. foreign policy is to explore the 'boundaries of the expressible' or range of permitted opinion on central topics.[49] A first order prediction of the propaganda model is that media interests and choices will reflect the myriad political, economic and ideological interests of power. The model's thesis, that consent in a free society is manufactured via the manipulation of public opinion, challenges the mythology that media are dedicated to the public interest and bespeaks journalistic self-censorship in an era in which corporate ownership and advertising values are increasingly prevalent influences on news production processes.

The propaganda model implies that media serve a legitimizing function on a range of issues: globalization, domestic social and economic policies, distribution of power and resources, and systematic structural inequalities pervading a range of central issues and topics that are generally speaking of wide concern. The model highlights fundamental inequalities deriving from unequal distribution of resources and power within democratic societies and stresses that media can be seen to facilitate specific interests, such that *MediaThink* (James Winter's phrase) becomes akin to 'commonsense.'[50]

In the original preface to *Animal Farm*, penned in the 1940s, George Orwell had reflected upon literary self-censorship within Great Britain. 'Anyone who challenges the prevailing orthodoxy finds himself silenced with surprising effectiveness. A genuinely unfashionable opinion is almost never given a fair hearing, either in the popular press or in the highbrow periodicals,' Orwell wrote at the time.[51] This was the case, he reasoned, precisely because media ownership within Britain was highly concentrated. Again, to quote Orwell directly: 'The British press is extremely centralized, and most of it is owned by wealthy men who have every motive to be dishonest on certain important topics.'[52] Chomsky often cites a statement made by John Jay—'Those who own the country ought to govern it'—to illustrate the conception of democracy which underlies neo-conservative dogmas prevalent today.[53] Hence, the need for what Chomsky refers to as *necessary illusions*.[54] Chomsky comments, 'we're subject to the democracy of the marketplace.'[55]

> This is a game for elites, it's not for the ignorant masses, who have to be marginalized, diverted, and controlled—of course for their own good.[56]

Conclusion

Whereas the first order predictions of the propaganda model are concerned with observable patterns of media behavior, the second and third order predictions pertain to the ideologized spectrums of opinion within the broader intellectual culture.[57] Chomsky comments that the propaganda model will be excluded from scholarly debates on patterns of media performance because 'it questions the factual assumption that is most serviceable to the interests of established power: namely, that the media are cantankerous, perhaps excessively so. However well-confirmed the model may be, then, it is inadmissible, and, the model predicts, should remain outside the spectrum of debate over media. Note that the model has a rather disconcerting feature. Plainly, it is either valid or invalid. If invalid, it may be dismissed; if valid, it will be dismissed.'[58]

That the propaganda model typically *is* assailed, mis-characterized and often excluded from scholarly debates on media would appear to be supportive of the model's second and third order predictions. Chomsky comments that 'By and large, the possibility of studying the functioning of the media in terms of a propaganda model is simply ignored.'[59] Again, to quote Orwell's original preface to *Animal Farm*, 'Unpopular ideas can be silenced, and inconvenient facts kept in the dark, without the need for any official ban.'[60] Orwell was referring to Great Britain and wrote this in the 1940s.[61] Chomsky remarks that the propaganda model refers to 'a stage of propaganda well beyond anything that Orwell imagined.'[62] 'What you face here is a very different kind of ideological control, because one can remain under the impression that censorship does not exist, and in a narrow technical sense that is correct,' Chomsky[63] comments: 'You will not be imprisoned if you discover the facts, not even if you proclaim them whenever you can. But the results remain much the same as if there were real censorship.'[64]

In replying to several critiques that have been leveled against the propaganda model, this chapter has sought to bring the model firmly into the realm of scholarly debate, to dispel various antiquated *(and decidedly unnecessary)* illusions, and, of course, to facilitate and encourage further discussion on the topic.

NOTES

1. First published in *Journalism Studies*, Volume 4, Number 3, 2003, 359-369. Reprinted with permission. http://www.tandf.co.uk/journals/titles/1461670X.asp
2. Milan Rai, *Chomsky's Politics* (New York: Verso, 1995), 42.
3. Edward S. Herman and Noam Chomsky, *Manufacturing Consent: The Political Economy of the Mass Media* (New York: Pantheon, 1988, 2002), xii.
4. See Rai, 43.
5. Dr. Peter Archibald, Sociology, McMaster University, Hamilton, Ontario. Personal correspondence, Nov 2001.
6. Noam Chomsky, *Towards a New Cold War: Essays on the current crisis and how we got there* (London: Sinclair Brown, 1982), p. 94.
7. Noam Chomsky. Personal correspondence, Dec 8, 1998.
8. Ed Herman, 'The Propaganda Model Revisited,' *Monthly Review* (July); reprinted online at http://musictravel.free.fr/political/political7.htm
9. For instance, Archibald writes that Herman and Chomsky 'themselves claim that micro theorizing about the beliefs and motivations of editors and reporters and empirical studies to verify one of another set of intervening processes are of little interest to them, because their model is a structural model which does not depend upon any one of these sets of comments. To wit,

the individuals who, in Althusserian terminology, "carry" or "bear" the structured social processes may deliberately avoid topics or only give one point of view on them; they may instead genuinely believe in what they are doing; or they may believe otherwise, but feel they have no choice but to do what business, governments, etc., want them to do. This is not inferring structural processes from social psychological ones; rather, it says the latter are irrelevant for the former, or, at least, that any one of the three types of intervening processes just outlined will produce the same, structured outcome. In other words, it may be intentional, unintentional, or even counter-intentional. At a minimum, I would argue, and others as well, that such an explanation is incomplete, since there has to be some way that humans make structured outcomes occur, but the PM neither tells us which is most important, nor provides evidence for the answer.' Personal correspondence, Nov 2001. It bears noting, in translation, again, that any model within the social sciences may be criticized for providing 'explanations' which are in some fashion 'incomplete.' That is, no one model or theoretical perspective, even the most powerful and compelling, capture, account for, define or 'explain' every aspect of social life. Indeed. Postmodern theorists have developed a whole school of thought around this axiom. This is to say, simply, that the utility of various schools of thought within the disciplines is not commonly seen to be contingent upon how well the theoretical model in question explains 'everything,' in every context. Such criticism is simply a straw person. Moreover, Chomsky and Herman quite clearly detail those (structural) elements that [in their view] are the most central determinants in shaping patterns of media behavior. These are the five inter-related 'filter' constraints outlined in the first chapter of the first edition of *Manufacturing Consent*. Insofar as the matter of 'evidence' is concerned, an intellectually honest assessment would at least acknowledge that the authors provide a plethora of evidence, in the form of often exhaustively footnoted text, in support of the various hypotheses which they first advanced in *Manufacturing Consent*.

10. Robert Hackett, *News and Dissent: the press and the politics of peace in Canada* (Norwood, N.J.: Ablex, 1991), 98.

11. James Winter, *Common Cents: Media Portrayal of the Gulf War and Other Events* (Montreal: Black Rose, 1992), 44.

12. Herman and Chomsky, 1988, 2.

13. See H. Gans, *Deciding What's News* (New York: Pantheon, 1979); Gaye Tuchman, *Making News: a study in the social construction of reality* (New York: Free Press, 1978); Gadi Wolfsfeld, *Media and Political Conflict* (Cambridge: Cambridge University Press, 1997); Rai, 44.

14. Edward S. Herman, *Triumph of the Image: Essays on Economics, Politics and the Media* (Boston: South End, 1995); Jeffery Klaehn, 'A Critical Review and Assessment of Herman and Chomsky's "Propaganda Model"' in the *European Journal of Communication* (Sage), 2002, Vol. 17(2):147-182; Jeffery Klaehn, 'Corporate Hegemony: A Critical Assessment of the *Globe and Mail's News Coverage of Near-Genocide in Occupied East Timor 1975-1980*' in *Gazette: The International Journal of Communication Studies* (Sage), 2002, Vol. 64(4):301-321; James Winter, *Common Cents: Media Portrayal of the Gulf War and Other Events* (Montreal: Black Rose, 1992); James Winter, *Democracy's Oxygen: How the Corporations Control the News*. Second edition. (Montreal: Black Rose, 1998); James Winter, 'Media Think: The Role of the Media in Supporting the Establishment' in *Canadian Communications: Issues in Contemporary Media and Culture*. Edited by Bohdan Szuchewycz and Jeannette Sloniowski (Toronto: Prentice Hall, 2000); James Winter, *MediaThink*. (Montreal: Black Rose, 2002).

15. J. Curran and J. Seaton, *Power Without Responsibility: The Press and Broadcasting in Britain*, Second edition (London: Methuen, 1985); John Fiske, (1987) 'British Cultural Studies and Television' in *Channels of Discourse: Television and Contemporary Criticism*, R. Allen, ed. (North Carolina: University of North Carolina Press, 1987), ch. 8; L. C. Grossberg, Nelson, and P. Treichler (eds.), *Cultural Studies* (New York: Routledge, 1991); S. J. Sherwood, P. Smith, and J.C. Alexander "The British Are Coming...Again! The Hidden Agenda of 'Cultural Studies.' " *Contemporary Sociology*, 1993, 22, 3 (May):370-375; G. Turner, *British Cultural Studies: An Introduction* (Boston: Unwin Hyman, 1990).

16. Dr. Graham Knight, Sociology, McMaster University, Hamilton, Ontario. Personal correspondence, Feb 2, 2001.

17. G. C. Gunn, *A Critical View of Western Journalism and Scholarship on East Timor* (Sydney: Journal of Contemporary Asian Studies, 1994); Edward S. Herman and Gerry O'Sullivan, " 'Terrorism' as Ideology and Cultural Industry" in *Western State Terrorism*. Alexander George, ed. (New York: Routledge) 1991), 39-75; John McMurtry, *Unequal Freedoms: The Global Market as an Ethical System* (Toronto: Garamond Press, 1998); Joyce Nelson, *Sultans of Sleeze: Public Relations and the Mass Media* (Toronto: Between the Lines, 1989); Sharon Scharfe, *Complicity: Human Rights in Canadian Foreign Policy - The Case of East Timor* (Montreal: Black Rose, 1996); Katherine Sender and Sut Jhally, *The Myth of the Liberal Media: The Propaganda Model of News.* [Film] Produced and directed by Katherine Sender. Executive Producer and director, Sut Jhally (Media Education Foundation: North Hampton, Massachussetts, 1997), Winter, *Common Cents*; Winter, *Democracy's Oxygen*; Winter, *MediaThink*.

18. Dr. Valerie Scatamburlo-D'Annibale, Communications, University of Windsor, Personal correspondence, Nov 8, 2001.

19. See Wallace Clement, *Canadian Corporate Elite: Analysis of Economic Power* (Toronto: McClelland and Stewart, 1975), 278-1; Bernard Cohen, *The Press and Foreign Policy* (Princeton, N.J.: Princeton University Press, 1963), 15; Murray Dobbin, *The Myth of the Good Corporate Citizen: Democracy Under the Rule of Big Business* (Toronto: Stoddart, 1998); Teun Van Dijk, *Ideology: a multi disciplinary approach* (London: Sage, 1998); Klaehn, 'Corporate Hegemony'; Klaehn, 'A critical review and assessment of Herman and Chomsky's Propaganda Model'; Winter, *Democracy's Oxygen*.

20. Winter, *MediaThink*, xxvii.

21. Dr. Graham Knight. Personal correspondence, Jan 1999.

22. Knight. Personal correspondence, Jan 1999.

23. Herman, 'The Propaganda Model revisited,' cited in Jeffery Klaehn, 'Behind the Invisible Curtain of Scholarly Criticism: revisiting the propaganda model,' *Journalism Studies*, Volume 4, Number 3, 2003, p. 363.

24. See Wolfsfeld, Media and Political Conflict; S. Dale, *McLuhan's Children: The Greenpeace Message and the Media* (Toronto: Between the Lines, 1996).

25. Herman, 'Postmodernism triumphs' in *Z Magazine* (Jan 1996), 15-17.

26. William G. Domhoff, *The Powers That Be: Processes of Ruling Class Domination in America* (New York: Viking, 1979).

27. Clement, *Canadian Corporate Elite*, 364; McMurtry, *Unequal Freedoms*; Tom Bottomore, *Elites and Society*, Second edition (New York: Routledge, 1993), 119; Dobbin, *Myth of the Good Corporate Citizen.*

28. Ed Finn, *Who Do We Try To Rescue Today? Canada Under Corporate Rule*. Ottawa, Ontario, Canada (Canadian Centre for Policy Alternatives, 2000); Klaehn, 'Corporate Hegemony'; Winter, *Common Cents*; Winter, *Democracy's Oxygen*; Winter, *MediaThink*.

29. Herman, 'The Propaganda Model revisited.'

30. Herman and Chomsky, *Manufacturing Consent* (1988), xiii.

31. Herman and Chomsky, *Manufacturing Consent*, 298; also see Klaehn, 'A Critical Review and Assessment...,' 172.

32. See Klaehn, 'A Critical Review and Assessment...,' 172-173.

33. Herman and Chomsky, *Manufacturing Consent*, 306.

34. Noam Chomsky, *Necessary Illusions: Thought Control in Democratic Societies* (Toronto: CBC Enterprises, 1989), vii; also see Klaehn 'A Critical Review and Assessment...,' 173.

35. Noam Chomsky, *Media Control: The Spectacular Achievements of Propaganda*. Open Media Pamphlet Series (New York: Seven Stories Press, 1997).

36. See Herman, 'The Propaganda Model revisited'; also see Klaehn, 'Corporate Hegemony'; Winter, *Common Cents*.

37. Philip Schlesinger, 'From production to propaganda' in *Media, Culture and Society: A Reader* (London: Sage, 1992), 306, 308.

38. Herman, 'The Propaganda Model Revisited.'

39. Aaron Doyle, Brian Elliot and David Tindall, 'Framing the Forests: Corporations, the B.C. Forest Alliance, and the Media,' in *Organizing Dissent: Contemporary Social Movements in Theory and Practice*. Second ed. William K. Carroll, ed. (Toronto: Garamond Press, 1997), 243.

40. The volume in question was edited by William Carroll, who is the current editor of the *Canadian Review of Sociology and Anthropology*.

41. This, apparently, is scholarship.

42. Hackett, 278.

43. Cited in McMurtry, 199.

44. Conrad Black, cited in McMurtry, 199.

45. Doyle *et al*, 266.

46. Hackett, 280.

47. Hackett, 281.

48. For a detailed discussion of these techniques, see Klaehn, 'A Critical Review and Assessment...,' 165-170.

49. Chomsky, *Necessary Illusions*, 59.

50. Winter, *MediaThink*.

51. Orwell, cited in Winter, *MediaThink*, xxvi.

52. Orwell, cited in Winter, *MediaThink*, xxvi; also see Chomsky, *Necessary Illusions*, 22; Domhoff, 169; Klaehn, 'A Critical Review and Assessment...,' 153; Rai, 23; Winter, *Democracy's Oxygen*; Peter Wintonick and Mark Achbar, *Manufacturing Consent: Noam Chomsky and the Media* (Montreal: Black Rose, 1994), 40-1.

53. Noam Chomsky, *Language and Politics* (Montreal: Black Rose, 1988), 679.

54. Chomsky, *Necessary Illusions*; see also Noam Chomsky, *Class Warfare*, Interviews with David Barsamian (Vancouver: New Star, 1997); Noam Chomsky, *Perspectives on Power: Reflections on Human Nature and the Social Order*. (Montreal: Black Rose, 1997); Noam Chomsky, *The Common Good*. Interviews with David Barsamian (Berkeley, CA: Odonian, 1998); M. Lee and N. Solomon, *Unreliable Sources: A Guide to Detecting Bias in the News Media* (New York: Carol, 1990).

55. Chomsky, cited in Klaehn, 'A Critical Review and Assessment...,' 164.

56. Chomsky, cited in Wintonick and Achbar, 40.

57. Chomsky makes the point that 'The general prediction, at each level, is that what enters into the mainstream will support the needs of established power.' See Chomsky, *Necessary Illusions*, 153.

58. Chomsky, *Necessary Illusions*, 11.

59. See Chomsky, *Necessary Illusions*, 145; see also, Rai, 22-23; for discussion of Chomsky's critique of intellectuals see Chomsky, *Necessary Illusions*, 151; Russell Jacoby, *The Last Intellectuals: American culture in the age of the academe* (New York: Noonday, 1987), 182-200; Klaehn, 'Behind the Invisible Curtain...,' 367.

60. Orwell, cited in Winter, *MediaThink*, xxvi.

61. See Winter, *MediaThink*, xxvi.

62. Chomsky, cited in Rai, 33.

63. Chomsky, cited in Rai, 33.

64. Herman addresses the enhanced relevancy of the PM today in Herman, 'The Propaganda Model Revisited'; see also Edward S. Herman, 'The Propaganda Model: a retrospective,' *Journalism Studies*, 2000, 1, 101-12. The case studies presented herein afford further support.

BEYOND HYPOCRISY: Decoding the News in an Age of Propaganda, Including a Doublespeak Dictionary for the 1990s

Edward S. Herman, Illustrations by Matt Wuerker

This spirited book offers abundant examples of duplicitous terminology, ranging from the crimes of free enterprise to media coverage of political events.

> Rich in irony and relentlessly forthright. —*Montréal Mirror*

> Makes us think and thinking is what protects our minds, otherwise we are going to join Orwell's characters. —*Times-Colonist*

> A hard-hitting and often telling critique of American public life. —*Ottawa Citizen*

EDWARD S. HERMAN is Professor Emeritus of Finance at the Wharton School, University of Pennsylvania and author of *Triumph of the Market* (Black Rose Books).

239 pages ❖ paper 1-895431-48-4 $19.99 ❖ cloth 1-895431-49-2 $48.99

ISLAMIC PERIL: Media and Global Violence

Karim H. Karim

Explores the lack of historical and cultural understanding with regard to coverage of conflicts involving Muslims. Winner of the 2001 Robinson Book Prize for excellence.

> If the importance of this kind of scholarship was evident prior to 9/11, such work has taken on added urgency since. —*Canadian Journal of Communication*

> An important addition to the critical literature. —*Choice Magazine*

> Karim should be applauded for his excellent analysis. A timely book...that makes a very important contribution. —*Middle East Journal*

KARIM H. KARIM, Ph.D., is an assistant professor at the School of Journalism and Communication, Carleton University in Ottawa.

224 pages ❖ paper 1-55164-226-3 $26.99 ❖ cloth 1-55164-227-1 $55.99

LIES THE MEDIA TELL US

James Winter

Records example after example, from major newspapers and televison programs, of the use, misuse, and abuse of information. Included is a scathing analysis of actions by the U.S. administration since 9/11; a look at how the corporate media demonize youthful protesters; fought the Kyoto Accord; and push pharmaceutical drugs. Understanding how media shape our thinking about social issues, Disney's animated feature films are scrutinized, as are a number of video games from which children as young as eight are learning violence, sexism and racism.

JAMES WINTER, is a professor of communication studies at the University of Windsor and author of *MediaThink*, *Democracy's Oxygen*, and *Common Cents*. He is also a contributor to *Filtering the News* and to *Radical Mass Media Criticism*.

256 pages ❖ paper 1-55164-252-2 $24.99 ❖ cloth 1-55164-253-0 $53.99

RADICAL MASS MEDIA CRITICISM: A Cultural Genealogy
David Berry, John Theobald, editors
Since the beginning of the media age, there have been thinkers who have reacted against the increasing power of the mass media. This book examines those early mass media critics, and their controversial writings, and links them with their contemporaries to demonstrate the relevance of their legacy for today's debates on media power and media ethics.

DAVID BERRY is Senior Lecturer in Journalism, Culture and Mass Communications and JOHN THEOBALD is Associate Professor in Modern Languages, both of whom are at the Southampton Institute, UK.

256 pages ❖ paper 1-55164-246-8 $24.99 ❖ cloth 1-55164-247-6 $53.99

For a complete list of books on the media, see: http://www.web.net/blackrosebooks.

PARTICIPATORY DEMOCRACY: Prospects for Democratizing Democracy
Dimitrios Roussopoulos, C.George Benello, editors
This wide-ranging collection probes the historical roots of participatory democracy in our political culture, analyzes its application to the problems of modern society, and explores the possible forms it might take on every level of society. Apart from the editors, contributors include: George Woodcock, Murray Bookchin, Don Calhoun, Stewart Perry, Rosabeth Moss Kanter, James Gillespie, Gerry Hunnius, John McEwan, Arthur Chickering, Christian Bay, Martin Oppenheimer, Colin Ward, Sergio Baierle, Anne Latendresse, Bartha Rodin, and C.L.R. James.

DIMITRIOS ROUSSOPOULOS is an author, activist and political economist. C.GEORGE BENELLO taught sociology at Goddard College in Vermont until his untimely death.

380 pages ❖ paper 1-55164-224-7 $24.99 ❖ cloth 1-55164-225-5 $53.99

send for a free catalogue of all our titles

C.P. 1258, Succ. Place du Parc
Montréal, Québec
H2X 4A7 Canada

or visit our website at http://www.web.net/blackrosebooks

to order books
In Canada: (phone) 1-800-565-9523 (fax) 1-800-221-9985
email: utpbooks@utpress.utoronto.ca
In United States: (phone) 1-800-283-3572 (fax) 1-651-917-6406
In UK & Europe: (phone) London 44 (0)20 8986-4854 (fax) 44 (0)20 8533-5821
email: order@centralbooks.com

Printed by the workers of
MARC VEILLEUX IMPRIMEUR INC.
Boucherville, Québec
for Black Rose Books